THE NEXT CHRISTENDOM

THE NEXT
CHRISTENDOM

The Coming of Global Christianity

PHILIP JENKINS

OXFORD
UNIVERSITY PRESS

OXFORD
UNIVERSITY PRESS

Oxford   New York
Auckland   Bangkok   Buenos Aires   Cape Town
Chennai   Dar es Salaam   Delhi   Hong Kong   Istanbul   Karachi
Kolkata   Kuala Lumpur   Madrid   Melbourne   Mexico City   Mumbai   Nairobi
São Paulo   Shanghai   Taipei   Tokyo   Toronto

Copyright © 2002 by Philip Jenkins

Published by Oxford University Press, Inc., 2002
First issued as an Oxford University Press paperback, 2003
198 Madison Avenue, New York, New York 10016

www.oup.com

Oxford is a registered trademark of Oxford University Press

Library of Congress Cataloging-in-Publication Data
Jenkins, Philip, 1952–
The next Christendom : the coming of
global Christianity / Philip Jenkins.
p. cm   Includes bibliographical references and index.
ISBN-13 978-0-19-514616-5 (cloth)   ISBN-13 978-0-19-516891-4 (pbk.)
ISBN 0-19-514616-6 (cloth)   ISBN 0-19-516891-7 (pbk.)
1. Christianity—Forecasting.
2. Church membership.
I. Title.
BR121.3 .J46 2002
270.8'3'0112—dc21   2001047554

Book design by Helen B. Mules

Printed in the United States of America
on acid-free paper

CONTENTS

LIST OF TABLES

ACKNOWLEDGMENTS

Among the friends and colleagues I want to thank for assistance along the way, I would particularly acknowledge Kathryn Hume, On-Cho Ng, Susan O'Brien, and Gregg Roeber. As so often in the past, I thank Cynthia Read of Oxford University Press for all her encouragement and support.

I am grateful for permission to use portions of my article "That New Time Religion," which first appeared in August 1999 in *Chronicles: A Magazine of American Culture*. *Chronicles* is a publication of The Rockford Institute (928 N. Main St., Rockford, IL 61103; www.ChroniclesMagazine.org).

This book went to press in September 2001, at very much the same time as the terrorist outrages that, among other things, destroyed the World Trade Center in New York City. These and subsequent events have had a profound impact on American ideas of Islam and the Middle East. Even so, nothing that has happened recently changes the fundamental argument of my book, and in fact, these developments only strengthen my concerns about possible future confrontations between "jihad" and "crusade." Still, I wanted to add this brief explanation as to why my book, as it stands, makes no mention of these tumultuous events. The world is simply changing too quickly for printed books to keep pace.

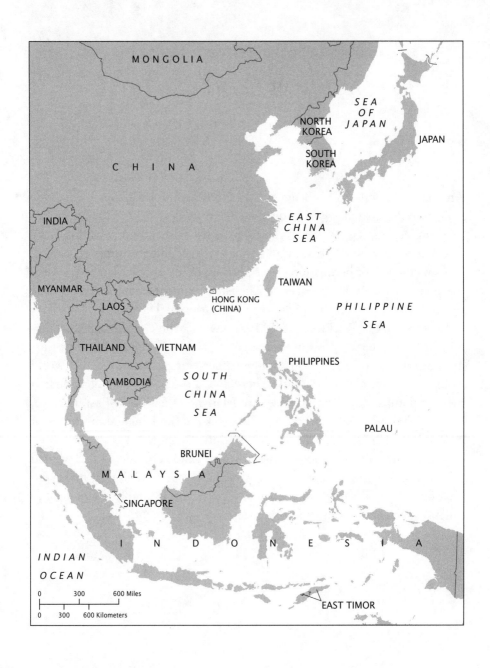

MONGOLIA

CHINA

NORTH
KOREA

SEA
OF
JAPAN

SOUTH
KOREA

JAPAN

INDIA

EAST
CHINA
SEA

MYANMAR

LAOS

HONG KONG
(CHINA)

TAIWAN

PHILIPPINE
SEA

THAILAND

VIETNAM

PHILIPPINES

CAMBODIA

SOUTH
CHINA
SEA

PALAU

BRUNEI

MALAYSIA

SINGAPORE

INDONESIA

INDIAN

OCEAN

EAST TIMOR

0   300   600 Miles

0   300   600 Kilometers

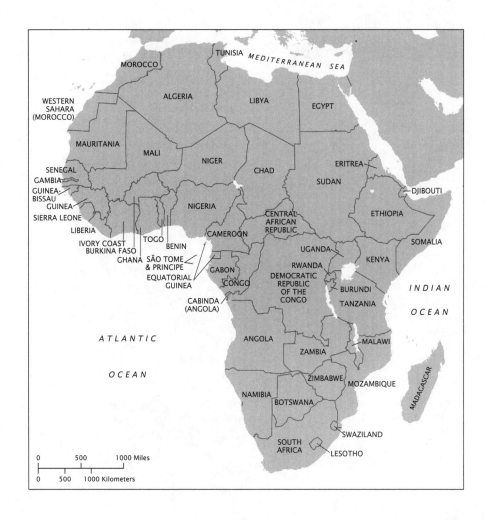

TUNISIA

MEDITERRANEAN SEA

MOROCCO

WESTERN
SAHARA
(MOROCCO)

ALGERIA

LIBYA

EGYPT

MAURITANIA

MALI

NIGER

CHAD

ERITREA

SUDAN

DJIBOUTI

SENEGAL

GAMBIA

GUINEA-
BISSAU

GUINEA

SIERRA LEONE

LIBERIA

NIGERIA

CENTRAL
AFRICAN
REPUBLIC

ETHIOPIA

SOMALIA

IVORY COAST

BURKINA FASO

TOGO

CAMEROON

GHANA

BENIN

UGANDA

KENYA

SÃO TOME
& PRINCIPE

EQUATORIAL
GUINEA

GABON

RWANDA

DEMOCRATIC
REPUBLIC
OF THE
CONGO

CONGO

BURUNDI

INDIAN

CABINDA
(ANGOLA)

TANZANIA

OCEAN

ATLANTIC

ANGOLA

MALAWI

OCEAN

ZAMBIA

MADAGASCAR

ZIMBABWE

MOZAMBIQUE

NAMIBIA

BOTSWANA

SWAZILAND

SOUTH
AFRICA

LESOTHO

0   500   1000 Miles

0   500   1000 Kilometers

ATLANTIC

OCEAN

Gulf of Mexico

BAHAMAS

MEXICO

DOMINICAN REPUBLIC

CUBA

ST. KITTS AND NEVIS
BARBUDA
BELIZE   ANTIGUA
JAMAICA   PUERTO RICO   DOMINICA
HAITI   GUADELOUPE   MARTINIQUE
GUATEMALA   CARIBBEAN SEA   ST. LUCIA   BARBADOS
EL SALVADOR   GRENADA   ST. VINCENT AND THE GRENADINES
HONDURAS   TRINIDAD AND TOBAGO
NICARAGUA
COSTA RICA   VENEZUELA   GUYANA
PANAMA   SURINAME
                                                FRENCH GUIANA
COLOMBIA

ECUADOR

PACIFIC

OCEAN

PERU   B R A Z I L

BOLIVIA

PARAGUAY

CHILE   ARGENTINA

URUGUAY

ATLANTIC

OCEAN

| 0 | 500 | 1000 Miles |

| 0 | 500 | 1000 Kilometers |

BELIZE

GUATEMALA

HONDURAS

EL SALVADOR

NICARAGUA

COSTA
RICA

PANAMA

CARIBBEAN

SEA

PACIFIC

OCEAN

| 0 | 100 | 200 Miles |

| 0 | 100 | 200 Kilometers |

THE NEXT CHRISTENDOM

The Christian Revolution

Europe is the Faith.
—*Hilaire Belloc*

The end of the twentieth century was marked by an obsessive compilation of retrospective lists, which assessed the greatest moments and the most important individuals of the previous hundred years. Some observers, still more ambitious, tried to identify the high and low points of the whole millennium then passing. Yet in almost all these efforts, religious matters received remarkably short shrift. When religious individuals were highlighted, they were usually those most closely identified with secular political trends. Martin Luther King Jr. is an obvious example. After all, the attitude seemed to be, what religious change in recent years could possibly compete in importance with the major secular trends, movements like fascism or communism, feminism or environmentalism? To the contrary, I suggest that it is precisely religious changes that are the most significant, and even the most revolutionary, in the contemporary world. Before too long, the turn-of-the-millennium neglect of religious factors may come to be seen as comically myopic, on a par with a review of the eighteenth century that managed to miss the French Revolution.

We are currently living through one of the transforming moments in the history of religion worldwide. Over the past five centuries or so, the story of Christianity has been inextricably bound up with that of Europe and European-derived civilizations overseas, above all in North America. Until recently, the overwhelming majority of Christians have lived in White nations, allowing theorists to speak smugly, arrogantly, of "European Christian" civilization. Conversely, radical writers have seen Christianity as an ideological arm of Western imperialism. Many of us share the stereotype of Christianity as the religion of the "West" or, to use another popular metaphor, the global North. It is self-evidently the religion of the haves. To adapt the phrase once applied to the increasingly conservative U.S. electorate of the 1970s, the stereotype holds that Christians are un-Black, un-poor, and un-young. If that is true, then the growing secularization of the West can only mean that Christianity is in its dying days. Globally, the faith of the future must be Islam.

Over the past century, however, the center of gravity in the Christian world has shifted inexorably southward, to Africa, Asia, and Latin America. Already today, the largest Christian communities on the planet are to be found in Africa and Latin America. If we want to visualize a "typical" contemporary Christian, we should think of a woman living in a village in Nigeria or in a Brazilian *favela*. As Kenyan scholar John Mbiti has observed, "the centers of the church's universality [are] no longer in Geneva, Rome, Athens, Paris, London, New York, but Kinshasa, Buenos Aires, Addis Ababa and Manila."[1] Whatever Europeans or North Americans may believe, Christianity is doing very well indeed in the global South—not just surviving but expanding.

This trend will continue apace in coming years. Many of the fastest-growing countries in the world are either predominantly Christian or else have very sizable Christian minorities. Even if Christians just maintain their present share of the population in countries like Nigeria and Kenya, Mexico and Ethiopia, Brazil and the Philippines, there are soon going to be several hundred million more Christians from those nations alone. Moreover, conversions will swell the Christian share of world population. Meanwhile, historically low birth rates in the traditionally Christian states of Europe mean that these populations are declining or stagnant. In 1950, a list of the world's leading Christian countries would have included Britain, France, Spain, and Italy, but none of these names would be represented in a corresponding list for 2050.

Christianity should enjoy a worldwide boom in the new century, but the vast majority of believers will be neither white nor European, nor Euro-American. According to the respected *World Christian Encyclopedia,* some 2 billion Christians are alive today, about one-third of the planetary total. The largest single bloc, some 560 million people, is still to be found in Europe. Latin America, though, is already close behind with 480 million.

Africa has 360 million, and 313 million Asians profess Christianity. North America claims about 260 million believers. If we extrapolate these figures to the year 2025, and assume no great gains or losses through conversion, then there would be around 2.6 billion Christians, of whom 633 million would live in Africa, 640 million in Latin America, and 460 million in Asia. Europe, with 555 million, would have slipped to third place.[2] Africa and Latin America would be in competition for the title of most Christian continent. About this date, too, another significant milestone should occur, namely that these two continents will together account for half the Christians on the planet. By 2050, only about one-fifth of the world's 3 billion Christians will be non-Hispanic Whites.[3] Soon, the phrase "a White Christian" may sound like a curious oxymoron, as mildly surprising as "a Swedish Buddhist." Such people can exist, but a slight eccentricity is implied.

This global perspective should make us think carefully before asserting "what Christians believe" or "how the church is changing." All too often, statements about what "modern Christians accept" or what "Catholics today believe" refer only to what that ever-shrinking remnant of *Western* Christians and Catholics believe. Such assertions are outrageous today, and as time goes by they will become ever further removed from reality. The era of Western Christianity has passed within our lifetimes, and the day of Southern Christianity is dawning. The fact of change itself is undeniable: it has happened, and will continue to happen. So little did we notice this momentous change that it was barely mentioned in all the media hoopla surrounding the end of the second millennium.

LOOKING SOUTH

The idea of Christianity literally "going South" is not unfamiliar, at least to religious studies scholars.[4] The theme is well-established in Europe, where African affairs are more attended to than they are in the United States. As long ago as the 1970s, this global change was discussed in well-known works by European scholars like Andrew Walls, Edward Norman, and Walbert Buhlmann, and the theme was consecrated by its inclusion in the *World Christian Encyclopedia,* first published in 1982. It was Buhlmann who coined the term "the Third Church," on the analogy of the Third World. The phrase suggests that the South represents a new tradition comparable in importance to the Eastern and Western churches of historical times. Walls sees the faith in Africa as a distinctive new tradition of Christianity comparable to Catholicism, Protestantism, and Orthodoxy; it is "the standard

Christianity of the present age, a demonstration model of its character."
When in 1998 the World Council of Churches commemorated the fiftieth
anniversary of its founding, it decided to meet in Zimbabwe, as an explicit
recognition of the growing significance of Africa in world Christianity.[5]

Yet outside the ranks of scholars and church bureaucrats, few commentators have paid serious attention to these trends, to what I will describe as
the creation of a new Christendom, which for better or worse may play a
critical role in world affairs. In the catalogues of North American religious
publishers, materials either from or about Africa or Asia are rarely in evidence. This does not mean that publishers willfully refuse to present the
information for sinister motives, but they know from experience that Third
World topics rarely attract a general audience of the sort that would make
a new title profitable. For whatever reason, Southern churches remain
almost invisible to Northern observers. When in 2000, the popular evangelical magazine *Christian History* listed the "hundred most important
events in Church history," the only mention of Africa, Asia, or Latin America involved the British abolition of the slave trade. Missing from this top
hundred was church growth in modern Africa, where the number of Christians increased, staggeringly, from 10 million in 1900 to 360 million by
2000. Nor were there any Southerners among the same publication's list of
the ten most important Christians of the passing century. (In fairness, the
list did include two African Americans, Martin Luther King Jr. and Pentecostal pioneer William Seymour.) An evangelical-oriented survey of *100 Christian Books That Changed the Century* featured three or four books about
missions in Africa and Asia, but scarcely a word about Latin America. The
only work actually *by* a Southern writer was *Cry the Beloved Country,* by
White South African Alan Paton.[6]

The imbalance is just as evident in the Western academic world, in which
published studies of Third World religion represent only a tiny fraction of
scholarship on Christianity. At the same time, the volume of academic studies coming out of Africa and Latin America has shrunk as universities in
those regions have been crippled by lack of resources. To quote John Mbiti
once more, "It is utterly scandalous for so many Christian scholars in [the]
old Christendom to know so much about heretical movements in the second and third centuries, when so few of them know anything about Christian movements in areas of the younger churches." Matters have changed
somewhat since Mbiti wrote in the 1970s. Some excellent books are now
available on Southern religion, notably Harvey Cox's influential *Fire from
Heaven* (1995), and we have some fine studies on Latin American Pentecostalism.[7] But the general observation about what most Western religious

studies scholars actually work on is still applicable. While we can endorse Walls' remark that "anyone who wishes to undertake serious study of Christianity these days needs to know something about Africa," it scarcely reflects common scholarly perceptions.[8]

If most writers are neglecting the present-day realities of Christianity, they are still worse on projecting the future. In North America at least, most visions of the coming century are based firmly on extrapolating familiar domestic conditions. The imagined future looks a lot like the American present, only with Western liberalism ever more in the ascendant. Robert Wuthnow's *Christianity in the 21st Century* has basically nothing to say about conditions in the Third World. There is only a little more in a book with the promising title *Toward 2015: A Church Odyssey,* although one of its co-authors is an Episcopal bishop. Not even Anglicans and Episcopalians are looking South, although that is where virtually all of the growth is occurring in their Communion.[9]

If the religious world, the old Christendom, is so cavalier about these epoch-making changes, it is not surprising that secular commentators are largely oblivious.[10] Nobody, for instance, has asked the crucial question of just what Western civilization means when what were once its critical religious aspects are now primarily upheld outside the "West." One key exception is Samuel P. Huntington's book, *The Clash of Civilizations and the Remaking of World Order,* one of the most widely read analyses of current global trends, which does pay serious attention to changing religious patterns. Even Huntington, though, understates the rising force of Christianity. He believes that the relative Christian share of global population will fall steeply in the new century, and that this religion will be supplanted by Islam: "In the long run . . . Muhammad wins out." But far from Islam being the world's largest religion by 2020 or so, as Huntington suggests, Christianity will still have a massive lead, and will maintain its position into the foreseeable future. By 2050, there should still be about three Christians for every two Muslims worldwide. Some 34 percent of the world's people will then be Christian, roughly what the figure was at the height of European world hegemony in 1900.[11]

Huntington's analysis of the evidence is misguided in one crucial respect. While he rightly notes the phenomenal rates of population growth in Muslim countries, he ignores the fact that similar or even higher rates are also found in already populous Christian countries, above all in Africa. Alongside the Muslim efflorescence he rightly foresees, there will also be a Christian population explosion, often in the same or adjacent countries. If we look at the nations with the fastest population growth and the youngest populations, they are evenly distributed between Christian- and Muslim-dominated societies. I dispute Huntington's assertion that "Christianity spreads primarily by conversion, Islam by conversion and reproduction." Huntington's lack of interest in the epoch-making Christian growth in Africa is odd because elsewhere he has written so knowledgeably about the role of the Catholic Church in promoting democratic movements across the continent. Throughout his *Clash of Civilizations*, though, he refers to "Western Christianity" as if there could be no other species. The same kind of tunnel vision affects another recent work on global mega-trends, Benjamin Barber's *Jihad vs. McWorld*. For Barber, Third World religion is discussed chiefly in terms of Islam, and Christianity just means North American fundamentalism. There is no recognition that the gravest challenge to "McWorld" might not come from Jihad, but rather from what we might call the forces of Crusade, from the Christian Third World.[12]

BACK TO THE FUTURE

The numerical changes in Christianity are striking enough, but beyond the simple demographic transition, there are countless implications for theology and religious practice. To take a historical parallel, Christianity changed thoroughly when a movement founded in a Jewish and Hellenistic context moved into the Germanic lands of Western Europe during the early Middle Ages. Although it is only a symbolic example, we can learn something from the way in which the English language imported its large Christian vocabulary. Familiar words like "church" or "bishop" are borrowed from Greek originals, although in radically mutated forms. "Church" derives from *kyriakos oikos* (house of the Lord), "bishop" from *episkopos* ("supervisor," or one who watches over the community). We can imagine the Roman and Greek missionaries to the Anglo-Saxons confronting the notorious English incapacity to deal with foreign tongues, and hearing their elegant terms butchered into the words we have today.

In this instance, the substance of the words survived the cultural transition intact, but in other vital ways, a largely urban Mediterranean Christianity was profoundly changed by the move to the Northern forests. In art and popular thought, Jesus became a blond Aryan, often with the appropriate warrior attributes, and Christian theology was reshaped by West European notions of law and feudalism.[13] European Christians reinterpreted the faith through their own concepts of social and gender relations, and then imagined that their culturally specific synthesis was the only correct version of Christian truth. In fact, it was about as far removed from its origins as the word "church" is from *kyriakos oikos*. As Christianity moves southward, the religion will be comparably changed by immersion in the prevailing cultures of those host societies.

But what would this new Christian synthesis look like? One obvious fact is that at least for the foreseeable future, members of a Southern-dominated church are likely to be among the poorer people on the planet, in marked contrast to the older Western-dominated world. For this reason, some Western Christians have since the 1960s expected that the religion of their Third World brethren would be fervently liberal, activist, and even revolutionary, the model represented by liberation theology. In this view, the new Christianity would chiefly be concerned with putting down the mighty from their seats, through political action or even armed struggle. All too often, though, these hopes have proved illusory. Frequently, the liberationist voices emanating from the Third World proved to derive from clerics trained in Europe and North America, and their ideas won only limited local appeal. Southern Hemisphere Christians would not avoid political activism, but they would become involved strictly on their own terms.[14]

At present, the most immediately apparent difference between the older and newer churches is that Southern Christians are far more conservative in terms of both beliefs and moral teaching. The denominations that are triumphing all across the global South are stalwartly traditional or even reactionary by the standards of the economically advanced nations. The churches that have made most dramatic progress in the global South have either been Roman Catholic, of a traditionalist and fideistic kind, or radical Protestant sects, evangelical or Pentecostal. Indeed, this conservatism may go far toward explaining the common neglect of Southern Christianity in North America and Europe. Western experts rarely find the ideological tone of the new churches much to their taste.

Southern Christians retain a very strong supernatural orientation, and are by and large far more interested in personal salvation than in radical politics. As Harvey Cox showed in *Fire from Heaven,* Pentecostal expansion across the Southern Hemisphere has been so astonishing as to justify claims of a new reformation. In addition, rapid growth is occurring in non-traditional denominations that adapt Christian belief to local tradition, groups that are categorized by titles like "African indigenous churches." Their exact numbers are none too clear, since they are too busy baptizing newcomers to be counting them very precisely. By most accounts, membership in Pentecostal and independent churches already runs into the hundreds of millions, and congregations are located in precisely the regions of fastest population growth. Within a few decades, such denominations will represent a far larger segment of global Christianity, and just conceivably a majority. These newer churches preach deep personal faith and communal orthodoxy, mysticism and puritanism, all founded on clear scriptural authority. They preach messages that, to a Westerner, appear simplistically charismatic, visionary, and apocalyptic. In this thought-world, prophecy is an everyday reality, while faith-healing, exorcism, and dream-visions are all basic components of religious sensibility. For better or worse, the dominant churches of the future could have much in common with those of medieval or early modern European times. On present evidence, a Southernized Christian future should be distinctly conservative.

The theological coloring of the most successful new churches reminds us once more of the massive gap in most Western listings of the major trends of the past century, which rightly devoted much space to political movements like fascism and communism, but ignored vital religious currents like Pentecostalism. Yet today, Fascists or Nazis are not easy to find, and Communists may be becoming an endangered species, while Pentecostals are flourishing around the globe. Since there were only a handful of Pentecostals in 1900, and several hundred million today, is it not reasonable to identify this as perhaps the most successful social movement of the past century? According to current projections, the number of Pentecostal believers should surpass the one billion mark before 2050. In terms of the global religions, there will by that point be roughly as many Pentecostals as Hindus, and twice as many as there are Buddhists. And that is just taking one of the diverse currents of rising Christianity: there will be even more Catholics than Pentecostals.[15]

THE DEATH OF CHRISTIANITY?

As Southern Christianity continues to expand and mature, it will assuredly develop a wider theological spectrum than at present, and stronger liberal or secularizing tendencies may well emerge. For the foreseeable future, though, the dominant current in emerging world Christianity is traditionalist, orthodox, and supernatural. This would be an ironic reversal of most Western perceptions about the future of religion. As I have worked on this book over the past few years, I have described its general theme to friends and colleagues, most of whom are well-educated and widely traveled. When I say, though, that my theme is "the future of Christianity," a common follow-up question is, in effect, "So, how long do you think it will last?" or specifically, "How long can the Catholic Church survive?" In their own way, secular, liberal Americans have a distinctly apocalyptic view of the future, with a millenarian expectation of the uprooting of organized religion. At the least, there is a widespread conviction that Christianity cannot survive in anything like its present form.

For over a century, the coming decline or disappearance of religion has been a commonplace assumption of Western thought, and church leaders have sometimes shared this pessimistic view. Every so often, some American or European writer urges the church to adjust itself to present-day realities, to become "relevant" by abandoning outmoded supernatural doctrines and moral assumptions. In 1998, the Episcopal Bishop John Spong of Newark advocated just such a skeptical and secularist New Reformation in his book *Why Christianity Must Change or Die*. More recently, Templeton Prize-winning scholar Arthur Peacocke has urged that the church abandon the "incomprehensible and unbelievable" teachings of supernaturalism, and present the faith in a "credible" manner. (Peacocke, like Spong, is also a senior cleric of the Anglican Communion.) Not long ago, the *New York Times* popularized these ideas in a now-notorious review in which Brent Staples proclaimed the imminent demise of American Christianity. "Visit a church at random next Sunday," Staples wrote, "and you will probably encounter a few dozen people sprinkled thinly over a sanctuary that was built to accommodate hundreds or even thousands. The empty pews and white-haired congregants lend credence to those who argue that traditional religious worship is dying out." Staples was arguing that Christianity had failed and was collapsing, and would continue to do so unless and until the religion came to terms with liberal orthodoxies on matters of sex and gender.[16]

Viewed from Cambridge or Amsterdam, such pleas may make excellent sense, but in the context of global Christianity, this kind of liberalism looks distinctly dated. It would not be easy to convince a congregation in Seoul or Nairobi that Christianity is dying, when their main concern is building a worship facility big enough for the 10,000 or 20,000 members they have gained over the past few years. And these new converts are mostly teenagers and young adults, very few with white hair. Nor can these churches be easily told that, in order to reach a mass audience, they must bring their message more into accord with (Western) secular orthodoxies.

In contemplating this shift to traditionalism, a historical analogy comes to mind. In eighteenth-century Europe and America, secular Enlightenment ideas made enormous progress among social elites. Few traditional bastions of Christian belief escaped attack. The Trinity, the divinity of Christ, the existence of hell, all fell into disfavor, while critical Bible scholarship undermined the familiar bases of faith. Thomas Jefferson was confident that rational Unitarianism was destined to be the dominant creed of the new United States, and generously offered his version of the New Testament shorn of miracles and supernatural intervention. Under heavy assault from the European kingdoms, the Roman Catholic Church was forced to dissolve the Jesuit order, which represented the aggressive confidence of bygone days. In 1798, the anti-religious French revolutionaries captured the pope himself.[17]

Any knowledgeable observer in the 1790s would have concluded that orthodox Christianity had reached its last days. Of course, this sensible opinion would have been absolutely wrong. In the early nineteenth century, orthodoxy and tradition made a comeback, as did the papacy and, indeed, the Jesuit order. The rationalism prevailing in many Protestant churches was overwhelmed by a new evangelical revivalism. Far from dominating the American scene, Unitarian-Universalists today comprise around 0.2 percent of the U.S. population. So thoroughly was eighteenth-century liberalism obliterated that many modern writers tend to assume that its ideas were invented anew by Victorian skeptics and rationalists, or perhaps grew out of the controversies over Darwinian evolution. Then as now, the triumph of secular liberalism proved to be anything but inevitable.

THE RISE OF CHRISTENDOM

In describing the rising neo-orthodox world, I have spoken of a "new Christendom." The phrase evokes a medieval European age of faith, of passionate spirituality and a pervasive Christian culture. Medieval people spoke readily of "Christendom," the *Res Publica Christiana*, as a true overarching unity and a focus of loyalty transcending mere kingdoms or empires. Kingdoms like Burgundy, Wessex, or Saxony might last for only a century or two before they were replaced by new states and dynasties, but any rational person knew that Christendom simply endured. This perception had political consequences. While the laws of individual nations lasted only as long as the nations themselves, Christendom offered a higher set of standards and mores, which alone could claim to be universal. Although it rarely possessed any potential for common political action, Christendom was a primary form of cultural reference.[18]

Ultimately, Christendom collapsed in the face of the overwhelming power of secular nationalism. Later Christian scholars struggled to live in this new age of "post-Christendom," when one could no longer assume any connection between religion and political order.[19] By the start of the 21st century, however, the whole concept of the nation-state was itself under challenge. Partly, the changes reflected new technologies. According to a report by the U.S. intelligence community, in the coming decades, "governments will have less and less control over flows of information, technology, diseases, migrants, arms, and financial transactions, whether legal or illegal, across their borders. . . . The very concept of 'belonging' to a particular state will probably erode." To use Benedict Anderson's famous phrase, nation-states are imagined communities of relatively recent date, rather than eternal or inevitable realities. In recent years, many of these communities have begun to reimagine themselves substantially, even to unimagine themselves out of existence. In Europe, loyalties to the nation as such are being replaced by newer forms of adherence, whether to larger entities (Europe itself) or to smaller (regions or ethnic groups). It remains to be seen whether or not the nation-state will outlive the printed book, that other Renaissance invention that may also fade away in the coming decades.[20] If even once unquestioned constructs like Great Britain are under threat, it is not surprising that people are questioning the existence of newer and still more artificial entities in Africa or Asia, with their flimsy national frontiers dreamed up so recently by imperial bureaucrats. As Paul Gifford notes, many Africans live in mere quasi-states: "though they are recognized legal entities, they are not, in a functional sense, states."[21]

For a quarter of a century, social scientists have been analyzing the decline of states in the face of globalization, and have noted parallels with the cosmopolitan world of the Middle Ages. Some scholars have postulated the future emergence of some movement or ideology that could in a sense create something like a new Christendom. This would be what political scientist Hedley Bull called "a modern and secular equivalent of the kind of universal political organization that existed in Western Christendom in the Middle Ages." Might the new ideological force be environmentalism, perhaps with a mystical New Age twist?[22] Yet the more we look at the Southern Hemisphere in particular, the more we see that while universal and supranational ideas are flourishing, they are not secular in the least. The centers of gravest state weakness are often the regions in which political loyalties are secondary to religious beliefs, either Muslim or Christian, and these are the terms in which people define their identities. The new Christian world of the South could find unity in common religious beliefs.

That many Southern societies will develop a powerful Christian identity in culture and politics is beyond doubt. Less obvious is whether, and when, they will aspire to any kind of global unity. In this matter, the Atlantic Ocean initially seems to offer a barrier quite as overwhelming as it was before

Columbus. Very soon, the two main centers of Christianity will be Africa and Latin America, and within each region, there is at least some sense of unity. Latin American ecclesiastics meet periodically, scholars treat the region as a whole (albeit a diverse one), and a similar canon of authors is read widely. The same can be said of Africa in its own way. However, next to no common sense of identity currently unites the churches and believers of the two continents. Even in terms of worldwide Christian networks, the two continents belong almost to different planets. For many Protestant Africans, the World Council of Churches offers a major institutional focus of unity, but because the Roman Catholic Church abstains from membership in the Council, this forum is closed to the majority of Latin Americans. When African and Latin American church leaders and scholars do meet, all too often it is at gatherings in Europe or the United States, following agendas conceived in the global North.

The resulting segregation of interests and ideas is remarkable, since the churches in Africa and Latin America share so many common experiences. They are passing through similar phases of growth, and are, independently, developing similar social and theological worldviews. Both also face similar issues, of race, of inculturation, of just how to deal with their respective colonial heritages. All these are common hemispheric issues that fundamentally separate the experiences of Northern and Southern churches.[23] Given the lively scholarly activity and the flourishing spirituality in both Africa and Latin America, a period of mutual discovery is inevitable. When it begins—when, not if—the interaction should launch a revolutionary new era in world religion. Although many see the process of globalization as yet another form of American imperialism, it would be ironic if an early consequence was a growing sense of identity between Southern Christians. Once that axis is established, we really would be speaking of a new Christendom, based in the Southern Hemisphere.

The archaic term "Christendom" conjures some potential nightmares about the future we are imagining. The last Christendom, in the Middle Ages, was anything but an unmixed blessing for either Church or society. While it offered a common culture and thought-world, the era was also characterized by widespread intolerance, symbolized at its very worst by aggressive Crusades, heresy hunts, and religious pogroms. Critically, Christendom was defined in terms of what it was not, since the Christian world existed in unhappy conjunction with neighboring Muslim states.

This Christian-Muslim conflict may in fact prove one of the closest analogies between the Christian world that was, and the one coming into being. No less than Christians, Muslims will be transformed by the epochal demographic events of the coming decades, the shift of gravity of population to the Two-Thirds World. Muslim and Christian nations will expand adjacent to each other, and often, Muslim and Christian communities will both grow within the same country. Based on recent experiences around the world—in Nigeria and Indonesia, the Sudan and the Philippines—we face the likelihood that population growth will be accompanied by intensified rivalry, by struggles for converts, by competing attempts to enforce moral codes by means of secular law. Whether Muslim or Christian, religious zeal can easily turn into fanaticism.

Such struggles might well provoke civil wars, which could in turn become international conflicts. This development is quite likely when one of the competing ideologies is shared passionately by a neighboring country, or by an international religious-oriented alliance. Across the Muslim world, many believers have shown themselves willing to fight for the cause of international Islam with far more enthusiasm than they demonstrate for any individual nation. Putting these different trends together, we have a volatile mixture that could well provoke horrific wars and confrontations.

Worldwide, religious trends have the potential to reshape political assumptions in a way that has not been seen since the rise of modern nationalism. While we can imagine any number of possible futures, a worst-case scenario would include a wave of religious conflicts reminiscent of the Middle Ages, a new age of Christian crusades and Muslim jihads. Imagine the world of the thirteenth century armed with nuclear warheads and anthrax. In responding to this prospect, we need at a minimum to ensure that our political leaders and diplomats pay as much attention to religions and to sectarian frontiers as they ever have to the distribution of oilfields.

USING THE FUTURE

This scenario may well be too pessimistic, but there can be no doubt about the underlying realities, demographic and religious, which ensure that Christianity will flourish in the new century. The question is just how to respond to that fact. While political leaders must make their own agendas, current changes also pose questions for anyone interested in the state of religion.

The greatest temptation—and maybe the worst danger—is to use future projections as a club in present-day arguments. Northerners rarely give the South anything like the attention it deserves, but when they do notice it, they tend to project onto it their own familiar realities and desires. If in fact the global South represents the future, then it is tempting to claim that one's own ideas are more valid, more important, because they coincide with those of the rising Third World. For the Left, the rise of the South suggests that Northern Christians must commit themselves firmly to social and political activism at home, to ensuring economic justice and combating racism, to promoting cultural diversity. Conservatives, in contrast, emphasize the moral and sexual conservatism of the emerging churches, and seek to enlist them as natural allies. From this point of view, the churches that are doing best in the world as a whole are the ones that stand farthest from Western liberal orthodoxies, and we should learn from their success. For both sides, the new South is useful, politically and rhetorically. Even if an activist holds an unusual or unpopular position, it can be justified on the basis that it represents the future: if they wait long enough, they will be vindicated by the churches of Africa (or Asia, or Latin America). Like any true-believing Marxist, one is claiming to be on the side of history, which will absolve its faithful disciples.

The difficulty, of course, is deciding just what that vast and multifaceted entity described as the Third World actually does want or believe. As Southern churches grow and mature, they will increasingly define their own interests in ways that have little to do with the preferences and parties of Americans and Europeans. We can even imagine Southern Christians taking the initiative to the extent of evangelizing the North, in the process changing many familiar aspects of belief and practice, and exporting cultural traits presently found only in Africa or Latin America. We can only speculate what this future synthesis might look like. But underlying all these possibilities is one solid reality. However partisan the interpretations of the new Christianity, however paternalistic, there can be no doubt that the emerging Christian world will be anchored in the Southern continents.

Disciples of All Nations

> As I travel, I have observed a pattern, a strange
> historical phenomenon of God "moving"
> geographically from the Middle East, to Europe
> to North America to the developing world. My
> theory is this: God goes where he's wanted.
> —*Philip Yancey,* Christianity Today,
> *February 5, 2001*

As Christianity moves South, it is in some ways returning to its roots. To use the intriguing description offered by Ghanaian scholar Kwame Bediako, what we are now witnessing is "the renewal of a non-Western religion."[1] Founded in the Near East, Christianity for its first thousand years was stronger in Asia and North Africa than in Europe, and only after about 1400 did Europe (and Europeanized North America) decisively become the Christian heartland. This account challenges the oddly prevalent view of Christianity as a White or Western ideology that was foisted on the rest of an unwilling globe, under the auspices of Spanish galleons, British redcoats, and American televangelists.

In this popular image, Christianity becomes not just an aspect of Western imperialism, but an essential justification for that whole era. When twentieth-century African Americans sought religious roots distinct from the mainstream culture that spurned them, a substantial minority opted for the Muslim faith, which they regarded as authentically African. Christianity, in contrast, was seen as the tool of the slave-masters. (Few Westerners pay any attention to the long history of Arab Muslim slaving enterprises in Africa.)[2] As "everyone knows," the authentic religions of Africa and Asia are faiths like Hinduism, Buddhism, animism, and, above all, Islam. Not just among Blacks, a common assumption holds that when we do find

Christianity outside the West, it must have been brought there from the West, probably in the past century or two. Images of Victorian missionaries in pith-helmets are commonly in the background.

The power of this hostile picture is all the more surprising when we realize how easily available are the historical sources and modern scholarly studies that utterly contradict it. We do not have to excavate obscure schol-arly collections in order to read the rich and ancient histories of African and Asian Christianity. Based on this very large literature, we can see that at no point did the West have a monopoly on the Christian faith. And even at the height of the missionary endeavor, non-Western converts very soon absorbed and adapted the religion according to their own cultural needs.

THE MYTH OF WESTERN CHRISTIANITY

The whole idea of "Western Christianity" distorts the true pattern of the religion's development over time. The conventional picture of Christian origins, presented in any number of popular history books and television documentaries, is commonly illustrated by a graphic of the Mediterranean world and Europe, with Jerusalem at an eastern extreme. Christianity grows from its roots in Palestine, spreads through Asia Minor and Greece, and ultimately arrives in Italy, the center of the map and presumably of the world. The faith then spreads through the Roman world, until by the fourth cen-tury, it becomes coterminous with the Roman Empire.

Tracing later developments from the seventh century on, animations or sequences of maps show Eastern Christianity being overwhelmed by the forces of Islam. As Muslim forces conquer each territory of the eastern or southern Mediterranean, the land affected is often depicted, literally, fad-ing into darkness. For a modern viewer, it is easy to understand why lands like Egypt, Syria, and Palestine would quickly be lost to the faith, since any-one can see that they were only clinging lightly to the far skirts of the Roman (and Christian) world. After the rise of Islam, maps generally shift their focus to the lands of Western Europe, especially to what will later become France and Britain. The Christian center of gravity shifted decisively from the Jordan to the Rhine, from Antioch to Chartres. In the east, all that remains by this point is the long-enduring, if ultimately doomed, presence of the Byzantine Empire, based in Constantinople. Barring this single bas-tion, the usual graphic representation implies that by 800 at the latest, the time of Charlemagne, Christianity was more or less synonymous with Western Europe, and grew or shrank with European fortunes. Long before this point, Christians had abandoned their perverse habit of writing sacred texts in Greek, Syriac, and Coptic, and confined themselves to good, Christian, Latin.

Popular histories always oversimplify, but in this instance, the inaccuracies are serious. To imagine the early history of Christianity, we would do much better to use the standard map of the world that was regularly offered in medieval times. In these older pictures, the then known continents of Europe, Africa, and Asia all appeared as more or less equal lobes conjoined at a central location, which was Palestine, with Jerusalem at its center. This image made splendid theological sense, in that Jesus' sacrificial self-giving occurred at the very center of the world that he was saving. Theology apart, the tripartite model is far more useful for understanding Christian expansion, which occurred simultaneously into the three continents.[3] When we think of the missionary endeavors of the early apostles, we look first at Paul's career in the eastern Mediterranean, because this happened to be recorded in the Acts and Epistles that form so large a part of the New Testament. Appropriately enough for the modern Europe-centered view, the book of Acts ends once St. Paul established himself in Rome. This Pauline movement became all the more important in hindsight because of the relative success of the Gentile churches after the Jewish revolt of 66–73. At the time, though, the richest fields for missionary expansion were unquestionably in Africa and Asia, rather than Europe. During the first century or two of the Christian era, Syria, Egypt, and Mesopotamia became the Christian centers that they would remain for many centuries. Christian art, literature, and music all originated in these lands, as did most of what would become the New Testament. Monasticism is an Egyptian invention.

By the time the Roman Empire granted the Christians toleration in the early fourth century, there was no question that the religion was predominantly associated with the eastern half of the empire, and indeed with territories beyond the eastern border. Of the five ancient patriarchates of the church, only one, Rome, clearly stood in the west. The others were at Constantinople, Antioch, Jerusalem, and Alexandria—three on the Asian continent, one in Africa. If we can imagine a Christian center of gravity by around 500, we should still be thinking of Syria rather than Italy. Africa, too, had its ancient Christian roots. Apart from Egypt, much early Christian history focuses on the Roman province known as Africa, roughly modern Tunisia. This was the home of such great early leaders as Tertullian, Cyprian, and Augustine, the founders of Christian Latin literature.[4]

THE EASTERN CHURCHES

Christianity has never been synonymous with either Europe or the West. In fact, theological controversies of the fourth and fifth centuries tended to isolate European or Western Christianity from the traditional Christian lands, and leave it out on a geographical and cultural limb. Repeatedly, Christians engaged in furious debates over the nature of Christ, debates that seem arcane to most modern observers but would be crucial for defining cultural frontiers. The core question was the relationship between the divine and human natures of Christ. The Catholic or Orthodox position, which ultimately triumphed, held that there were indeed two natures, which were conjoined and commingled. Most Egyptians and Easterners, however, accepted the Monophysite teaching that Christ had only one nature, and was purely divine. Nestorians accepted the two natures, but held that these were not absolutely united, so that it was blasphemous nonsense to speak of the Virgin Mary as "Mother of God." Following violent controversies, the Nestorians were cast out of the fold in 431, while the Monophysites were deemed heretical at the great ecumenical council at Chalcedon, in 451. This left the Orthodox in command of the empire and the mainstream church apparatus. Over the next two centuries, many of the traditional centers of Christianity saw themselves as oppressed by the tyrannical rulers of Rome and Constantinople. Already, Christianity was bitterly divided between Western (European) and Eastern (Asian and African) models. Denominations arising directly from these theological squabbles survive today, and have only barely patched up their differences.[5]

This mutual hostility helps to explain why European Christians had little sympathy for or knowledge of some of the truly ancient Christian societies of the East, and why our historical view of the Eastern churches is often blinkered. When we refer to Christianity forming a relationship with the secular state, Western historians think first of Constantine, who granted toleration within the Roman Empire in 313. Far less celebrated are the other early states that established Christianity as their own official religion in the fourth century, namely Ethiopia and Armenia. Almost certainly, Armenia was the first state anywhere to establish Christianity as an official faith, which it did around the year 300. Armenian Christianity became increasingly separated from the Western tradition in the fifth century after it adopted the Monophysite position. Even so, Christianity survived and has flourished there up to the present day, developing a rich literary, musical, and architectural culture.[6]

The Ethiopian church is equally ancient, and an Ethiopian court official is one of the first Gentile converts identified in the book of Acts. Like its Armenian counterpart, the organized church in Ethiopia also owed much to Syrian missionaries of the third and fourth centuries. By the time the first Anglo-Saxons were converted, Ethiopian Christianity was already in its tenth generation. Although scarcely known by Westerners, the Ethiopian church offers one of the most heroic success stories in Christianity. Not surprisingly given its location, the church drew heavily on Egyptian influence. Through the Middle Ages, the symbolic center of the Christian kingdom was at the ancient capital of Aksum, long a point of contact with Pharaonic Egypt. An episcopal see was founded here around 340, and this remained the "home. of the Ark of the Covenant, Ethiopia's original New Jerusalem." The Egyptian connection created a potent monastic tradition that endures to this day. It also meant that, like the Armenians, the Ethiopians followed the Monophysite teaching, which reinforced their separation from European Christianity. Far from being concerned with the opinions of Rome, the story of the Ethiopian church for most of its history constitutes a battle between local control (the monastic leadership) and the *abunas,* the representatives of the Coptic patriarchs in Alexandria. On every side, this was a wholly African affair.[7]

The Ethiopian church has many aspects that would surprise a Westerner, including practices that stem from Judaism.[8] Believers practice circumcision, some keep a Saturday Sabbath, and many churches feature an ark. Claiming Solomonic tradition, the kings practiced polygamy. We really do not know whether early Ethiopians had been converted to Judaism before they found Christianity, or if (more likely) they just treated Old Testament models with much more reverence than would European Christians. As we will see, many modern-day African Christians likewise feel very comfortable with the world of the Old Testament, and try to revive ancient Hebrew customs—usually to the horror of European Christians.

But for all the Ethiopian church's quirks, it would be a daring outsider who would venture to suggest that the faith for which Ethiopians have struggled and died over 1,700 years is anything less than a pure manifestation of the Christian tradition. In 1970, in the last days of the old royal regime, the church had "61,000 priests, 12,000 monks, 57,000 deacons, 31,000 *debteras* (choir leaders) and 827 monasteries."[9] Even today, after lengthy conflicts with Muslims and, more recently, anti-clerical Marxists, the church claims some 25 million members. To put this in Western terms, that is roughly the number of North American Methodists of all denominations combined.

SURVIVAL

Both Armenia and Ethiopia maintained a stubborn independence for most of their history. Ethiopia was one of the last portions of Africa to be swallowed by European imperialism, and even then only briefly, during the 1930s. Yet these nations were far from unusual in keeping their distinctive religious identity alive through the Middle Ages. Even in those African and Asian regions subjugated by Islam, Christian loyalties survived for centuries.

Contrary to the historical maps with which we are familiar, Christian lights did not just fade out following the arrival of the Muslims. Initially, Muslim rulers made little effort to encourage conversion, partly for the solid practical reason that converts to Islam ceased to pay the special taxes levied on unbelievers, so that it literally paid to keep Christian subjects Christian. The persecutions that did occur were sporadic, and usually directed against monks and clergy rather than ordinary believers. Not until the later Middle Ages did the mystical Sufi orders begin the process of popular evangelism for Islam, and they did this by offering former Christians a package of familiar practices that included saints, shrines, relics and pilgrimages, and a veneration for the ascetic Prophet Jesus. The genius of the Sufis was to present the Muslim faith in catholic forms.[10]

Under Muslim rule, patriarchates like Alexandria, Constantinople, and Antioch continued to be vital centers of ecclesiastical authority, still commanding the allegiance of millions of followers. Through the tenth century, the patriarchs of Alexandria occupied a powerful role under the Muslim rulers, and when the royal capital moved to the upstart city of Cairo, so did the patriarch's residence. Christian primates "were often used as ambassadors, consulted for political advice, or even solicited for prayer." Muslim rulers respected the countless distinctions they found among their Christian subjects. They recognized each denomination or theological tradition as a separate *millet,* a community under its own laws and courts and governed by its own particular clerical structures.[11]

Christians enjoyed nothing like what modern Americans construe as religious liberty, and there were stringent limits on any kind of Christian expansion. Seizures of church property are painfully symbolized by the fate of Constantinople's church of Hagia Sophia, once the greatest church in the world, which in the fifteenth century became a mosque. (Today, it is secularized as a museum.) Still, most Christian groups survived quite successfully into modern times. For many so-called heretics, like the Monophysites, Muslim rulers were no worse than Christian Byzantine emperors, and were less intrusive.

Egypt offers a telling example of Christian persistence. Partly, the Egyptian church retained such a mass following because of its enthusiastic adoption of the native Coptic language. At least the gospels and psalter were already available in Coptic by around 300. Elsewhere in North Africa, the church's insistence on speaking Latin meant that it never evangelized far beyond the cities, so that Christianity did not long survive the Muslim conquests. But Egypt offered a very different picture. At the start of the twentieth century, Coptic Christians here comprised 10 or 20 percent of that nation's people. Today, the official figure is around 5 percent, but most observers believe that is a serious underestimate. The modern Coptic Church claims 10 million members.[12]

The fact of Coptic survival is all the more remarkable when we recall just who these "Copts" are. Their name is a corruption of *Aigyptos,* that is, native Egyptians, and their language descends from the tongue of the pyramid-builders. When modern scholars translated the hieroglyphics on the Rosetta Stone, they did so by using the language they found spoken in the liturgies of the Coptic Church. The Syrian Orthodox churches, similarly, still use a kind of Syriac that is close to the Aramaic spoken by Jesus himself. At so many points, the living Christianity of Egypt, Syria, Palestine, Ethiopia, and Armenia takes us back to the earliest centuries of the faith, a time when the followers of Jesus were developing cells of believers within a still vibrant Roman Empire.

Far from being merely a tattered remnant, Christian communities would on occasion emerge as leaders within the Middle East, and seldom more so than in the twentieth century. As Arab countries struggled to respond to the dual challenges of modernization and Western domination, it was mainly Christian activists who created a ferment of ideas and policies, who initiated the various nationalist and socialist movements that swept the region in mid-century. Christians founded the Arab nationalist Ba'ath movement that still rules Syria and Iraq. Writing of Syria in the mid-1990s, William Dalrymple observed that "Five of [President] Asad's seven closest advisers are Christians." Christians led the Arab Communist parties, which have always had their strongest support in the Christian areas of countries like Palestine and Iraq. Christians founded and led many of the most militant groups in the Palestinian nationalist cause. Across the nationalist and socialist spectrum, we regularly find Arab leaders bearing characteristically Christian names like Michael, Anthony, and George. Edward Said, probably the best-known Arab intellectual in the Western world, comes from a Palestinian Christian family. Arab Christians remained politically powerful until the rise of a new Muslim fundamentalism in the 1980s.[13]

NUMBERS

Just how numerous were the Christian communities that survived under Muslim rule? As late as the twelfth and thirteenth centuries, Christians still made up a large proportion of most former Roman territories that had fallen under Muslim rule, in societies like Syria, Mesopotamia, and Egypt, and it is not easy to tell when Muslims actually gained majority status in these communities. A reasonable guess would place the transition around the time of the Crusades, about 1100 or 1200. As late as 1280, the patriarch of the (Monophysite) Jacobite sect still "oversaw 20 metropolitans and about 100 bishops from Anatolia and Syria to lower Mesopotamia and Persia." By way of comparison, the English church at the same time had just two metropolitans (Canterbury and York) and twenty-five bishops. And the Jacobites were just one Christian denomination among several.[14]

As in Egypt, large Christian communities survived until modern times in nations like Syria, Lebanon, Palestine, Iraq, and Turkey, indicating that they must have been still more numerous in bygone years. Even in 1900, Christians and Jews combined might have made up 30 percent of the total population of the Ottoman Empire. In the core Ottoman lands of Anatolia, the area that we today call Turkey, a substantial Christian population lasted until the early twentieth century, and Muslims were not even a majority in Constantinople itself. Christian communities survived until they were destroyed by a series of wars, expulsions, and population exchanges between 1915 and 1925. At the time of the establishment of the state of Israel, perhaps 20 percent of Palestinian Arabs were still Christian. Even today, after decades of decline and sporadic massacres, perhaps 10 percent of Syrians are Christian.[15]

Modern notions of medieval Christianity draw heavily on images of France and Western Europe, which are portrayed as priest-ridden, theocratic states, with little tolerance for Jews or heretics. We may be surprised to realize that through much of the Middle Ages, a large proportion of the world's Christians themselves lived under the political power of a hostile faith. Not just in Roman times, substantial numbers of Christians lived as despised minorities. In pre-revolutionary Russia, the common word for "peasant" was *Krest'ianin,* which derives from "Christian," recalling a time when the rural masses preserved their faith in the face of Tatar and Muslim invasion. As so often in medieval times, the Christians were the oppressed poor and ignorant, rather than the sophisticated town-dwellers.

In some areas, Eastern churches actually expanded through missionary successes beyond the bounds of the Muslim world. Most spectacular among the growing churches were the Nestorian Christians, who had been labeled as heretical in late Roman times. From their bases in Syria and Persia, Nestorian missionaries penetrated deeply into Central Asia and China by the seventh century, following the silk route. The Nestorians and their "luminous doctrine" were welcomed at the imperial court, and in 638, a church was erected in the capital of Ch'ang-an, then perhaps the largest city in the world. The church enjoyed 200 years of peace and toleration, before succumbing to persecution by the tenth century. Even so, the Nestorian church revived in China in the twelfth and thirteenth centuries, and launched missionary efforts still farther afield, probably into Southeast Asia. Christianity has been in China for a very long time—about as long, in fact, as Buddhism has been in Japan, or Christianity in England.[16]

Another mission field was in southern India, where the ubiquitous Syrian missionaries founded native Christian communities that claimed to follow St. Thomas, *Mar Thoma*. (Since long-established trade routes connected southern India with the Mediterranean world, Christianity may indeed have reached India as early as the second century, or even the first.) Reflecting the vast sphere of Eastern Christianity, these Indian Christians spoke Syriac and retained their links with the Nestorian patriarch of Babylon, who resided at Baghdad. Today, the Indian state of Kerala has some 7 million "Thomas Christians," divided among Catholic, Protestant, and Orthodox traditions. The oriental triumphs of the Nestorians gave rise to the persistent Western myth of Prester John, a great Christian priest-king dwelling beyond the Muslim world.[17]

The size of the Christian communities in the East is significant because in the Middle Ages, the Eastern lands were more densely populated than those of Europe. Medieval England and France were Christian states, while the regimes of Egypt and Syria were solidly Muslim, but there may have been more Christians all told in the Eastern states than the Western, and the Easterners possessed at least as active a cultural and spiritual life. When judging the population of "Christian Europe," we should also recall that large parts of Europe did not even nominally accept Christianity until well into the Middle Ages. Russia and the Scandinavian lands were both converted around 1000, but Lithuania, then a major state dominating much of Eastern Europe, did not formally accept Christianity until 1387. In the thirteenth century, the height of medieval Christian civilization in Europe, there may have been more Christian believers on the continent of Asia than in Europe, while Africa still had populous Christian communities.

My estimates differ from those of the standard reference source, namely the *World Christian Encyclopedia,* which has made a valiant effort to

TABLE 2.1
Distribution of Christians in Ancient and Medieval Times

Continent	Christians (in millions) Year			
	500	1000	1200	1500
Africa	8	5	2.5	1.3
Asia	21.2	16.8	21	3.4
Europe/Russia	14.2	28.6	46.6	76.3
GLOBAL TOTAL	43.4	50.4	70.1	81

Source: David B. Barrett, *World Christian Encyclopedia* (Nairobi, Kenya: Oxford University Press, 1982), 796.

quantify Christian strength through history (see table 2.1).[18] According to the first edition of this work, Europe gained its preeminence earlier than I have suggested, probably around the tenth century. It is hard to be certain about any of this. Historical demography is a painfully uncertain science, especially where religious minorities are concerned. Even today, governments underplay the size of inconvenient minorities, and in earlier times, it was much easier for dissidents to live far removed from centers of government, from elite agencies and census takers. But the figures offered by the *Encyclopedia* are multiply unlikely. The Christian population of Egypt alone in 1200 was probably around 3 million, and that takes no account of Ethiopia and Nubia, so the figures suggested for Africa probably understate Christian numbers by about half. The undercount for Asia may be just as serious. On balance, I would argue that at the time of the Magna Carta or the Crusades, if we imagine a typical Christian, we should still be thinking not of a French artisan, but of a Syrian peasant or Mesopotamian town-dweller, an Asian not a European.

The persistence of Christian communities under Islam challenges contemporary attitudes toward historical conflicts between the two faiths. In recent years, a powerful social movement has demanded that the West, and specifically the churches, apologize for the medieval crusading movement. In this view, the Crusades represented aggression, pure and simple, against the Muslim world, and nobody can deny the resulting wars involved their share of atrocities. Underlying the movement for apology, though, is the assumption that religious frontiers are somehow carved in stone, and that the Muslim-ruled states of the Near East must always and infallibly have been destined to form part of the world of Islam. An equally good case can be made that the medieval Middle East was no more inevitably Muslim than other regions conquered by Islam and subsequently liberated, like Spain and Hungary. Nor, curiously, do Westerners suggest that Muslims apologize for the aggressive acts that gave them power over these various lands in the first place. Westerners have simply forgotten the once-great Christian communities of the Eastern world.

RUIN

If Christians survived the Muslim conquests so successfully, then why are they such a small minority in the Middle East today? The answer must be sought in political events of the later Middle Ages, when interfaith relations were transformed, swiftly and horribly. The change was heralded promisingly enough in the early thirteenth century, when rumors told how Prester John's forces were on the march, and were on their way to assist the West against the Muslims. Great military forces were indeed operating in Asia, but they were in fact the Mongol hordes, the first of a wave of invasions that over the next 200 years would devastate most of the centers of civilization in the Middle East. In the process, some of the most ancient Christian communities would be eliminated. The ruin of Mesopotamia in the 1250s was a catastrophe for Christians no less than Muslims.

Yet Christians could still take hope from these events. Middle Eastern Christians initially saw the Mongol invaders as potential liberators from the Muslim yoke, and they took the opportunity to revenge themselves on their Muslim conquerors. The Mongol king who sacked Baghdad in 1258 had a Christian queen, and at her behest, the Mongols destroyed many mosques. There were prominent converts at the Mongol court, due in large measure to Nestorian efforts, and it was quite feasible that the whole nation could be converted. Seeing glorious prospects, the Western crusaders allied with these Asian invaders. Christian hopes culminated during the Mongol invasion of Palestine in 1260, which was led by a Christian Turkish warlord. This campaign ended though with the battle of 'Ayn Jalut, where the Muslim Mamluk Turks won decisively. Inexplicably, 'Ayn Jalut has escaped the attention of those counterfactual historians who like to ask "what if?" and who imagine alternate scenarios. Had the Mongols won, their victory could well have consolidated Christian power across much of Asia, virtually destroying Islam in the process.

In reality, it was the Christians who suffered ruin. The Mongols were driven out, and the last crusader states perished shortly afterward. Seeing the wave of Muslim victories, the Mongols came to believe that it was the

God of Islam who was favoring his worshipers, and they accepted conversion. Meanwhile, the remaining Middle Eastern Christians found their situation dreadfully changed, as they were persecuted as quislings for their actions during the Mongol onslaught. Since 'Ayn Jalut was such a decisive disaster for Asian Christianity, its location has an awful irony: it stands very close to the source of the faith, at Nazareth. Conditions grew still worse for Christians in the fourteenth century, when Asia was struck repeatedly by plague and a general population contraction. The cumulative disasters resulted in the rise of new regimes, which were intolerant and inward-looking. While European Christians blamed the Jews for the disasters of the age, Muslim governments turned against Christians, who suffered repeated pogroms and forced mass conversions.[19]

In China too, Christians were associated with the Mongol regime, and they fell victim to a nationalist reaction when the Ming dynasty came to power in 1368. This movement was disastrous for Christian communities, who at their height may have been several hundred thousand strong, counting both Nestorians and Roman Catholics. In the early fifteenth century, the bloody career of Timur (Tamerlane) uprooted Christian societies across Eurasia, marking the end of the great Nestorian adventure. By the sixteenth century, there is no evidence of any organized Christian activity in China, and precious few remnants of the faith anywhere in Central Asia. Table 2.1 indicates the catastrophic decline of Christian populations across the continent between 1350 and 1500. In Africa also, Christianity stood in deep peril. The Christian state of Nubia succumbed to Muslim pressure around 1450, and Ethiopia was almost wiped out in a deadly jihad in the early sixteenth century, "a systematic campaign of cultural and national genocide." Although the church and kingdom survived, Ethiopian culture was all but annihilated.[20]

Even in Europe, the late Middle Ages witnessed a steep decline in Christian power in the face of Muslim expansion under the Ottoman Turks. Ever larger numbers of Christians found themselves under Muslim rule, and the trend did not begin to be reversed until the 1680s. This point deserves stressing in view of the modern image of a predatory Christian West ever seeking to expand its dominion over an unsuspecting world. As late as the seventeenth century, Muslim power was still pressing hard on the frontiers of Germany; and in the age of Shakespeare, Muslim pirates regularly raided the coasts of northern and western Europe, taking tens of thousands of Christian slaves. If we want to picture the lights of Christianity fading on an imaginary map of the world, with the Christian faith largely confined to

Europe, then this is the point at which we should do so, a full thousand years after the fall of the Roman Empire in the West.

THE CATHOLIC MISSIONS

At this point, too, about 1500, we can first glimpse the pattern of Christian expansion familiar from popular stereotypes, namely a religion borne by European warships and muskets to vulnerable natives in Africa or South America. Yet even then, these missions (if we can so dignify them) succeeded only to the extent that they created a religious structure that meshed with local cultures and beliefs. Even when carried by the armed force of European empires, the newly planted Christianity in Africa, Asia, and South America swiftly acquired local roots.

From about 1500, western powers like Spain and Portugal began a global expansion, ostensibly under the flag of Christianity. By the end of the six- teenth century, the Roman Catholic Church looked more like a genuinely global institution than at any time in its history, and far more so than dur- ing the time of the Roman Empire, which it had long outlived. Whereas the Romans merely dominated the Mediterranean world, the standards of Catholic powers like Spain and Portugal were flying in Asia, Africa, and the Americas. By 1580, the Iberian powers had largely completed their conquest of the New World to the west, while soldiers and merchants were pushing eastward from Europe into the Indies. When the Spaniards established an imperial sea route from Mexico to Manila, the twin ventures were merging into a global strategy on a scale never before witnessed on the planet. The popes supported Iberian missionary endeavors, above all in South America and the Philippines. Manila had an archdiocesan see by 1595, and over the next century the nation would be extensively Christianized. To put this chronology in context, regions like Mexico, the Philippines and the Kongo first received their Christianity only a century or so after the conversion of Europe was completed by the submission of Lithuania.[21]

In religious terms, the greatest long-term Catholic successes would be in Central and South America, where the conquered peoples all accepted forms of Catholicism, heavily mixed with local beliefs. This particular expansion of Christianity remains one of the most controversial, since it was undoubtedly associated with a brutal conquistador regime at least as inter- ested in winning treasure as in saving native souls. When challenged with his failure to convert and teach the natives of Peru, the conquistador Pizarro replied, frankly enough, that "I have not come for any such reasons; I have come to take away from them their gold." As far as we can reconstruct the voices of the native peoples, they saw the coming of Christian civilization as an undiluted disaster. One Mayan prophetic book records of the coming of the Spanish: "Here they arrived, with the true God, the true Lord, the cause of our misery." When the conquerors tried to destroy every written remnant of the ancient Meso-American civilization, all its literature and science no less than its religious materials, they were perpetrating one of the gravest crimes in the history of civilization.[22]

It is a mild defense to say that at least some of the worst charges about the conquest are false. Twentieth-century scholars produced vastly inflated estimates of the pre-Columbian native population, which implied that the European contact had caused one of the worst acts of genocide in human history. More realistic population figures show that while the new Catholic world was initially founded upon conquest and exploitation, the "American genocide" charges are no more than a contemporary academic myth. Yet the new Christianity was unquestionably associated with robbery and tyranny, leaving a sinister heritage over the coming centuries.[23]

In formal terms, the conversion of Central and Southern America was steady and impressive. Already in the 1520s, there were eight bishoprics in the Antilles, and the first sees were appearing in Mexico itself. By the 1570s the continent had an extensive network of bishoprics looking to metropolitan sees at Mexico City and Lima, and Lima was ruling congregations spread over what would later be the nations of Peru, Ecuador, Bolivia, and Chile. Natives were baptized in vast numbers, on occasion running to thousands in a single day. Some religious orders, especially Dominicans and Jesuits, struggled heroically to prevent natives from being exploited by greedy European colonists.[24]

Yet at least in the initial decades, the depth of these conversions was questionable. For the first century or two after the conquest, the church made little effort to educate or evangelize, once native peoples had given formal assent to the faith. This severely limited penetration outside the cities and provincial towns. Moreover, native converts were granted admission to communion only on the rarest occasions, a policy that acknowledged the shallowness of conversions. Just as seriously, natives were almost never ordained to the priesthood. Learned councils reserved ordination for purebred Europeans, who were untainted by Indian or African blood. This excluded not just Indians but also the growing population of mixed-blood *mestizos*. Papal instructions tried to overrule these prohibitions, but in practice they were not entirely lifted until the end of the eighteenth century.[25]

Far from being a formula for effective conversion, the record of colonial Latin America sounds potentially like a story of disaster, so much so that it is baffling that Catholicism would ultimately plant such deep roots in this continent. Yet the ordinary people who were ignored and despised by the churches created their own religious synthesis, which became the focus of devoted loyalty. Lacking priests and access to church sacraments, Latin American people concentrated instead on aspects of the faith that needed no clergy, on devotions to saints and the Virgin, and they organized worship through lay bodies like confraternities, the *cofradías*. These practices flourished in the magnificent churches built by the conquerors at once to inspire and overawe their subjects. As a result, Catholicism not only established itself, but became an integral part of the cultural identity of Latin Americans, in all parts of that very diverse landscape. As an institution, the church made an impact that was partial and often inadequate, but Christianity itself flourished. It is a distinction we will often see.

BEYOND THE BORDERS

It is easy to see the Catholic expansion efforts in terms of imperial arrogance, of imposing European standards upon the rest of the globe, but in many cases, the missionaries found themselves in no position to enforce their will politically. Catholic missionaries also sought converts beyond the immediate reach of the European empires, in lands where they could not call on fleets and armies to protect them. Naturally, the Christianity of these other regions developed very differently from that of Peru or the Philippines.

Portuguese Catholics introduced Christianity into the territories they dominated along the western coast of Africa, but in most areas, European control was confined to trading and military centers. Yet missionaries also penetrated independent kingdoms inland, as in Angola. In the powerful realm of Kongo, a king was baptized in 1491. Observers over the next two centuries remarked on how widely the Kongolese people knew and accepted Catholic Christianity, at least as thoroughly as their South American counterparts. This was no mere conversion for convenience, for the purpose of securing European guns and gold. One of the first Christian Kongo rulers, Mvemba Nzinga, has been described as "one of the greatest lay Christians in African church history." In 1516, a Portuguese priest wrote of Kongo's king Afonso that "Better than we, he knows the prophets and the Gospel of our Lord Jesus Christ, and all the lives of the saints, and all things regarding our Mother the Holy Church."[26]

Already in the sixteenth century, a Kongo monarch received the papal title "Defender of the Faith," which had hitherto been bestowed on England's Henry VIII. Unlike Henry's family, though, the Kongolese monarchy devotedly upheld the Catholic religion. In 1596, São Salvador became a diocese in its own right. During the next century, Christianity thoroughly penetrated the local society and thought-world, although without supplanting traditional African lifestyles. The kingdom was dominated by "a literate elite, dressing partially in European clothes, and professing Catholicism." Native kings and dukes bore names like Andrew, Peter, John, and Afonso, and the state capital was named São Salvador, for the Holy Savior. By 1700, Kongolese Catholicism was already in its sixth generation.[27]

THE SILK STRATEGY

Catholic missionaries became particularly creative when they encountered the unfamiliar social environments of China, Japan, and the Indian states. Lacking imperial backing, the missionaries (above all, the Jesuits) had to insinuate themselves into local societies, and in so doing, they had to deal with many of the later dilemmas about adapting the traditions of a European church to a non-European reality. Christian leaders were forced to redefine the relationship between Christianity and Europeanness, and to ask whether accepting the faith implied a need to take on board the assorted cultural baggage. How far should strict ideals of orthodoxy be sacrificed in pursuit of a successful missionary strategy? And how many of the church's accepted practices were in reality reflections of European custom and prejudice, rather than essentials of the faith? All are, of course, very relevant questions today. Equally sensitive, then and now, was the matter of European political control. Time and again, missions collapsed when those being introduced to the new faith feared that they might be subjecting themselves to some kind of foreign imperial domination.

Issues of accommodating local customs and practices surfaced repeatedly. In seventeenth-century India, the Jesuit Robert De Nobili succeeded by effectively posing as a Hindu guru, who instructed his disciples in the mysteries of Christianity. He wore local dress and respected the complex Indian caste system. His doing so was controversial because caste symbols implied a belief in reincarnation and former lives. Also, acknowledging caste meant refusing to treat the poorest on terms of equality, violating the teachings of Jesus. Still, this represented a successful missionary strategy, and perhaps the only one that could have worked in the setting of the time.[28] For future missionaries, the lesson was obvious. Adapting the gospel to local cultures was the path to growth, while trying to force Asians or Africans into a Western straitjacket invited disaster. The enlightened Jesuit position was that as long as converts accepted Catholic Christianity, it could certainly be Catholicism of a Chinese, Indian, or Japanese variety, just as Europe had its French and Spanish species of the common truth.

A similar cultural dilemma arose in Japan, over the seemingly trivial issue of preference in dress: should Christian priests wear silk or cotton? If cotton, missionaries were identifying with the poorest and most despised, and following appropriate rules of Christian humility, but Fathers dressed thus would not be welcomed into the homes of the upper classes. If they chose silk—as they ultimately did—this identified them as members of the social elite, who could win the respect of lords and gentry. The silk strategy worked splendidly in gaining the adherence of Japanese elites, who would in turn order the conversion of their followers and tenants. For decades, success followed success, so that by about 1600, it seemed that Japan would soon be a Catholic nation. Nagasaki became a bishopric in 1596, and the first ordinations of Japanese priests followed in 1601. Hundreds of thousands of Japanese were baptized.[29]

Disastrously, though, the extent of Catholic successes provoked a nationalist reaction. Hostility was all the more intense when the Japanese heard some European Catholics talk wildly of turning the nation into a Spanish colony just as subservient as the Philippines. Catholic hopes of mass conversion were dashed by a severe persecution, which claimed thousands of lives. The story is familiar from the novels of Shusako Endo, creator of some of the greatest Christian writings of the past century. Japanese Catholicism survived clandestinely into the twentieth century, when its vestiges received a far greater blow than could have been inflicted by all the native regimes. In 1945, the second atomic bomb used against Japan destroyed the city of Nagasaki, the country's Catholic stronghold.

Despite the Japanese debacle, Catholics found that another door opened promptly as Jesuit missions began to achieve stunning successes in China, then as now the world's most populous nation. Here too, Catholics followed the silk approach, presenting themselves in the familiar garb of scholars, and converting nobles and intellectuals. They offered prospective converts whatever Western learning might be of interest to the highly developed Chinese civilization. The pivotal figure in the missions was the celebrated Matteo Ricci, who arrived in China in 1589. The Jesuit venture survived the collapse of the Ming regime in 1644, and won at least equal favor from the succeeding Manchu dynasty.[30]

The Jesuits were very sensitive to issues of cultural adaptation, and spurned attempts to impose European values. From the first, the missionaries tried to transform Christianity into a form that would be comprehensible and relevant to the Chinese. The liturgy and scriptures were translated into Chinese, which meant choosing one of several possible Chinese terms for God. In the event the missionaries chose *T'ien,* a term familiar in Chinese philosophy and usually translated as "heaven"; they addressed God as *Shang-ti,* Lord of Heaven. The Jesuits took a relaxed attitude to deep-rooted Chinese customs and practices, preferring to absorb peacefully anything not flagrantly contrary to Christian teaching. The missionaries were supported by the Vatican and its *Propaganda* office, which in 1659 asked, perceptively, "What could be more absurd than to transport France, Spain, Italy or some other European country to China? Do not introduce all that to them but only the faith. It is the nature of men to love and treasure above everything else their own country and that which belongs to it. In consequence, there is no stronger cause for alienation and hate than an attack on local customs, especially when these go back to a venerable antiquity."[31] This principle meant respecting the Chinese veneration for ancestors and the philosophy of Confucius.

The late seventeenth century was a glorious time for the Chinese missions, as in 1692, Christians earned an edict of toleration from the ruling Emperor Kang Xi. The prospects were intoxicating: Kang Xi was arguably the most powerful ruler in the world at the time, ruling perhaps 150 million subjects, a population equivalent to that of the whole of Europe, including Russia. Historically minded Catholics recalled that the conversion of the Roman Empire had also begun with an edict of toleration from a friendly emperor. Yesterday, Rome; tomorrow, China? Winning many converts, the missionaries advanced Chinese clergy, and Luo Wenzao, the first Catholic bishop of Chinese origin, was consecrated in 1685. By 1700, China had around 200,000 Catholics, many of whom were well-placed politically.

The Catholic missions in China can be regarded as one of the great might-have-beens in world history. If China had been converted in the seventeenth century, the impact on the future history of Christianity would have been incalculable, as would the effects on the religious balance in Europe itself. A converted China would have provided a cultural beacon for Japan, Korea, Vietnam, and ultimately the whole of Asia. But of course, it was not to be.

The Jesuit cultural compromise fell apart at the end of the seventeenth century, when the Society's enemies succeeded in turning the popes against them. Within a few years, Jesuits came under repeated attack for permitting the Chinese to worship ancestors, canonizing Saint Confucius, and including the names of pagan gods in the translated scriptures. By 1704, the Vatican ruled decisively against the Society of Jesus, prohibiting the Chinese Rites and ordering the suppression of recent Bible translations. Henceforth, religious services were to be held strictly in Latin. Just as bad, the papal envoys who declared the new regulations also made high claims for the political role of the Vatican, a foreign presence that could not be tolerated by the Chinese emperors. As the emperor understood, prophetically, "I know that at the present time there is nothing to fear, but when your ships come by thousands, then there will probably be great disorder."[32] In 1724, the Chinese government responded to these accumulated insults by proscribing the Christian faith. As the Catholic Church became ostentatiously a foreign body, it invited persecution on a scale that eliminated most of the Jesuits' successes by the end of the eighteenth century.

The effects of the new policy were not confined to China. In the same years, the Church began to insist on similar conformity among the Catholic Christians of India, and the effects there were almost as severe. From about 1700 too, the Kongolese church now began a long period of decline, which represents one of the greatest wasted opportunities in the story of African Christianity. Political fragmentation in the Kongo state was partly to blame, but much more significant was the Church's refusal to approve native liturgies and its reluctance to ordain African clergy. Nor was the Vatican willing to grant other key concessions to African values, including a married clergy—a model that was accepted elsewhere, in parts of Eastern Europe and the Middle East. The Chinese Rites debacle, and the cultural rigidity it symbolized, crippled the progress of Catholic missions worldwide for over a century.

THE GREAT CENTURY

Up to the end of the eighteenth century, large-scale missionary efforts were strictly the preserve of the Catholic powers, a point of superiority proudly stressed by Catholic controversialists. How could the upstart Protestants claim to be a true church since they self-evidently neglected Jesus' Great Commission to preach the gospel to all nations? In the 1790s, however, Protestants took up this challenge. This was partly a consequence of the evangelical revival and partly due to the unprecedented power and reach of the British Empire. Protestants, particularly from the British Isles, now entered the missionary movement in earnest. In the space of a decade, global missions acquired the kind of enthusiastic backing that they would retain through the colonial era. In 1792, modern missionary work began with the formation of London's Baptist Missionary Society, a venture that was soon challenged by the London Missionary Society (Congregationalist, 1795) and the Anglican-sponsored Church Missionary Society (1799). The new United States shared in the missionary excitement, with its own newly founded missionary Boards and Societies.[33]

Missions now became a major focus for Protestant activists. In 1793, William Carey began his fanatical campaign to convert India, under the famous slogan that would inspire countless successors: "Expect great things from God, and attempt great things for God." China, too, attracted the rapt attention of European evangelicals. By 1807, the first Protestant missionary had set up shop in Canton. Africa also attracted fervent interest, partly due to the greatly enhanced knowledge of the continent's geography. In 1799, Mungo Park's *Travels in the Interior Districts of Africa* alerted European Protestants to the vast mission field awaiting harvest in the western parts of the continent. Also, new political footholds now developed. Colonies for freed slaves were created—at Sierra Leone in 1787 and Liberia in 1821—and in each case, the new settlers had had extensive firsthand contact with Christianity. When the British established themselves at the Cape of Good Hope in 1806, Protestant mission work began in earnest across southern Africa.[34]

These events began what is justifiably regarded as the great missionary century. As we have seen, though, this was quite different from the sudden Christian expansion so often portrayed in modern accounts of European imperialism. In many cases, as in India, China, and large parts of Africa, Christian missionaries were not so much breaking new ground as reopening ancient and quite familiar mines. In the 1880s, missionaries in the Kongo met with mass enthusiasm that would be difficult to explain if we did not realize that the people were rediscovering what had been the national religion only a century or so earlier.[35]

Undeniably, the Christian missions of this historical phase were intimately connected with political and imperial adventures, and Protestant and Catholic fortunes followed the successes of the different empires. Protestant expansion across Africa neatly followed the spreading rule of the Union Jack, while the French led the way for the Catholic cause in both Africa and Asia. The linkage between religion and empire is neatly epitomized by the experience of southern Uganda, where Catholics were colloquially known as *baFaransa* ("the French") and Protestants were *baIngerezza* ("the English").[36] Both British and French colonial authorities combined missionary endeavors with struggles against African slavery, so that imperial power was justified by both religious and humanitarian activities.

By the mid-nineteenth century, the missionary impulse reached new heights as most of the African continent came within European reach and the military defeat of China opened that country to new activity. In 1858, a new generation of prospective missionaries was inspired by the appearance of David Livingstone's book, *Missionary Travels and Researches in South Africa*. Many of the legendary missionaries of this era began their career in mid-century, while whole new areas of Africa were opened in the 1870s by the establishment of missions around Lake Malawi and in Uganda. Catholic evangelism also flourished, institutionalized in new orders like the Holy Ghost Fathers (Spiritans) and the White Fathers. The French even tried to evangelize in the Muslim world, and a bishopric was created at Algiers in 1838. It was an archbishop of Algiers, Cardinal Charles Lavigerie (1865– 92), who had the most systematic vision of a concerted imperial campaign to convert the whole of Africa. For Lavigerie, Christianity was resuming its ancient dominance in Africa, in which the Muslim age had been merely an unhappy interval, a thousand-year night that was now ending. Reinforcing this claim to ancient continuity, the pope gave him the title of Archbishop of Carthage and primate of Africa. Lavigerie dreamed of a kind of modern-day crusading order, a well-armed *militia Christi,* which would wander Africa defending pilgrims and fighting slave-traders.[37]

In later decades, these Anglo-French successes attracted jealous imitators. Across Africa, each new entrant into the imperial stakes sought to justify its existence by the rhetoric of missionary endeavor: Germans, Italians, Belgians, all were ostensibly there to convert the poor heathen. Elsewhere in the world, American Christians in particular saw their destiny in China. By the 1920s, at the height of the Euro-American adventure in China, perhaps 8,000 Western missionaries were active in that country. Americans claimed their nation had a special role in the divine plan. In 1893, a World Parliament of Religions that met in Chicago was intended to celebrate the imminent global triumph not just of Christianity but of that religion in its liberal, Protestant, and quintessentially American form. In this view, the age to come would be the American century, and also, inevitably, the Christian century (the magazine of that name was founded in 1902). If anyone doubted the truth of this vision, they would be reassured by the vast achievements of American missionaries throughout Africa and Asia, and especially in China. By the 1950s, the United States was supplying two-thirds of the 43,000 Protestant missionaries active around the world.[38]

For all the hypocrisy and the flagrantly self-serving rhetoric of the imperial age, the dedication of the missionaries was beyond question. Knowing
as they did the extreme dangers from violence and tropical disease, it is
inconceivable that so many would have been prepared to lay down their
lives for European commerce alone, and many certainly viewed missionary
work as a ticket to martyrdom. Their numbers and their zeal both grew
mightily after each successive revival in the West, especially when such an
event coincided with a spectacular tale of exploration and martyrdom.

Also, for all their association with imperialism, nineteenth-century missionaries did make important concessions to native cultures. Crucially,
Protestants from the very first recognized the absolute necessity of offering
the faith in local languages, so the Bible was now translated, in whole or in
part, into many African and Asian tongues. In many ways, Protestant missionaries were just as shortsighted as the Catholics in their willingness to
respect colonized peoples, but in the matter of language, Protestants had a
clear advantage.

Both Protestants and Catholics were often realistic about the cultural
problems they faced in presenting a universal faith in a colonial European
guise. In fact, they faced exactly the same debates that their predecessors
had encountered over how far they should go native in order to win converts. Particularly when venturing into dangerous territories, the temptation was to rely on the protection of European bureaucrats and soldiers, but
a Christianity established by those means was not likely to gain many converts. At its worst, this policy threatened to create a segregated veranda
Christianity, in which paternalistic European clergy literally refused to admit
native converts into their houses.[39] Farsighted evangelists recognized this
peril. The founder of the Holy Ghost Fathers warned trainee missionaries
that "You are not going to Africa in order to establish there Italy or France
or any such country. . . . Make yourselves Negroes with the Negroes. . . .
Our holy religion has invariably to be established in the soil."[40] On the same
principle, some Protestant missionaries in China abandoned the European
clothing and lifestyle that gave them protection and prestige, but also separated them from ordinary people. One of the great Protestant movements
of this period was the China Inland Missions (CIM), founded in 1865.
Members wore Chinese dress, and sported the pigtail or queue that symbolized submission to the imperial dynasty: they were to be "all things to
all men." By 1900, the CIM was directing some 800 missionaries.[41]

In their openness to native cultures, missionaries were sometimes far in
advance of secular politicians. Imperialist statesmen were slow to imagine
a future in which the colonized peoples might be emancipated to indepen-

dence. Even as late as the 1950s, few British or French leaders thought they would live to see the end of direct European control of Africa. In contrast, at least some early missionaries happily accepted that their own contributions only represented a temporary historical phase. Even in the 1850s, Henry Venn of the Church Missionary Society knew that missions would give way to churches on the banks of the Niger or the Congo, just as they once had in the lands of the Rhine and the Thames. Venn spoke, unforgettably, of the coming "euthanasia of the mission." The transition would come through a "three self" policy, in which the church should be built on principles of self-government, self-support, and self-propagation. The result would be "a native church under native pastors and a native episcopate."[42] These visions became clouded during the years of highest imperialist fervor, when, drunk with sight of power, some church leaders were speaking of an indefinite period of global white supremacy. Even so, ideas of future native autonomy never vanished entirely.

For any missionary venture, the ordination of native clergy must be the acid test of commitment to moving beyond an imperial context, to leaving the veranda. In this regard, the churches of the Great Century offered a mixed picture. Some bodies recorded early successes. In 1765, the Church of England ordained Philip Quaque of the Gold Coast as its first African priest. A century later, in the 1860s, the same church chose the Yoruba Samuel Adjai Crowther as its first non-European bishop, and deputed this learned "black Englishman" to found a missionary diocese in West Africa. Other churches followed suit in their respective territories, particularly the Protestant missions, and Chinese clergy were being ordained by the 1860s. Yet although the principle of native leadership was well established, it was not followed with any consistency. In 1914, the Roman Catholic Church worldwide had no bishops of non-Euro-American origin, except for a handful serving the Indian Thomas Christians in communion with Rome. In the whole of Africa, the Catholic Church ordained only a handful of native priests before 1920.[43]

Yet for all the uncertainties about native clergy, all the mixed messages about presenting Christianity in native terms, the successes were very striking. In 1800, perhaps one percent of all Protestant Christians lived outside Europe and North America. By 1900, that number had risen to 10 percent, and this proved enough of a critical mass to support further expansion. Today, the figure stands around two-thirds of all Protestants. Catholics also reaped their harvest. In 1914, the Catholic Church in Africa had 7 million baptized believers and a further million catechumens; these figures doubled by 1938. Put another way, in the late nineteenth century, Africa had about

10 million Christians of all denominations, including the Copts, about 9 percent of the continental total. By 1950, that figure had risen to 34 million, or 15 percent; by 1965, there were 75 million Christians, a quarter of the whole.[44] And although less spectacular, expansion in China nevertheless achieved more than in any previous age of Christian evangelization. Taking Protestants and Catholics together, China's Christian population stood at around 1.2 million in 1900, but 5 million or so by 1949.

Most modern Europeans or Americans cringe at the claims their ancestors made about their "civilizing mission" to the rest of the world. Still, where the Victorian enthusiasts proved more right than they could have dreamed was in their belief that Christianity would indeed make enormous strides in the years to come. In most ways, the twentieth century was anything but a Christian Century, since the horrors of those years made it look more like a new dark age than a golden age for any religion. Even so, Christianity would indeed enjoy worldwide success. To quote the late Stephen Neill, one of the great historians of the missionary movement, "in the twentieth century, for the first time, there was in the world a universal religion—the Christian religion."[45] In the third millennium, like the first, the faith would once again be a truly transcontinental phenomenon.

Missionaries and Prophets

> The three combined bodies—missionaries, government
> and companies, or gainers of money—do form the
> same rule to look upon the native with mockery eyes.
> It sometimes startles us to see that the three combined
> bodies are from Europe, and along with them there is
> a title "Christendom." And to compare or make a
> comparison between the Master of the title and his
> servants, it pushes any African away from believing
> the Master of the title. If we had power enough to
> communicate ourselves to Europe we would advise
> them not to call themselves 'Christendom' but
> 'Europeandom.'
> —*Charles Domingo, 1911, quoted in Adrian Hastings,*
> The Church in Africa, 1450–1950

It is one thing to talk about missionary successes and numbers, but quite another to determine the nature of the religious changes involved. The act of joining a church or sect is not necessarily the same as the internal process of conversion. While we can more or less measure the numbers declaring themselves Christian, the inner dynamics of religious change do not lend themselves to counting of any kind. Missions succeeded for different reasons in different times and places, and some new churches planted much deeper roots than others.[1] Yet many of these churches enjoyed remarkable success, to a degree that is impossible to understand if the new Christians were responding only out of fear or envy of the imperial conquerors. Amazing as it may appear to a blasé West, Christianity exercises an overwhelming global appeal, which shows not the slightest sign of waning.

"THE FAITH OF EUROPE"

The runaway successes of Christian missions to Africa or Asia are all the more striking in view of the extraordinarily poor image that such activities possess in Western popular thought. For many contemporary observers, the whole missionary enterprise epitomizes so much of what is wrong with Western culture. At their worst, missions are presented as a cynical arm of ruthless, racist, colonial exploitation. In 2000, U.S. television's Arts and Entertainment network showed a major documentary on the second millennium of Christianity, A.D. 1000–2000.[2] In the segment on the sixteenth century, the narration recounted how "Europeans sail the world, and wherever they go, whatever they explore, they bring with them the faith of Europe—Christianity. . . . However, Christian explorers bring more than just their faith. They also bring a profound sense of cultural superiority, and a lust for wealth." By the nineteenth century, "the missions became inseparable from the expanding western empires and their seemingly insatiable desire for profit."

Plenty of modern observers share this view. Kenyan leader Jomo Kenyatta complained that "When the missionaries came to Africa they had the Bible and we had the land. They said 'Let us pray.' We closed our eyes. When we opened them we had the Bible and they had the land." (The remark has been quoted by Archbishop Desmond Tutu, who is usually assumed to have originated it.) The Gikuyu people in Kenya had a saying that states, "There is no difference between missionary and settler."[3] For novelist Chinua Achebe too, Christianity was part of a larger package of colonial intrusion. As one of Achebe's characters remarks, "The white man, the new religion, the soldiers, the new road—they are all part of the same thing." Achebe's books often play on the idea of "whiteness," which in traditional African thought was an inauspicious color, connected with leprosy: "But now Ezeulu was becoming afraid that the new religion was like a leper. Allow him a handshake and he wants an embrace."[4]

Many Westerners sympathize with these views, seeing missionary Christianity as a kind of cultural leprosy. As European colonial empires were collapsing in the mid-twentieth century, it was fashionable for Third World writers to dismiss the Christian venture solely as misguided imperialism, and to argue that the effects were barely skin-deep. Christianity, it seemed, could make little impact on African social and especially sexual mores. To quote the disillusioned narrator of Mongo Beti's classic novel of colonial religion, *The Poor Christ of Bomba,* "I'm beginning to wonder myself whether the Christian religion really suits us, whether it's really made to the measure of the Blacks." In her scathing account of Western cultural imperialism, *The Almanac of the Dead,* Native American novelist Leslie Marmon Silko writes that "The Europeans . . . had gone through the motions with their priests, holy water, and churches built with Indian slave labor.

But their God had not accompanied them. The white man had sprinkled holy water and had prayed for almost five hundred years in the Americas, and still the Christian God was absent."[5]

At best, in the suspicious modern view, the missionary impulse manifested ignorant paternalism. Discussion of missions today is all too likely to produce lame sexual jokes about "the missionary position." The phrase conjures a whole mythology, of deeply repressed young Victorians attempting to spread their corrosive moral and sexual notions among a more liberated native population, who do not need such Western inhibitions, and would only be harmed by them. For a modern secular audience, the notion that the missionary enterprise might involve any authentically religious content, or might in fact be welcomed, seems ludicrous. When in 1995, journalist Christopher Hitchens published his snide attack on Mother Teresa of Calcutta, he chose the title *The Missionary Position,* since that phrase so effectively proclaimed what every educated Westerner is presumed to believe about Christian activities in the Third World.[6]

Of course, it is not long since that missionaries attracted deep respect, and even veneration: recall the heroic accounts of Dr. Livingstone. Twentieth-century stories in this tradition included *The Inn of the Sixth Happiness* (1958) and the fictional portrait of the China missionary played by Gregory Peck in the classic 1944 film *The Keys of the Kingdom.* In stark contrast to these works, we think of the many negative depictions of missionaries in recent film and fiction. Movies in this hyper-critical tradition include *Hawaii* (1966), *The Mission* (1986), *Black Robe* (1991), and *At Play in the Fields of the Lord* (1991).[7]

These recent works all offer a broadly similar view of the missionary enterprise. Above all, missions are wrongheaded, since all religious traditions are of roughly equal value, so what is the point of visiting the prejudices of one culture upon another? The vision of perfect relativism breaks down somewhat when Western Christianity is concerned, since it is seen as ipso facto a less valid and desirable model than those which it is seeking to replace. Commonly, Christianity is less an authentic religion than a package of Western prejudices and inhibitions. In Barbara Kingsolver's hugely successful novel *The Poisonwood Bible,* a missionary girl in the Belgian Congo recollects how "We came from Bethlehem, Georgia, bearing Betty Crocker cake mixes into the jungle." The overtly religious content of such missions is minimal—one girl "prayed the dumb prayers of our childhood: 'Our Father which art in heaven,' . . . I could not remotely believe any Shepherd was leading me through this dreadful valley, but the familiar words stuffed my mouth like cotton." Like the rest of her family, she is in Africa solely to humor her fanatical preacher father.[8]

Western attempts to export their own cultural sickness are all too obvious in matters of sexuality. In *Black Robe,* a young French Jesuit struggles with massive temptation after watching the healthy and frank sexual activities of the Native Canadian people he is trying to convert. When the missionary's daughter of *The Poisonwood Bible* arrives in the Congo, she is appalled by the overt sexuality she finds. African women sing joyous hymns of welcome, "with their bosoms naked as a jaybird's egg . . . all bare-chested and unashamed. . . . Am I the only one getting shocked to smithereens here?" Her father denounces "Nakedness and darkness of the soul! For we shall destroy this place where the loud clamor of the sinners is waxen great before the face of the Lord."[9] In these fictional works, this latter-day Dark Legend, the missionaries are so obsessed with their losing battles against temptation that they float on the edge of insanity. In *At Play in the Fields of the Lord,* the religious fanaticism and sexual repression of missionary Hazel Quarrier (played by Kathy Bates) bring her to psychic collapse.

Hostility to missionary activities is quite as intense within the churches themselves, or at least most of the liberal mainstream bodies. Whereas successful missions were once considered the richest ornament of an American or European church, the whole endeavor had become deeply suspect by the 1960s, the years of fastest decolonization. By 1970, African churches in particular were calling for a moratorium on Western missions because they stunted the growth of local initiatives. The equation seemed clear: missions were an arm of colonialism, and once the colonial governments were withdrawn, so also should their religious manifestations. Mainstream U.S. churches like the Lutherans and Episcopalians severely pruned their funds for missionary work, preferring to spend money on social programs at home.[10]

SOMETHING FELT IN THE MARROW

If the modern missionary stereotype had any force, we can scarcely understand why the Christian expansion proceeded as fast as it did, or how it could have survived the end of European political power. There must have been a great deal more to Southern Christianity than the European-driven mission movement. In some cases, the appeal of Christianity might indeed have been linked to a desire to emulate the West. Christianity was inextricably bound up with the all-conquering imperial nations, and thus with an image of success and modernity. This appealed to local elites, who could begin the conversion of their societies from the top down. Around the world, even cultures that rejected the full religious package tried to absorb some aspects of Christianity as part of a wider effort to modernize, and thus better to compete with the West. Nineteenth-century Hinduism was revolutionized by reform movements that explicitly borrowed from Christian thought, practice, and worship styles.[11]

But emulation cannot be the whole answer. If the faith had been a matter of kings, merchants, and missionaries, then it would have lasted precisely as long as the political and commercial order that gave it birth, and would have been swept away by any social change. Commonly, though, Christianity grew as a grassroots movement, appealing to a rich diversity of groups. In some cases, this might mean those on the margins of traditional societies. In his nuanced account of the conversion of the Igbo people of eastern Nigeria, Chinua Achebe describes how the faith gained its initial successes among the marginalized: "None of the converts was a man whose word was heeded in the assembly of the people. None of them was a man of title. They were mostly the kind of people that were called *efulefu,* worthless, empty, men. . . . Chielo, the priestess of Agbala, called the converts the excrement of the clan, and the new faith was a mad dog that had come to eat it up." Gradually, though, an increasing number of converts were drawn in from major families. (Today, the Igbo are overwhelmingly Christian.)[12]

In its early days, African Christianity was conspicuously a youth movement, a token of vigor and fresh thinking. Commonly, the key African converts were the younger members of society, teenagers and young adults, the ones most likely to travel to cities, ports, or trading posts during the first great age of globalization between about 1870 and 1914. These were the migrants, laborers, traders, and soldiers. In these border communities, they encountered the Christian faith that they subsequently brought home to their villages. Whatever the initial audience, what made Christianity succeed was the networking effect, as the word was passed from individual to individual, family to family, village to village. In their epic survey of African Christianity, Sundkler and Steed repeatedly stress the role of African converts themselves in passing on what they had received: "The new convert did not keep the discovery for individual consumption but took the message to others. . . . Thus it was that the message could spread as rings on the water."[13]

We can suggest all sorts of reasons why Africans and Asians adopted

Christianity, whether political, social, or cultural; but one all-too-obvious explanation is that individuals came to believe the message offered, and found this the best means of explaining the world around them. Achebe, again, describes the impact of the new preaching on one young Igbo man: "It was not the mad logic of the Trinity that captivated him. He did not understand it. It was the poetry of the new religion, something felt in the marrow.... He felt a relief within as the hymn poured into his parched soul. The words of the hymn were like the drops of frozen rain melting on the dry palate of the panting earth. Nwoye's callow mind was greatly puzzled."[14] For the fictional Nwoye, and for millions of his real-life counterparts, Christianity was accepted because it spoke to them, because they found it to be true. In Kenyatta's parable, quoted earlier, we recall that it is the African, not the European, who ends up owning the Bible.

Just how deeply, and how quickly, the new Christians appropriated the religion can be illustrated from the many stories of zeal in the face of persecution. In Madagascar in the 1850s, perhaps 200 Christians were "speared, smothered, starved or burned to death, poisoned, hurled from cliffs or boiled alive in rice pits."[15] We can also look at the British colony of Uganda, where Anglicanism was established in 1877 and African clergy were being ordained by the 1890s. Also in this decade, Roman Catholic missionaries started making their own converts. From its first days, Ugandan Christianity has produced its share of martyrs, whose stories demonstrate how firmly the faith has rooted itself in African soil. Some of the worst persecutions occurred in the kingdom of Buganda, which was later absorbed into the British colony.[16] Christianity made rapid progress at the royal court, to the horror of the king. Among other things, he found that his Christian male courtiers now refused his sexual demands. He ordered his subjects to renounce the new faith upon pain of death, and hundreds of native Bugandans were executed in 1885 and 1886. On a single day, thirty-two Christians were burned alive. With such examples in mind, it was ludicrous to claim that the new religion was solely for white people, and the faith spread quickly in both Uganda and Madagascar. In the 1890s, Buganda experienced a mass conversion of astonishing speed. Today, perhaps 75 percent of Ugandans are Christian, as are 90 percent of the people of Madagascar. Nor are such modern stories of persecution confined to Africa. In terms of the number of victims, the bloodiest persecution of these years was probably that which occurred in the native-ruled states of Indo-China during the mid- and late nineteenth century. The purge claimed the lives of a hundred or so Catholic priests, but as in Africa, ordinary lay believers made up the vast majority of the tens of thousands of victims.[17]

CROSSING THE RIVER

Once the religion was accepted, what remained was to purge away from that essential truth the foreign cultural trappings with which it was originally presented, and to let the message speak in intelligibly African (or Asian) terms. This process has been a lively theme for the rich tradition of fiction writing that has emerged in postcolonial Africa. One of the continent's most powerful writers is Kenya's Ngugi wa Thiong'o, whose book *The River Between* describes the conversion of his own Gikuyu people during the 1920s. The river in question refers to the literal and symbolic water dividing two villages, one newly converted, the other staunchly traditional-minded. At first, the book looks like a simplistic night-and-day account of how intrusive colonialist Christianity ruthlessly destroys the ancient way of life. The leading Christian convert, Joshua, is depicted in the most bigoted and fanatical terms, while traditionalist Waiyaki is a noble pagan, perhaps a native messiah.

As the story develops, though, matters become more complex. One of Joshua's daughters rebels against her father by demanding the pagan circumcision that marks her entry into womanhood. Although the ritual causes her death, her last vision is of Jesus. Joshua's other daughter falls in love with Waiyaki, and their union suggests the need for a cultural synthesis, in which Christianity would be acclimatized to African ways. For all its failings, there was something true in the white man's religion, but it "needed washing, cleaning away all the dirt, leaving only the eternal. And that eternal that was the truth had to be reconciled to the traditions of the people. A people's traditions could not be swept away overnight." A religion that failed to synthesize old and new "would only maim a man's soul." Joshua had erred when he "clothed himself with a religion decorated and smeared with everything *white*."[18]

From the earliest days of the missionary enterprise, indigenous peoples found aspects of Christianity exciting, even intoxicating, to the extent that they tried to absorb them into local culture, without waiting for the blessing of the European churches. In some instances, the zeal to accept and naturalize Christianity resulted in movements far removed from any customary notion of Christianity. I do not wish to exaggerate their numerical importance, since so much of the Christian history in Africa and Asia was, is, and shall be bound up with mainstream churches, Catholic and Protestant, rather than with the newer indigenous movements. The independent churches are critical, though, in demonstrating the real spiritual hunger that Christianity encountered and sought to fill.

To illustrate the passionate response to early Christian contacts, we might look at the Taiping movement, which won enormous influence in nineteenth-century China. This might seem an unprepossessing example to illustrate Christian successes, since the movement became so deeply involved in politics and failed so thoroughly. It launched a rebellion that resulted in tens of millions of deaths, and set the stage for the ultimate destruction of the imperial regime. Although Chinese communist historians prize the movement as a precursor to national liberation, the Taiping's roots were unmistakably Christian. The movement was founded by Hong Xiuquan, who experienced a visionary ascent to heaven—the same story told by so many other first-generation converts. Here Hong met his true family, which included God, the Virgin Mary, and his elder brother, Jesus. His prophetic mission to redeem China was institutionalized in a new Society of Worshippers of Shang-ti (God). The group launched a rebellion intended to establish a regime of perfect communism, known as the Taiping, or "Great Peace." To put this term in its Chinese biblical context, the angels had proclaimed the birth of Christ with the words "Glory to God in the highest, and on earth, *Taiping* and good will towards men."[19] Throughout its brief history, the movement maintained aspects of Christianity, although in a curious and deviant form. Recruits were required to learn the Lord's Prayer within a set period, upon threat of death.

Visionary movements like this have been remarkably common in world history, and not just within the bounds of Christianity. Visionary prophets and messiahs were a frequent occurrence in medieval Europe, while similar stories have erupted regularly in Southern lands during the process of Christianization. Arguably, such charismatic prophets are an inevitable by-product of the conversion process, and their appearance in large numbers marks the transition from a grudging and formal acceptance of Christianity to the widespread internalization of Christian belief among the common people.

Going back to the early colonial period, Latin America has a long tradition of messianic, millenarian, and utopian movements, many of which appealed to dispossessed natives. Against this background, frequent reports of miracles and Marian visions could scarcely be politically neutral, and colonial regimes rightly suspected that desperate native peoples saw their best hope for liberation in the Virgin and saints, viewed in Indian guise. In the eighteenth century, native revolts in Central America usually took the form of apocalyptic "Virgin movements."[20]

Many such movements have used the idea that God's purposes would be fulfilled on the frontiers of this new continent rather than in corrupt Europe.

This idea is far from extinct today, not least in contemporary liberation theology. One Latin American messiah was Antônio Conselheiro, who led an apocalyptic social movement on the Brazilian frontier of the 1890s. The revolt has entered continental mythology, to the point of being commemorated by two of the region's greatest writers, Euclides Da Cunha (*Rebellion in the Backlands*) and Mario Vargas Llosa (*The War at the End of the World*).[21] Another figure from the region's revolutionary canon is the Nicaraguan revolutionary leader Augusto Sandino. In the 1920s, he was driven by a classic millenarian belief that the old order of the world would soon perish in fire and blood, to be replaced by a new system of justice and equality. He wrote that "The oppressed people will break the chains of humiliation. . . . The trumpets that will be heard will be the bugles of war, intoning the hymns of the freedom of the oppressed peoples against the injustice of the oppressors." In his vision, oppressed Indian, Latino, and *mestizo* peoples would serve a messianic role in the struggle against North American oppression.[22]

No religious denomination traces its roots to these various revolts, although the Sandinistas survived as a major thorn in the flesh of successive U.S. governments. Other movements, though, which developed on or beyond the Christian fringe would grow into thriving independent churches. Under various names, these newer autonomous churches represent one of the most notable aspects of Southern Christianity. It is above all in Africa that such groupings would gain most significance. Often, the new indigenous denominations arose exactly in those regions that are likely to be experiencing the most striking population growth in the near future, so their traditions can be expected to play an increasing role in world Christianity.

OUT OF AFRICA

If the rising independent churches ever decide to identify a patron saint, they could do no better than to choose a seventeenth-century woman named Kimpa Vita, who was baptized by Italian Capuchin missionaries in the kingdom of Kongo.[23] Renamed Beatrice, she began her life as a Christian in the mode preached by the European Fathers, but she became disturbed as the priests attacked traditional ritual societies and initiations. She herself was a *Nganga,* a medium to the Other World, what colonial administrators might have called a medicine woman or witch doctor. About 1703, in a dream, she received a vision from St. Anthony, one of the most beloved saints in the Kongo, who warned her that the colonial churches were deeply in error. Jesus, she now learned, was a Black Kongolese, as were the apostles and popular saints like Saint Francis. In fact, Jesus had been born in the Kongo capital of São Salvador. Kimpa Vita's overarching message was that African Christians needed to find their own way to God, even if that meant using traditional practices condemned by the White priests. Kimpa Vita came to identify herself with St. Anthony, "the restorer of the kingdom of Kongo . . . the second God," whose spirit possessed her.

As so often in the African churches, a dream served as the conduit for a transforming spiritual message, with profound political implications. Kimpa Vita led a movement to reconcile the warring factions in her country, and she struggled to support the Kongolese monarchy. Time and again, we see analogies to Joan of Arc. And, as in Joan's case, such a revelation led to a tragic encounter with the colonizers: in 1706, Dona Beatrice Kimpa Vita was burned as a heretic and witch. Her "Antonian" followers were suppressed, and many thousands were sent as slaves to the New World, chiefly to Brazil and South Carolina. Millions of North and South Americans alive today can trace some degree of descent from this pioneering form of indigenous African Christianity.

Although her sect would not long outlive her, Kimpa Vita would have many successors who tried to translate Christianity into terms intelligible to the Two-Thirds World.[24] Across Africa, a common prophetic pattern has recurred frequently since the late nineteenth century. An individual is enthusiastically converted through one of the mission churches, from which he or, commonly, she, is gradually estranged. The division might arise over issues of church practice, usually the integration of native practices. The individual receives what is taken as a special revelation from God, commonly in a trance or vision. This event is a close imitation of one of the well-known New Testament scenes in which God speaks directly to his people, as at Pentecost or on the road to Damascus. The prophet then begins to preach independently, and the result might well be a new independent church. Particularly where the movement originates from a founder's revelation, such churches place a heavy premium on visions and charismatic gifts.[25]

One of the greatest of these prophets was William Wadé Harris, a potent figure in modern African religion. He might in fact be one of the most glaring omissions from the various lists of the world's great Christian leaders drawn up over the past few years. Harris was a Liberian, who in the early years of the last century was instructed by the angel Gabriel in a vision that had strong physical manifestations. He received "a triune anointing by God: he was tapped three times on the head and the spirit descended upon his head, feeling and sounding like a jet of water." Now, he was a prophet, the watchman of the apocalyptic dawn, he was Elijah. The angel also ordered him to abandon his prized European clothing. In so doing, he was rejecting not just the power of White colonialists, but also of the Americanized Black elite that monopolized power in his homeland. In 1913, clad in a white robe and turban, Harris began his wildly successful preaching journeys across West Africa: symbolizing the African nature of his mission, he bore a bamboo cross, a Bible, and a gourd rattle. Reportedly, he converted 100,000 people over a two-year period. His message was largely orthodox Christianity, teaching obedience to the Ten Commandments and demanding strict observance of the Sabbath.[26]

What made Harris particularly African was his emphasis on dealing with the people's ancient cult-figures or fetishes, which European missionaries had scorned or ignored. Harris, on the other hand, like his listeners, believed that the fetishes contained vast spiritual force, which he combated by burning the objects. Legend tells how pagan shrines actually burst into flames as he approached, and their priests fled before the coming of such supernatural power. Unlike the White missionaries, who called witchcraft a delusion, Harris knew its power all too well, and called upon his hearers to spurn occult practices. Nor did Harris condemn polygamy, and he traveled in the company of several wives. Although many of his followers eventually joined conventional mission churches like the Methodists, Harrist churches survive in West Africa. Today, they often appeal to transient immigrant communities like Ghanaian workers in the Ivory Coast, truly the poorest of the poor.[27]

The second decade of the century was fertile for the creation of such movements. The intensity of religious activism in these years suggests how wholeheartedly, how impatiently, the new African-Christian communities tried to absorb the message into their own societies. We recall the stubborn faith of the Ugandan martyrs, just a decade or so after the arrival of Christianity in that country. In 1915, Baptist missionary John Chilembwe launched an armed revolt against British rule in the province of Nyasaland (later Malawi). This was the first modern African challenge to imperial rule presented in terms of nationalism and social justice, and it was built firmly upon Christian foundations. One of the movement's goals was the creation of a National African Church.[28]

Another contemporary prophet was Simon Kimbangu, who lived in what was then the Belgian Congo. At the time of the worldwide influenza epidemic in 1918, he received visions calling him to be a prophet and healer. Although he tried to resist his call, he ultimately began his preaching and healing ministry in 1921, attracting such a vast following that the terrified

Belgian authorities sentenced him to be flogged and executed. Although the death sentence was commuted, he remained in prison until his death in 1951. Kimbangu preached an orthodox puritanical Christianity, but was distinctively African in his invocation of the help of the ancestors and his focus on himself as a charismatic leader and mediator between God and the people. He also preached an African political message. One of his prayers promises, "The Kingdom is ours. We have it! They, the Whites, no longer have it." Many of his followers regarded him as an African savior and messiah, whose hometown of Nkamba was seen as a New Jerusalem. His church's calendar commemorates the key dates of his life, including the beginning of his ministry and the day of his death in prison. The more extreme messianic claims were not accepted by the official Kimbanguist Church that flourished after his death, the Church of the Lord Jesus Christ on Earth of the Prophet Simon Kimbangu, the EJCSK (*Église de Jesus Christ sur la terre par son Envoyé Spécial Simon Kimbangu*). Believers do, however, see him as fulfilling Jesus' prophecy that "one who believes in me will also do the works that I do and will do greater works than these." The current size of this organization is very uncertain, but some claim numbers as high as 6 or 8 million.[29]

Harris and Kimbangu were by no means isolated figures. With their stress on spiritual healing, the new African churches gained strength because of the wave of epidemic diseases that swept most parts of Africa in the early years of the century, claiming millions of lives. In the Yoruba lands of Nigeria, the dreadful influenza epidemic led to the foundation of the faith-healing churches known as *Aladura* (the "Owners of Prayer"). From the 1920s on, the *Aladura* movement spawned many offshoots, usually under the leadership of some new charismatic leader or prophet. Such were the Cherubim and Seraphim Society, Christ Apostolic Church, and the Church of the Lord, Aladura. In some cases, the new bodies saw the divine messages received in trances and dreams as equal to the inspired word of the Bible.[30]

The tide of prophetic gifts was not confined to the 1910s and 1920s, the astonishingly creative years during and after the First World War. Over the past century, many African believers have announced that God has chosen them for a special prophetic mission, and most have sought to Africanize the Christianity that they received from European sources. As a final representative of this tradition, we might take Alice Lenshina.[31] While a candidate for baptism in the Presbyterian church of Northern Rhodesia in 1953, Alice received visions in which she was taken up to heaven and ordered to destroy witchcraft, which was seen as so pressing a danger in many African societies. She formed a church, the *Lumpa* ("better than all others"), of which she became Lenshina or queen. The group attracted hundreds of thousands of followers, who formed a utopian community in order to await the Second Coming of Christ. As they rejected worldly regimes to the point of refusing to pay taxes, *Lumpa* members were persecuted by the newly independent Zambian regime, and a small war ensued between church and government. Alice died in 1978, and while her church seems to have died with her, nobody would be surprised if clandestine followers reemerged someday.

Reading all the seemingly endless stories of Africa's modern-day prophets and visionaries, and the revivals they are credited with, we are tempted to identify certain decades as ages of revival, ages of prophecy. The decade after 1910 certainly seems to fit this profile. The problem is that really no era since the 1890s has lacked this kind of passionate prophetic activism, so there are no real troughs to set besides the peaks. We can usefully draw parallels with American religious history. Traditionally, the nation's religious past has been interpreted as a series of great revivals, the first in the 1730s, the second in the 1790s, and so on, right up to the present day, but these events can also be seen as convenient historical fictions. In reality, we can always find some kind of revival or great evangelical movement at work somewhere in North America, and only in retrospect do historians tie together a few of these events to portray them as "great revivals." In Africa similarly, it is more helpful to see the various revivals and prophetic movements as overlapping, more or less continuous events. To use the language of revivalism, Africa has now for over a century been engaged in a continuous encounter with Pentecostal fires, and the independent churches have been the most obvious products of that highly creative process. In American terms, much of the continent has served as one vast burnt-over district.

AFRICAN AND INDEPENDENT

The various new congregations are today described as the African independent churches (AICs), which collectively represent one of the most impressive stories in the whole history of Christianity (in some accounts, the acronym stands for African initiated churches, or else "African indigenous"). The term covers a wide range of groupings, from highly Africanized variants of recognizably European or American churches, all the way to tribal groups that borrow loosely and selectively from Christian thought and language. Although very diverse in ideas and practices, African independent churches use certain common themes, above all, the adaptation of Christianity to local cultures and traditions. They are African churches with African leaders for African people.[32]

Independent denominations sprang up in many parts of Africa from the late 1880s on, as racial segregation in European-founded churches drove many activists to defect. For many, the age of the so-called Scramble for Africa marked a scramble out of inhospitable White churches, with the resulting formation of new independent denominations. Many used words like "Native" or "African" in their titles, and some claimed a distinct Ethiopian heritage. One of the earliest was the Ethiopian Church founded in Pretoria, South Africa, in 1892: this was the work of Mangena Mokone, a refugee from Wesleyan Methodism. This Ethiopian connection needs some explanation. African churches since Mokone's time are fond of quoting a verse from Psalm 68, which proclaims, "Let Ethiopia hasten to stretch out her hands to God." In North America, Black churches were already claiming an "Abyssinian" identity from the start of the nineteenth century, and Black American missionaries spread these ideas to Africa. Ethiopia gained a still greater appeal following that nation's resounding victory over an Italian colonial force in 1896, one of the few examples of a native African country successfully repelling a European invasion. By describing themselves as Ethiopian, the new denominations were not only justifying departures from White Christian models, but also claiming a pan-African Christian identity.[33]

Apart from the Ethiopian groups, some other independent churches are termed "prophetic" because they follow modern-day charismatic leaders like Kimbangu, Harris, and the rest. Finally, there are the important Zionist churches, which grew ultimately from charismatic sects in late-nineteenth-century North America, and which practiced faith-healing and speaking in tongues. They take their name indirectly from Mount Zion in Jerusalem, but more immediately from Zion City, Illinois, the headquarters of an influential American charismatic movement. Zionist churches were already operating in southern Africa in the 1890s, and they enjoyed a boom in the early twentieth century. It was in 1910 that Engenas Barnabas Lekganyane established what would be one of the most successful, South Africa's Zion Christian Church (ZCC).[34] Despite the American influences in their origin, Zionist and other independent churches soon developed purely African leaderships. They adopted African customs, including polygamy, and in some cases, observed ritual taboos. They also resemble traditional native religions in their beliefs in exorcism, witchcraft, and possession. Some follow the customs of particular tribes, like the Zulus, and have to some extent become tribally based churches. Many groups practice distinctive pilgrimages and ritual calendars, which intertwine with older tribal cycles.[35]

The grievances that gave rise to the new African churches are generally long gone, but the churches themselves are flourishing. Just how significant these groups might become, we will see in the following chapter. For present purposes, though, churches like the Harrists and Kimbanguists, the Zionist and Aladura traditions, are significant because they suggest the real fervor that Christianity inspired outside the West. They confound the standard modern mythology about just how Christianity was, and is, exported to a passive or reluctant Third World. Over the past two centuries, at least, it might have been the European empires that first kindled Christianity around the world, but the movement soon enough turned into an uncontrollable brushfire.

Standing Alone

We carry with us the wonders we seek
without us; there is all Africa and her
prodigies in us.

—*Sir Thomas Browne*

Since the spread of Christianity had closely coincided with imperial
expansion, it seemed certain that the fate of the religion would be
affected by the breakup of the old European empires. Just as these
empires were built up in a slow and piecemeal fashion, so they did not disintegrate overnight. Although decolonization was at its most rapid in the
late 1950s and early 1960s, the process extended for about half a century
after the end of the Second World War, which so weakened the European
powers. The era of imperial collapse began when the British withdrew from
India and Pakistan in 1947 and the Dutch recognized Indonesian sover-
eignty in 1949. It was in 1955 that the Bandung conference symbolized the
emergence of a Third World, the community of new nations that aspired to
be independent of both capitalist West and communist East. In sub-Saharan
Africa, the decisive phase began with the independence of Ghana in 1957,
and proceeded rapidly over the next decade. Some of the landmarks in this
process included the independence of Zaire and Nigeria in 1960 and of
Algeria in 1962. However, the process continued long after this date. The
Portuguese empire did not disintegrate until 1975, Zimbabwe gained its
independence in 1979, and White rule survived in South Africa until 1994.
The Soviet empire in Central Asia continued as the last great vestige of European colonialism until the U.S.S.R. collapsed in 1991.

Particularly during the heady years of decolonization in the 1950s and 1960s, Western Christians were concerned about how the new African and Asian churches would survive the rapid transition. After all, Southern Christianity had developed its essential framework by mid-century, but it was still "a skeleton without flesh or bulk, a mission-educated minority who were leading nascent Christian institutions."[1] There were also some severe political tests. In Kenya during the 1950s, Mau Mau rebels targeted the Anglican Church as an arm of the imperial regime, and anarchy in the Belgian Congo during the 1960s led to widespread violence against believers and clergy. The mainly Muslim insurgency in Algeria all but uprooted the old-established Catholic missions. Churches also suffered under new Asian communist regimes.

Yet with a few exceptions, the new churches survived and flourished. Since mid-century, "The skeleton . . . had grown organs and sinew," as millions of new members poured into the churches. It was precisely as Western colonialism ended that Christianity began a period of explosive growth that still continues unchecked, above all in Africa. Just since 1965, the Christian population of Africa has risen from around a quarter of the continental total to about 46 percent, stunning growth for so short a period. To quote the 2001 edition of the *World Christian Encyclopedia*, "The present net increase on that continent is 8.4 million new Christians a year (23,000 a day) of which 1.5 million are net new converts (converts minus defections or apostasies)." Sometime in the 1960s, another historic landmark occurred, when Christians first outnumbered Muslims in Africa. Adrian Hastings has written that "Black Africa today is totally inconceivable apart from the presence of Christianity."[2]

Whatever their image in popular culture, Christian missionaries of the colonial era succeeded remarkably. Much of this growth could be explained in terms of the churches' elastic ability to adapt to local circumstances. Across the global South, we see a common pattern of development. Initially, Westerners try to impose their own ideas of Christianity as it should be, often backed up by the force of colonial political power. This evangelism gains some followers, usually for an approved or state-run church, and a striking number of believers are content to remain within that fold. Gradually, though, other people move beyond the colonial matrix, as they demand ever more accommodation with local ways: this is what happened with prophets like William Wadé Harris. This pressure can have various outcomes, depending on just how flexibly the old bottles can accommodate the new wine. In many cases the major European-oriented churches successfully adapt and incorporate native ways into local liturgies and worship styles.

In other instances, though, the result is the formation of wholly new churches, in a way that might have horrified the missionary founders. This can mean adopting some rival established denomination, as when millions of Latin American Catholics began converting to Protestantism and Pentecostalism. In yet other cases, believers form wholly new churches, so different from existing models that traditional-minded observers debate worriedly whether these upstarts have moved beyond the bounds of Christianity itself.

THE MISSION CHURCHES

Some of the greatest triumphs have been enjoyed by precisely those structures created by colonial authorities, which retain the passionate loyalty of indigenous peoples long after the empires themselves have dissolved. Despite all the scholarly attention justifiably paid to the distinctive Pentecostal and African indigenous churches (Zionist, Ethiopian, prophetic), the most successful structures across the global South are still easily recognizable to any North American. After decades of Protestant growth in Latin America, the Roman Catholic Church is still overwhelmingly the largest single religious presence on that continent, and the great majority of people still define their religious life in Catholic terms. If 50 million Latin Americans are Protestant (a fair estimate), then 420 million are not: most are, at least nominally, Catholic. In Africa, likewise, the leading churches are Catholic, Anglican, Methodist, and so on, and will be so for the foreseeable future.

The continuing power of the mainstream churches must be emphasized because many Westerners are understandably fascinated by the insurgent movements. Kenneth Woodward, for instance, writes that "In Africa alone, the collapse of European colonialism half a century ago saw the wild proliferation of indigenous Christian cults inspired by personal prophecies and visions."[3] That is true as far as it goes, but the overall statistics must be borne in mind. Although African independents today claim an impressive 35 million members, that represents less than one-tenth of all African Christians. Africa's Roman Catholics alone outnumber its Independents by better than three to one. Members of Africa's mainstream Catholic and Protestant churches often resent the attention that European and American academics pay to the independent churches. It is far easier to find scholarly studies of the independent or prophetic churches than of the Catholic or Anglican congregations that define religious life for hundreds of millions. However well-intentioned, this slant tends to make African Christianity look more far exotic and even syncretistic than it really is. All the emphasis on "independents" also suggests that the other churches are somehow dependent, lying under the neo-colonial yoke. In Latin America similarly, books on Pentecostal congregations are now commonplace, but we have few descriptions of everyday life in a regular Catholic parish. For academics and journalists alike, the ordinary is just not interesting.

The European colonial empires that flourished in the nineteenth century have left a global religious heritage. The idea that religions might actually represent the afterlife of dead empires is scarcely new. In the seventeenth century, Thomas Hobbes described the papacy as "no other than the ghost of the deceased Roman Empire, sitting crowned upon the grave thereof: for so did the papacy start up on a sudden out of the ruins of that heathen power." Another historical parallel is offered by the Hellenistic empire founded by Alexander the Great. Although this political entity lasted only briefly, it left a millennium-long heritage in terms of the widespread dispersion of Greek language, thought, and culture. Unwittingly, the Greek dynasts created the world in which early Christianity could spread so quickly.[4]

The present map of Catholicism around the world can be seen as a ghostly remnant of several empires—the French and Portuguese, but above all, the Spanish. According to official Catholic figures, the countries with the largest numbers of believers are Brazil (137 million), Mexico (89 million), the Philippines (61 million), the United States (58 million), and Italy (55 million). Brazil was once the crown jewel of the Portuguese empire, while Mexico and the Philippines owe their Catholic roots to Spain. Today, Latin America has 424 million baptized Catholics, 42 percent of the global total, more than in the whole of Europe and North America. A good number of North American Catholics are also of Latino heritage.[5]

Catholic growth has been particularly dramatic in Africa, usually in former French and Belgian territories. As recently as 1955, the church claimed a mere 16 million Catholics in the whole of Africa, but the growing availability of air travel permitted missionaries access to whole areas of the continent that were hitherto beyond reach. Today, there are 120 million African Catholics, and the number is growing daily: there could be 230 million by 2025, which would represent one-sixth of all Catholics worldwide. Although the expansion can be illustrated by any number of countries, Tanzania offers a good example. The number of Catholics here has grown by 419 percent since 1961, and the country has developed a strong ecclesiastical structure. By the 1990s, Tanzania had 4 provinces incorporating 29 dioceses, and in 8 of these, Catholics represented a majority of the population. Whereas in 1965, less than one-quarter of Tanzania's bishops were native Africans, by 1996 local men headed all the dioceses.[6] During the 1960s, archbishops of African stock emerged in many of the new nation-states. Somewhere, the shade of Cardinal Lavigerie is smiling contentedly.

The church's message has an appeal completely separate from the imperial power by which it was originally carried. There are eerie parallels here to the original spread of Christianity in Europe, which enjoyed its greatest successes after the collapse of the Roman political regime. To quote Kenneth Woodward, some church historians now "see history doing a second act: just as Europe's northern tribes turned to the church after the decay of the Roman Empire, so Africans are embracing Christianity in face of the massive political, social and economic chaos."[7] In modern Africa, as in medieval Europe, the religion of the old master races became most attractive when the formal political bonds were severed, so that accepting Christianity did not imply submission to a foreign political yoke. At that point, subject peoples were delighted to appropriate not just the beliefs but also the old administrative and cultural forms of empire.

World Christianity is also haunted by the specter of the defunct British Empire. The Anglican Communion now claims over 70 million members worldwide, a figure that significantly overestimates the number of practicing church members in the United Kingdom proper. By more plausible estimates, Anglicans in the British Isles are massively outnumbered by those overseas, and the so-called Anglican (literally, "English") Communion looks ever more African. Nigeria alone claims 20 million baptized Anglicans. The world's best-known Anglican cleric is former Cape Town Archbishop Desmond Tutu, who (alongside Nelson Mandela) became the symbol of the South African liberation movement. By 2050, the global total of Anglicans will be approaching 150 million, of whom only a tiny minority will be White Europeans. The imperial heritage is evident from other British-derived churches like Methodists and Presbyterians, which similarly used the imperial framework to spread their distinctive messages.[8]

The process of autonomous growth is illustrated by the church in the former British colony of Uganda. This promises to be an enormously significant development, since Uganda is one of the fastest-growing countries in Africa, with a present-day population of around 23 million. We have seen how Ugandan Christianity established its local credentials during the great persecutions of the 1880s. Anglicanism easily survived the transition from imperial rule, and the church became a separate province in 1961, a year before national independence. Christianity's role as a truly native faith was reinforced again in 1977, when Anglican Archbishop Janani Luwum was martyred for opposing the dictatorship of General Idi Amin.[9] Today, Anglicans make up 35 or 40 percent of the total population. There are twenty dioceses and 7,000 parishes, and by any measure of church attendance and participation, Anglicanism is considerably healthier in Uganda than in what was once the mother country.

The Ugandan story also suggests how the old colonial churches succeeded in adapting to local styles of worship and belief, which made the transition to political independence much easier. As early as the 1920s, the East African "mission churches" were transformed by a strongly evangelical revival movement which had its heart in Uganda and Rwanda, but which affected many neighboring states. (This was also the time of the great West African revivals that gave rise to the Aladura churches.) In East Africa, followers were known as the *balokole,* the "saved ones," and the *balokole* became a major force in the new church: one disciple became the first archbishop of the Ugandan Anglican Church after that nation's independence. The *balokole* movement gave the East African churches a Pentecostal tone, which reduced the boundaries dividing the established churches from the newer independents, and it endures to the present.[10] The revivalist emphasis on healing and visionary experience made the churches attractive to members of traditional animist faiths. Although older and newer churches disagree on issues of theology and structure, they share many common cultural assumptions.

SECESSION

Across the South, the older churches and missions remain the primary fact in the Christian story, yet they do not represent the whole picture. In many areas, older groupings proved inadequate for a changing society. Much of the most spectacular Christian expansion in recent decades has occurred not within either the Protestant or Catholic realms, but in new independent denominations. We can see a proliferation of churches with affiliations that might be termed "none of the above." According to the *World Christian Encyclopedia,* membership of Christian denominations in the 1990s could be listed as in table 4.1.

While we can place little confidence in the precision of any of these figures, we must be struck by the fact that almost one Christian in five worldwide is neither Protestant, nor Catholic, nor Anglican, nor Orthodox. For the average Western Christian, this idea is puzzling: apart from Mormons, possibly, what else is there? Just what is an "independent"? In some sources,

TABLE 4.1
Strength of Christian Denominations in 2000

Christian Denomination	Adherents (in millions)
Roman Catholics	1057
Independents	386
Protestants	342
Orthodox	215
Anglicans	79
Marginal Christians	26
TOTAL	2105

Source: David B. Barrett, George T. Kurian, and Todd M. Johnson, eds., *World Christian Encyclopedia,* 2nd ed. (New York: Oxford University Press, 2001), 4.

the same figure is given even more confusingly as "Other." These Other churches represent a wide variety of denominations, often (but not always) included under the general label of Pentecostal. Some are affiliated with Northern Hemisphere denominations like the (Pentecostal) Assemblies of God, but many are not. Some of these Other congregations are indigenous churches with roots entirely in Africa, Asia, and Latin America, sometimes in regions where Christianity was planted within the past century or so.[11]

Growth outside the traditional churches has been very evident in Latin America. Roman Catholicism represented the religion of the overwhelming majority of the people as recently as forty years ago, but since that time, there has been a major defection to Protestantism. (I am here including Pentecostals as a subset of Protestants, although as we will see, the two terms are not identical.) In 1940, barely a million Protestants were recorded in the whole of Latin America. Since 1960, though, Protestant numbers in the region have been growing at an average annual rate of 6 percent, so that today Protestants make up around one-tenth of the whole population, some 50 million people. In terms of their share of the population, Protestants or *evangélicos* are strongest in Guatemala and Chile, in each case representing around one-quarter of the whole.[12] Brazil alone has perhaps 20 to 25 million *crentes* or believers—that is, Protestants. If it were a separate country, then the most Protestant region of Latin America would be the U.S. territory of Puerto Rico, where numbers stand at around 35 percent. These proportions are so important because Protestants also tend to be more religiously committed, more likely to be active churchgoers, than most of their nominally Catholic neighbors. Just how much stronger the new churches can become remains a matter of alarm for the Catholic hierarchies of the region.[13]

We have to be careful about judging the exact scale of the movement to Protestantism, which has in recent years been described in rather inflated terms. In the 1980s, it was common to read claims that Protestantism was sweeping the continent, that many countries would be half Protestant by the year 2000, and so on. In 1990, David Stoll published a carefully argued book that sought to answer the question *Is Latin America Turning Protestant?*[14] Evangelicals were certainly making great strides, but the more extreme claims stemmed from partisan agencies with a strong theological agenda. One influential trend was known as "Discipling the Nations," and advocates had an apocalyptic commitment to achieving evangelical majorities in previously non-Protestant countries by the end of the second millennium. This optimism did much to shape statistical estimates. We can also discern an element of anti-Catholicism, since the claim being made was that millions of new believers were being rescued from this supposedly non-biblical and non-Christian faith. Enthusiastic missionary agencies rarely paid enough attention to the chronic difficulties in measuring church membership, and relied on optimistic self-report data. Special problems apply to Third World societies in which it is difficult to collect information from remote rural areas. Figures claimed for Latin America relied too heavily on projections from major churches accessible to scholars, mainly in large urban concentrations. However transforming they may appear at the time, moreover, conversions are not always a permanent and life-changing event: Latin America has plenty of ex-evangelicals, as well as ex-Catholics. But even when we take account of these problems, evangelical achievements are remarkable enough, and we can properly see this religious shift as one of the great religious revolutions over the past few centuries. Its importance is all the greater given population growth rates in Latin America, and the likely significance of the region in decades to come.[15]

Mexico illustrates the upsurge of Protestant practice over the past half-century. Mexico traditionally was divided between a vigorous Catholicism and an equally dedicated current of secularism and anti-clericalism. For much of the century, successive Mexican governments were deeply hostile to the Catholic Church, and there were periods of intense persecution: we recall Graham Greene's novel of a martyred priest, *The Power and the Glory*. While not actually favored by the authorities, Protestants were relatively free to operate, and by 1970 they were about a million strong, representing 2 percent of the population. Since that date, Protestants have flourished by appealing to two quite different constituencies, respectively urban and rural. In the cities, like elsewhere in Latin America, Protestantism particularly appeals to migrants and the marginalized. One remarkable development is the conversion of rural Indian communities in southeastern Mexico, among the Maya peoples in Chiapas and Tabasco. Of about 100 million Mexicans today, around 6 percent are Protestants, compared with 89 percent who nominally identify themselves as Roman Catholic.[16]

THE DAY OF PENTECOST

In addition to growing in overall numbers, Protestantism has changed substantially in nature, with the expansion of Pentecostal sects over the past half-century. The Pentecostal boom worldwide was little known to the general public in the West before the publication of Harvey Cox's important book *Fire from Heaven* in 1995, but the "rise of Pentecostal spirituality" has to be seen as truly epoch-making. According to reputable observers, by 2000, Pentecostal numbers worldwide were increasing at the rate of around 19 million each year.[17]

A word about definition is in order here. Historically, the chief religious division in the Western world was between Roman Catholics and Protestants, the latter term including all those groups that descended from the great ideological split of the Reformation. The key difference is that Protestants rely on the Bible alone as the source of religious authority, rather than on tradition or the institutional church. In this broad division, the Pentecostal movement should logically be considered Protestant, since it grew out of other Protestant churches, namely Methodism and the Holiness tradition, and it preaches a fundamentalist reliance on scriptural authority. Across Latin America, the term *evangélico* refers indiscriminately to both Protestants and Pentecostals. Increasingly, though, observers differentiate Pentecostals from Protestants because of growing divergences between the two in matters of faith and practice. One central division is that Pentecostal believers rely on direct spiritual revelations that supplement or even replace biblical authority. Across the continent, Protestants and Pentecostals remain at arm's length, chiefly because they appeal to different audiences. While Protestants serve a largely middle-class audience, Pentecostals derive their support mainly from the poor, indeed from the very poorest sections of society.[18]

Pentecostalism has deep roots in Latin America, where some independent churches were founded before the First World War. Their numbers were tiny until the 1950s, when growth began in earnest. Since that date, Pentecostals account for 80 or 90 percent of Protestant/Pentecostal growth across Latin America. Chilean Protestantism has a heavy Pentecostal majority, and this tradition has also become very strong in Central America. Some of the new Pentecostals adhere to international denominations, like the U.S.-based Assemblies of God. Today, this church claims at least 12 million members in Brazil, in contrast to only 2 or 3 million in the United States. The same denomination is now the largest non-Catholic community in Guatemala. However, much of the Pentecostal growth has occurred in wholly new denominations, with roots in Latin America itself. Chile is home to the Jotabeche Methodist Pentecostal Church, which boasts 80,000 members, and its "cathedral" in Santiago can seat 18,000.[19]

Brazil represents a particular success story for Pentecostals. The movement here was founded in the early twentieth century by missionaries of the Assemblies of God. Pentecostal conversions surged during the 1950s and 1960s, when native Brazilians began founding autonomous churches. The most influential included *Brasil Para o Cristo,* Brazil for Christ, founded in 1955 by Manoel de Mello. His spiritual roots lay in the Assemblies of God, and his colorful evangelization tactics included American-style mass rallies and crusades.[20] Today, the movement's main Temple claims a million members. Other groupings from this time include God is Love, founded in São Paulo in 1962, and the Church of the Four Square Gospel (*Igreja do Evangelho Quadrangular*). A third wave of Pentecostal evangelism has made massive gains over the past twenty years, and again, it clearly builds on local foundations. Of the fifty-two largest denominations in the Rio de Janeiro area in the 1990s, thirty-seven were of local Brazilian origin. Their successes have been striking—they would say, miraculous. Harvey Cox cites a study of Rio de Janeiro in the early 1990s, where over a three-year period, no less than 700 new Pentecostal churches opened. In the same period, an impressive 240 Spiritist temples also appeared, mainly of the African-derived Umbanda tradition—and only *one* new Roman Catholic parish. According to a recent estimate, some forty new Pentecostal churches are opening in Rio each and every week.[21]

One controversial example of the new Pentecostalism is the Brazilian-based Universal Church of the Kingdom of God, the *Igreja Universal do Reino de Deus* (IURD).[22] The Universal Church was founded by Edir Macedo de Bezerra only in 1977, but at its height in the mid-1990s, it claimed between 3 and 6 million members. Other estimates were much lower, in the hundreds of thousands, but in any case the expansion was awe-inspiring. After so brief an organizational existence, the IURD now controls one of the largest television stations in Brazil, has its own political party, and owns a Rio de Janeiro football team. (In the Brazilian context, the football team may be the most valuable asset in terms of its potential influence.) The church has expanded its activities to forty countries besides Brazil. Much of its wealth comes from the fervent devotion of members, who tithe faithfully.

The IURD has been widely attacked, and it is classified as a cult by some European governments and by media exposés in the United States. The Universal Church has been criticized for superstitious practices that exploit its largely uneducated members. The church sells special anointing oil for healing, and television viewers are encouraged to place glasses of water near the screen so they can be blessed by remote control. The IURD's web site promises that "A miracle awaits you." Sometimes, this miracle takes the form of release from demonic powers. The church offers "strong prayer to destroy witchcraft, demon possession, bad luck, bad dreams, all spiritual problems" and promises that members will gain "prosperity and financial breakthrough." Believers are told, in effect, that prayer and giving operate on the same crass principle as secular investments: the more one gives to the church, the more material benefit can be expected in this life. Some of the church's supernatural claims have earned very bad publicity in Great Britain in recent years, during the national scandal surrounding a young African girl called Anna Climbie, who died from extreme physical abuse. Her family suspected she was bewitched, and took her to a wide range of churches offering healing and exorcism services, including the IURD. Reportedly, these exorcisms contributed to her injuries. Finally, critics denounce the IURD as an irresponsible money-making scheme. The *New York Post* once exposed the church under the headline "Holy-Roller Church Cashes in on Faithful." Some years ago, an embarrassing videotape showed Macedo gloating over his profits, and urging lieutenants to squeeze more out of the flock. When the video was aired, the scandal caused a major setback, and the church's previously astronomical growth faltered.[23]

It is all too easy to list the flaws of a group like the IURD, but we should not use this case to generalize about the possible defects of the rising churches, still less about religion in a Third World context. All organizations can become deviant or exploitative: witness the scandals in U.S. mainline churches over the past two decades, over financial fraud as well as sexual abuse.[24] From the nature of the mass media, we do not hear about the other responsible churches that are not involved in abuse and exploitation, and which work faithfully for their members. Whatever our view of the IURD, its amazing growth indicates that it is catering to a vast public hunger, so that even if this group were to disappear tomorrow, new movements would arise to take its place. In most cases, we would presumably hear nothing about them in the North unless they fell prey to outrageous scandal. Without this kind of reporting, we would remain unaware of the religious revolution that is in progress across the hemisphere.

The evangelical revival has also spread beyond Pentecostal ranks, through what some hard-line Northern observers would consider only a semi-Christian movement, namely the Latter Day Saints, or Mormons. This church represents another of the great success stories in modern Latin American religion. Only a generation ago, Mormons were mainly concentrated in the United States, but matters have now changed completely. Of 11 million Mormons today, less than half now live in the United States and Canada, while over one-third live in Central and South America: there could soon be twenty temples in Latin America. Mexico and the other nations of Central America account for 1.3 million church members. The church well recognizes its Southern markets, and its recruiting literature cleverly emphasizes the distinctive New World and native context of this faith. In keeping with the Mormon scriptures, the group's posters and videos depict Jesus preaching before what are clearly Meso-American and Maya pyramids, to awed native hearers. By present projections, the proportion of Mormons living in Europe and North America will fall steadily over the next thirty or forty years, while African and Latin American contingents will grow apace.[25]

THE CATHOLIC RESPONSE

In the long term, the Catholic response to these changes may be as far-reaching as Protestant expansion itself. The desperate lack of Catholic priests across the global South meant that the church initially failed to keep up with shifts in population and popular taste, and no amount of condemnations from the hierarchy could keep the faithful from drifting to the new sects. Once the evangelical churches began to flourish, though, Catholics themselves had to compete by developing alternatives offering a far greater sense of popular commitment and lay participation. These include the famous *comunidades eclesiales de base,* the base communities, which rely on heavy lay involvement and participation in liturgy and church life, and which are deeply involved in community organizing.[26] These groups have served as an inspiration for radical First World Christians. Also important have been charismatic Catholic groups, which revive the mystical and visionary aspects of the faith. In fact, conservative Catholics have been disturbed to note just how much these new institutions look like their Protestant counterparts, with the base communities attracting particular hostility.

Although they have received far less attention in the West than the base communities, Catholic charismatic organizations may well be more influential in the long run. One striking example is the El Shaddai movement in the Philippines, which takes its name from a Hebrew term for the face of God. However much this wildly successful group looks like a classic Pentecostal church, it is firmly rooted within Roman Catholicism. It is in fact a lay charismatic group designed to combat Protestant penetration in the Philippines. Protestants currently comprise around 8 percent of what was historically an overwhelmingly Catholic nation, and there are surging Pentecostal groups like the Jesus is Lord movement. In this case, though, the reformers have met their match.

El Shaddai was founded in 1984 by Brother Mike Velarde, who looks and behaves like a U.S. mega-star televangelist. The group's meetings, hundreds of thousands strong, look like nothing so much as a 1960s rock festival. Audiences are predominantly women, but many whole families are in evidence. As in Pentecostal churches, there is a firm belief in God's direct intervention in everyday life, which different observers interpret in different ways. Some see this belief as a childlike faith in the divine presence, while for others, the new groups are teaching a crass materialism. El Shaddai followers raise their passports to be blessed at services, to ensure that they will get the visas they need to work overseas. Many open umbrellas and turn them upside-down as a symbolic way of catching the rich material blessings they expect to receive from on high. This suggests a materialistic thought-world not too far removed from the Brazilian IURD. The movement probably has 7 million members across the Philippines, making them a potent political force, and it also has the nucleus for a truly global presence. The large army of expatriate Filipino workers worldwide permits El Shaddai to operate congregations or chapters in over twenty-five countries, including the United States and Canada, most nations in western Europe, and the Persian Gulf region.[27]

Occasional warnings about the group's possible excesses show that the Philippine Catholic hierarchy does not see El Shaddai as an unmixed boon, but there is little doubt that the movement has done much to prevent the kind of mass defections that have occurred in Brazil and elsewhere. This experience offers sobering lessons for other Catholic nations alarmed at an upsurge of "sects." One way or another, inside the Catholic Church or outside it, Third World Christianity is becoming steadily more Pentecostal.

AFRICAN INDEPENDENTS

The same lesson emerges from the success of the newer churches in Africa. In recent years, some of the most successful congregations have been Pentecostal, and here too the Assemblies of God are growing fast. Throughout, we can see many analogies to the new Pentecostalism of Latin America. In Tanzania, charismatic services are marked by "rapturous singing and rhythmic hand-clapping, with . . . prayers for healing and miraculous signs." "Announcements of the meetings and the so-called power crusades can be seen on more or less every second house in the larger cities." In most of Africa, Pentecostals have overtaken the independent or indigenous churches in popularity, but these groups remain powerful in some areas. The independents vary widely in their belief and practice, but these too should be comprehended under the very flexible label of "Pentecostal." Many indigenous churches do not like the Pentecostal title, which implies a reliance on American mission activities, rather than spontaneous local growth. The "independents" fully deserve their name: they are nobody's puppets. Still, Harvey Cox makes a convincing case that we should also place the AICs firmly within the Pentecostal landscape, on account of their "free wheeling, Spirit-filled" worship style. Their worship "exhibits all the features of Pentecostal spirituality we have found from Boston to Seoul to Rio de Janeiro." The founders of the various prophetic churches also fit well into the Pentecostal mode, and their conversion experiences are classic Pentecostal narratives.[28]

The new churches have thrived across Africa, although there are huge regional variations. In some countries, like Uganda, major traditional churches still predominate, while in West Africa, traditional "mission" churches coexist with indigenous groups like the Cherubim and Seraphim. In southern Africa, the independents seem to be carrying the day, although they face serious competition from the newer Pentecostal churches. Over the past half-century, the Zionist churches have been phenomenally successful in South Africa, above all in the poorest urban areas.[29] In the 1990s, there were 4,000 independent churches in South Africa, claiming five million adherents; 900 congregations operated in the city of Soweto alone. The largest such body, the Zion Christian Church, is a major religious and political force in the country, and its power is regularly demonstrated in its vast seasonal pilgrimages. Every Easter, more than a million ZCC pilgrims gather for several days of celebrations at Zion City, the church's chief shrine in South Africa. To put this in perspective, the crowd gathered at the ZCC's pilgrimage is larger than that which greets the pope in St. Peter's Square on

Easter morning. Another powerful independent group is the amaNazaretha, the Nazarite Baptist Church, founded by the messianic Zulu prophet Isaiah Shembe in 1912: this too has its great pilgrimage gatherings.[30]

The growth of independent churches in South Africa neatly corresponded with the growing political and racial crisis in this nation between the 1960s and the early 1990s, where Black–White tensions reached heights unknown in most of Africa. As a result, many Black Africans felt uncomfortable belonging to mission churches associated with a colonialist regime. This distaste may explain why the independents have done so well across the far southern nations. Significantly, another country in which AICs have enjoyed comparable success is Zimbabwe, which as "Rhodesia" was the scene of a bloody liberation war from 1965 to 1979. The newer churches have also done well in Botswana, which is presently half Christian. Only about 30 percent of Botswana's church members belong to familiar denominations like the Anglicans, Methodists, and Roman Catholics. Seven percent more adhere to Pentecostal groups, while the remainder, almost two-thirds of Christian believers, belong to AICs.[31] In this region at least, independent groups continue to grow quickly, while membership in the mission churches stagnates.

ASIAN DAWNS

These examples remind us that Protestant and Pentecostal expansion is not limited to Latin America. Christian numbers have also been growing apace in societies around the Pacific Rim, although the exact scale of this phenomenon is open to debate. As in Latin America, we have to be wary of overly-optimistic claims. But Asian churches too demonstrate a real excitement about the prospects for future growth, a sense of standing at the beginning of a new Christian epoch. To quote one enthusiastic observer of modern Asian missions, "Europe is in the times of Jesus with anti-establishment protests against an aging religious institution tottering under the weight of its wealth, property and privileges. Asia is in the times of Paul, planting a convert church in virgin soil."[32]

The greatest statistical mystery concerns the People's Republic of China, which prior to the communist victory in 1949 was seen as the world's richest single mission field. Conditions for Christians deteriorated sharply under a communist government that was both anti-religious and xenophobic. All foreign missionaries were soon (1951) expelled as agents of imperialism. While Chinese Christians were grudgingly tolerated, they were expected to join organizations officially registered with the government. Catholics were required to join a Catholic Patriotic Association, while Protestants were to accept the three-self principle, the goals of self-government, self-support, and self-propagation. That scheme was originally meant to create a tougher and more autonomous Chinese Christianity, and whatever the Communists may have wanted, that was exactly the effect.

Estimates of the number of Chinese Christians today range anywhere from 20 million to 50 million, and some observers suggest still higher totals. According to the Chinese government itself, perhaps 20 million people, 1.6 percent of the total population, worship in government-registered churches, but that figure is an absolute minimum, which takes no account of unapproved congregations and private house churches. In its annual survey of International Religious Freedom, the U.S. State Department suggests that the total Chinese Christian population may run as high as 8 percent of the whole, 100 million souls. If true, and this figure is probably too high, that would place the Christian population on a par with the far older-established Chinese religion of Buddhism.[33]

Let us for the sake of argument accept the middle range figure of 50 million Chinese Christians. If that is true, then Christians have not merely survived under such adverse conditions, but they have actually enjoyed something of a population boom through two generations of often fierce antireligious persecution. By this measure, China today has ten times as many Christians as it did when Mao Zedong's forces seized control of the country in 1949. In absolute terms, there are more Christians in the People's Republic than in either France or Great Britain. Patchy evidence also indicates very healthy Christian growth in certain areas, particularly during the growing disaffection with communism in the 1980s. Just in that decade, the number of Catholics in central Henan province reputedly grew from 400,000 to a million. For national authorities, one of the most alarming signs of this religious upsurge is the number of defections to Christianity by party cadres and even officials.[34]

Christianity has also made rapid progress in the Chinese diaspora, the flourishing network of Chinese communities scattered around the Pacific Rim, in nations like Indonesia, Malaysia, and Singapore. By no means are all Christians in these areas ethnic Chinese: Indonesia's large Christian minority is especially diverse. Even so, the assumed linkage between Chinese origins and Christianity has been apparent during episodes of anti-Chinese protest, when Muslim mobs have targeted both Chinese businesses and Christian churches. As we will see, the ethnic-religious equation potentially places religion at the heart of future conflict in nations like Malaysia and Indonesia.[35]

Churches are also flourishing elsewhere in Asia and the Pacific Rim, and given the vast populations of these regions, one needs only a small proportion of the population to constitute a Christian Asian community many millions strong. All these churches are now highly autonomous, far removed from any possible Euro-American origins. One of the great Christian success stories in Asia is South Korea.[36] Christianity first arrived in Korea in the 1590s, originally as part of the wider Catholic missions to the Far East. The first Catholics in Korea were invading Japanese soldiers, which hardly augured well for the faith's reception. Soon, though, Korean scholars encountered Catholicism in more promising circumstances at the Chinese court. Protestant missionaries appeared later, in the nineteenth century. The number of Christians in the whole of Korea was only 300,000 or so in 1920, but this has now risen to 10 million or 12 million, about a quarter of the national population. Christians represent a solid majority of those declaring any religious affiliation, quite an achievement for a society that for centuries defined its identity in terms of Buddhism and Confucianism.

Korean Protestants outnumber Roman Catholics by about three to one, and, as in Latin America, Protestant growth has been largely Pentecostal. At the time of the Korean War, the nation's Pentecostal believers could be counted only in the hundreds, but by the early 1980s, their ranks had swelled to almost half a million. The growth of individual congregations has been dazzling. The Full Gospel Central Church in Seoul now has over half a million members, earning it a place in the *Guinness Book of Records* as the world's largest single congregation. The Kwang Lim Methodist Church reported 150 members in 1971; 85,000 by the end of the century. Mainstream Protestant churches have also succeeded remarkably: today, there are almost twice as many Presbyterians in South Korea as in the United States.[37]

Even in the grimmest political circumstances the churches have been resilient. Communist Vietnam offers as powerful an example as China. Officially, 9 percent of the country's 80 million people are Christian, but as in China, this figure does not include Protestant churches that refuse to register with the government. The scale of these catacomb churches is open to debate, but internal government documents suggest mushroom growth in some areas, notably those inhabited by tribal minorities like the Montagnards. In the province of Lao Cai, Protestant numbers grew from zero in 1991 to between 50,000 and 70,000 by 1998. Recently, too, Christians have been accused of involvement with widespread rural unrest across the country. A generation after the communist victory, Christianity is still a force to be reckoned with.[38]

Christianity has made deep inroads into regions once closely associated with other religions like Hinduism, Buddhism, and Chinese traditional faiths. The great exception to this statement has been Islam, and the historically Muslim lands into which Christian missions have never penetrated. It is open to debate whether this situation might change if political conditions ever opened Muslim countries to Christian evangelism, but given that such a transformation seems impossible, speculation is a waste of time. Evangelical Christians sometimes speak of the great missionary territory of the future as "the 10–40 window," a vast and densely populated rectangle stretching across Africa and Asia, from 10 degrees north to 40 degrees north of the equator. In practice, Christianity has made huge strides in much of this so-called Resistant Belt, far more successfully than might once have been dreamed, but the Muslim world continues to remain impervious. As we will see, the definition of Islamic–Christian frontiers will be a vital and contentious matter in the political world of the new century. For present purposes, we should note that the current general advance of Christianity is not, for the foreseeable future, going to affect every part of the globe.

EXPLAINING SUCCESS

Christian numbers have been growing in many diverse cultures, and the reasons for this expansion are equally complex. Concepts like "South" and "Third World" are enormous generalizations, that ignore not just the distinctions between countries, but the regional differences within vast states like China or Brazil. What do new Protestant mega-churches in Brazil have to do with independent congregations in Africa or rising denominations in China? In Africa, the new Christianity defines itself against a pagan society, while Latin American Pentecostalism emerges from a matrix that is thoroughly Christian. In economic terms, too, the divergences are evident. A South Korean might have far more in common with a German or American, a member of an advanced industrial society, than with a Peruvian or Kenyan. In different regions, churches might appeal either to the very poor or to rising middle-class groups. Even so, many of the new churches do have certain features in common, which set them apart from the traditional Christianity of Europe and North America. In this regard, we can understand the African independent congregations in very much the same context as the Pentecostal movements of Asia and Latin America.

One common factor is that the various Southern churches are growing in response to similar economic circumstances. Their success can be seen as a by-product of modernization and urbanization. As predominantly rural societies have become more urban over the past thirty or forty years, millions of migrants are attracted to ever larger urban complexes, which utterly lack the resources or infrastructure to meet the needs of these "post-industrial wanderers." Sometimes people travel to cities within the same nation, but often they find themselves in different countries and cultures, suffering a still greater sense of estrangement. In such settings, the most devoted and fundamentalist-oriented religious communities emerge to provide functional alternative arrangements for health, welfare, and education.[39] This sort of alternative social system has been a potent factor in winning mass support for the most committed religious groups, and is likely to become more important as the gap between popular needs and the official capacities to fill them becomes ever wider.

Medieval Europeans developed the maxim that "town air makes free," and for all its horrors, urbanization today does promise a new political and religious autonomy. In Latin America especially, the move to the cities over the past half-century has liberated ordinary people from traditional religious structures. No longer were they restricted to the only churches that landowners would permit on their estates, which in virtually every case were Catholic. Yet while liberating themselves, people were also seeking social structures not so very different from what they had previously known when they had lived in small villages or on landed estates: there were features of village life that they missed badly. One theory holds that the new Latin American churches provide the uprooted with the kind of structure to which they were accustomed. In Africa too, the independent churches find their firmest support in the swollen cities, among migrants and the dispossessed. In both continents, the pastors of the new churches exercise a paternalistic role reminiscent of familiar figures from rural society, of landlords in Latin America, of tribal authorities in Africa. The congregations replace the family networks that prevailed in the older villages.

We have already seen the linkage between urban growth and church expansion in a megalopolis like Rio de Janeiro, but we could easily choose other examples, like Lima, São Paulo, or Santiago.[40] Africa offers similar stories. One of the most important, in terms of the future significance of the region, is the vast Nigerian city of Lagos. In 1950, Lagos was a ramshackle port community with around a quarter of a million people. The official population in 1990 was 1.3 million, but the surrounding metropolitan region had then grown to 10 million people, and by 2015 could be around 25 million. Today, the population density of Lagos is around 20,000 people per square kilometer, and the city suffers desperately from congestion and pollution. Although Lagos is deeply divided between Christians and Muslims, the city has played host to some of the largest evangelical gatherings in world history. In 1998, a revival organized by the Redeemed Christian Church of God gathered a congregation between one and 2 million strong. In 2000, comparable crowds turned out to hear German Pentecostal evangelist Reinhard Bonnke, who advertised through the enticing slogan "Come and receive your miracle." On a single night, the crowd reached 1.6 million.[41]

RADICAL COMMUNITY

Churches provide a refuge during a time of immense and barely comprehensible social change. Cox aptly writes of modern urban centers that "sometimes the only thriving human communities in the vast seas of tarpaper shanties and cardboard huts that surround many of these cities are the Pentecostal congregations." A study of new Pentecostal churches in the barrios of Bogotá, Colombia, notes that "The *compañerismo* (fellowship) of the believers is comparable to the intimacy of a large family gathering."[42]

This sense of family and fellowship is crucial for understanding the wide and remarkably diverse appeal of the new Christian congregations. As we have seen, by no means do all draw from the very poorest. The older Protestant denominations in Latin America and East Asia commonly appeal more to middle-class groups, who have expanded as a result of modernization but whose goals and aspirations were hard to fulfill within older social structures. For David Martin, the older Protestantism of Latin America "provided a vehicle of autonomy and advancement for some sections of the middle class, conspicuously so in Brazil, and provided channels of mobility for some who would otherwise have been condemned to poverty."[43]

Yet it is among the very poor that the churches have won some of their greatest recent victories. Pentecostalism in Latin America has appealed particularly to the very poorest groups, such as Brazil's Black population and Mexico's Mayan Indians, who find in the churches a real potential for popular organization. Based on his study of new churches in Belém, Brazil, Andrew Chesnut argues that "in late twentieth-century Brazil, Pentecostalism stands out as one of the principal organizations of the poor." The churches provide a social network that would otherwise be lacking, and help teach members the skills they need to survive in a rapidly developing society.[44]

Given the history of much of Latin America, any movement that makes inroads among the poorest must of necessity be crossing racial boundaries, and much of the recent revivalism in Brazil has occurred particularly among those of African descent. Despite the nation's vaunted multiracialism, Brazil's Blacks and *mestizo* people have been largely excluded from political and social power, and that fact has been reflected in religious institutions.[45] Broadly speaking, darkness of skin directly correlates with poverty and political weakness. Although Blacks make up about half the national population, they represent only 2 percent of congressional representatives and a tiny fraction of the corporate elite. In the Roman Catholic Church too, Afro-Brazilians supply only 1.5 percent of bishops and priests. Not surprisingly, Blacks provide willing recruits for new churches in which they can rise to leadership positions, and to which they can bring their own cultural traditions.[46] The growth of Black spirituality has powerful implications for the wider picture of world Christianity in the new century. Not only will Africa itself be the religion's spiritual center within a few decades, but hundreds of millions of other Christians will belong to the wider African diaspora in the Americas and the Caribbean, and on the soil of Europe itself. It may not be too long before some enthusiast modifies Belloc's celebrated phrase to boast that "Africa is the Faith."[47]

The new churches are succeeding because they fulfill new social needs, and this is as true in matters of gender as of race. No account of the new Southern movements can fail to recognize the pervasive role of women in these structures, if not as leaders then as the devoted core members. Carol Ann Drogus writes of Latin America that "most Pentecostal converts are women . . . women are crucial to the maintenance and expansion of Pentecostal churches." Especially on this continent, much of the best recent scholarship on Pentecostalism stresses the sweeping changes that religious conversion can make in the lives of women and their families. A North American audience is accustomed to seeing religious believers as reactionary on issues of women's rights, but the new churches play a vital role in reshaping women's lives, in allowing them to find their voices. As in nineteenth-century England or North America, evangelical religion has encouraged a new and exalted view of the family and of domesticity, placing much greater emphasis on male responsibility and chastity. The reshaping of gender roles echoes through Southern Hemisphere Christianity, and Latin American churches often present Jesus as divine Husband and Father. In practical terms, the emphasis on domestic values has had a transformative and often positive effect on gender relationships, what Elizabeth Brusco has memorably called a "reformation of machismo."[48] Membership in a new Pentecostal church means a significant improvement in the lives of poor women, since this is where they are more likely to meet men who do not squander family resources on drinking, gambling, prostitutes, and second households. Drogus quotes one Pentecostal woman who reports that "I met a wonderful man. He never drinks, never smokes, he is polite, and he has a good job."[49] As in matters of race, Christianity is far more than an opium of the disinherited masses: it provides a very practical setting in which people can improve their daily lives.

At so many points in our story, we can see impressive analogies to the rise of early Christianity in the days of the Roman Empire, and it is tempting to use the scholarship on the older period to help us interpret the present day. As historian Peter Brown observes of the third and fourth centuries, "The appeal of Christianity still lay in its radical sense of community: it absorbed people because the individual could drop from a wide impersonal world into a miniature community, whose demands and relations were explicit." Every word in this sentence could be wholeheartedly applied to modern Africa or Latin America. The provision of social services that were otherwise unobtainable also went far to explaining the growth of urban Christianity during Roman times, just like today. Brown believes that "The Christian community suddenly came to appeal to men who felt deserted. At a time of inflation, the Christians invested large sums of liquid capital in people; at a time of increased brutality, the courage of Christian martyrs was impressive; during public emergencies, such as plague or rioting, the Christian clergy were shown to be the only united group in the town, able to look after the burial of the dead and to organize food supplies. . . . Plainly, to be a Christian in 250 brought more protection from one's fellows than to be a *civis Romanus*."[50] To be a member of an active Christian church today might well bring more tangible benefits than being a citizen of Nigeria or Peru.

Other more recent historic analogies come to mind. What we are now witnessing in the global South is very much what occurred in the North when it was passing through a comparable stage of social development. We can trace countless parallels between Pentecostal growth today and the much-studied story of English Methodism in the century after 1760, the most rapid stage of British industrialization. Then, as now, popular sects arose to meet the needs that could be filled neither by secular society, nor by the established churches, which had scarcely a foothold in the burgeoning cities. The new Dissenting churches were a triumph of cooperative endeavor, at once providing material support, mutual cooperation, spiritual comfort, and emotional release in the bleak wastes of the expanding industrial society.[51]

RECEIVE YOUR MIRACLE

When trying to understand religious movements, scholars apply the familiar techniques of social science, and see change as a function of familiar categories like modernization, of race, class, and gender; but such an approach always runs the risk of missing the heart of the matter. People might join churches because, consciously or otherwise, they see these institutions as a way of expressing their social aspirations, but other elements also enter into the equation. People join or convert because they acquire beliefs about the supernatural realm and its relationship to the visible world.[52] Just what are these teeming masses seeking from their churches and revivals? What kind of miracle are they looking for?

The seemingly diverse Southern churches have in common many aspects of belief and practice, and these characteristics differentiate them from older Northern Christianity. Just what these distinctive beliefs are, we will explore in more detail in chapter 6, but for present purposes, we have to stress the critical idea that God intervenes directly in everyday life. For both Pentecostal and independent sects, and often for mainstream churches as well, the sources of evil are located not in social structures but in types of spiritual evil, which can be effectively combated by believers. Southern religion is not other-worldly in the sense of escapist, since faith is expected to lead to real and observable results in this world. The believer's life in this world is transformed through conversion, and the change echoes through every aspect of lives, from ethics of work and thrift to family and gender relations.

Audiences respond enthusiastically to a gospel that promises them blessings in this life as well as the next—recall the upturned umbrellas at El Shaddai meetings or the blessing of passports. To quote an observer of Brazil's emerging churches, "Their main appeal is that they present a God that you can use. Most Presbyterians have a God that's so great, so big, that they cannot even talk with him openly, because he is far away. The Pentecostal groups have the kind of God that will solve my problems today and tomorrow. People today are looking for solutions, not for eternity." As a Pentecostal pastor in the same country explained, "We have salvation, but salvation is in heaven. We are here on earth. Jesus will come but he's not here yet."[53] Much the same points could be made about the rising churches across most of Africa and Asia.

People want prosperity—or at least, economic survival—but just as critical is the promise of health, and the desperate public health situation in the new cities goes far toward explaining the emphasis of the new churches on healing of mind and body. Apart from the general range of maladies that affect North Americans and Europeans, the Third World poor also suffer from the diseases associated with poverty, hunger, and pollution, in what has been termed a "pathogenic society." Child mortality is appallingly high by Northern standards. The attacks of these "demons of poverty" are all the graver when people are living in tropical climates, with all the problems arising from the diseases and parasites found in those regions. As well as physical ailments, psychiatric and substance abuse problems drive desperate people to seek refuge in God. Taking all these threats together—disease, exploitation, pollution, drink, drugs, and violence—it is easy to see why people might easily accept the claim that they are under siege from demonic forces, and that only divine intervention can save them.[54]

At its worst, a Faith Gospel of success and health can promote abuses and materialism, and it is easily mocked. Nigerian author Wole Soyinka presents a memorable satire of such a health-and-wealth sermon in his play *The Trials of Brother Jero,* in which the preacher promises: "I say those who dey walka today, give them their own bicycle tomorrow . . . I say those who dey push bicycle, give them big car tomorrow. Give them big car tomorrow." The doctrine also excuses corruption. If a pastor lives luxuriously, if he owns a very big car, he is simply living proof of the wealth that God has given him, while presumably someone who remains poor is just lacking adequate faith. The moral difficulties are all too obvious. Yet a doctrine promising glory in this world as well as the next has undoubted appeal.[55]

For the foreseeable future, the characteristic religious forms of Southern Christianity, enthusiastic and spontaneous, fundamentalist and supernatural-oriented, look massively different from those of the older centers in Europe and North America. This difference becomes critically important in light of current demographic trends. In the coming decades, the religious life characteristic of those regions may well become the Christian norm.

The Rise of the New Christianity

> After this I looked, and there before me was
> a great multitude that no one could count,
> from every nation, tribe, people and
> language, standing before the throne and
> in front of the Lamb.
>
> —*Revelation 7: 9, NIV*

Projecting demographic changes as far ahead as fifty years in the future seems like a risky venture, and perhaps this chapter should really be entitled "Fools Rush In." Yet the process of Christian expansion outside Europe and the West does seem inevitable, and the picture offered here is based solidly on current trends, religious and demographic. In this instance, the foolishness seems justified.

One central fact in the changing religious picture is a massive relative decline in the proportion of the world's people who live in the traditionally advanced nations. If we combine the figures for Europe, North America, and the lands of the former Soviet Union, then in 1900, these Northern regions accounted for 32 percent of the world population. Viewed over the span of world history, that may have been an untypically large proportion, which reflected the explosive demographic growth of the industrial revolution years. Over the course of the twentieth century, matters reverted to what was likely a more typical preindustrial norm, as the proportion of peoples living in the advanced nations fell, slowly at first, but then more dramatically. By 1950, the share had fallen a little to 29 percent, but the rate of contraction then accelerated, to 25 percent in 1970, and around 18 percent by 2000. By 2050, the figure should be around 10 or 12 percent.[1]

Relative growth rates in the South have been just as impressive. Africa and Latin America combined made up only 13 percent of the world's people in 1900, but that figure has now grown to 21 percent. Every indication suggests that the rate of change is accelerating. By 2050, Africa and Latin America will probably be home to 29 percent of the world's people. In 1900, "Northerners" outnumbered these "Southerners" by about 2.5 to one; by 2050, the proportions will be almost exactly reversed. Overall, global population stands at 6 billion today, and should reach 9 billion around 2050, but that increase will not be equitably distributed around the globe. Southern nations are growing very rapidly, while their Northern neighbors are relatively static.

There are many ways to look at statistics of this sort, and one's use of language inevitably reflects value judgments. It is tempting to speak of European rates of population growth as "weak," "stagnant," or "anemic," while African rates are "strong" or "booming," implying that Europe is somehow losing a contest, or failing to achieve. We rarely speak of "decline" as a good thing. Yet one does not have to be a Malthusian to be alarmed by uncontrolled population growth, and most observers would praise the changes in social structure and gender relations that have permitted Europeans to achieve demographic stability. One person's "stagnation" is another's "stability."

Being one of the world's largest nations can be a mixed blessing. The fact of size offers the potential of a huge domestic market for goods and services, and implies political clout. A fast-growing population is also a young community, with a large labor force, a thriving pool of military recruits, and at least the potential of a solid tax base. At the same time, large countries face intense pressure on energy and natural resources, as well as the dangers of social and political turbulence. By the mid-twenty-first century, India could be facing a crushing population density of 1,200 people per square mile. Demographically stable nations like Britain or Italy face an exactly opposite range of costs and benefits, with declining markets and labor forces, and all the problems of an aging community requiring ever more expenditure on pensions and health care. It is an open question whether modern governments are worse prepared to face the emerging problems of the booming South or the stable North.

Predictions like these are open to detailed criticism, and the demographers who produce these figures make no claims about their absolute reliability. Projections work only so long as people maintain their present behavior and societies adapt to changing circumstances. Extrapolating present-day trends far enough down the road can lead to results that are simply ludicrous. Carrying current trends to their logical conclusion, the Japanese will literally have bred themselves out of existence by the year 2500. In reality, "logical" conclusions are far from inevitable. Populations can and do rebound from decline, while what seems like exponential growth can taper off. If the United States had maintained the growth rates of the eighteenth and early nineteenth centuries, then it would today be as populous as China, but of course it did not. In the same way, United Nations demographers predict that global population will eventually level off in the twenty-second century, at a new plateau of 10 billion or so.[2]

Crucially, population change is conditioned by economic circumstances. The history of the West indicates that as a community becomes more prosperous, people tend to have fewer children, and these trends should eventually be replicated in the global South. The decline in family size reflects greater confidence in the ability of medicine to keep children alive, and to ensure that the babies who are born will actually grow to adulthood. Also, couples who have faith in social welfare arrangements have less need to create large families who will maintain them in old age. Gender relationships play a critical role. As economies become more sophisticated, more women participate in the workplace, and employed women cannot afford to devote as much of their lives to bearing and rearing children as do women in traditional societies. This fact encourages a trend toward smaller family size. In the long run, feminism may be the most effective means of regulating population.

As Southern economies develop, their demographic patterns will presumably come to resemble those of the older industrial nations, but those changes will not take effect for some decades. For present purposes, we can be confident that in the middle term—say, the next fifty years—we will indeed be seeing a spectacular upsurge in Southern populations and a decisive shift of population centers to the Southern continents.

DECLINING EUROPE

The stagnation of Northern and particularly European populations will be one of the most significant facts of the twenty-first century. If we take what are currently the eight most populous nations of Europe, then their combined populations amount to 535 million. By 2025, that total will have fallen by 3 percent, to about 519 million, most of the reduction occurring in Russia and Ukraine. Western Europe will retain a fairly stable population. Then as now, there will be around 60 million Britons and 38 million Poles; there will be a couple of million more French people, and a couple of million fewer Italians and Spaniards. But the rate of decline becomes more marked in mid-century, when these major European nations will have shrunk to 465 million, 13 percent below their present figure.[3] If we expand our focus to the fifteen nations of the European Union as a whole, then their combined population would contract by about one-sixth between 2000 and 2050. In 1950, a list of the world's twenty most populous states would have included six European nations, apart from the Soviet Union; on a comparable list in 2025, only Germany would still be ranked among the leaders.

In order to keep a population stable, a nation needs an overall fertility rate of 2.1 children per woman (the rate would have to be higher in countries with worse infant mortality rates). Today, many countries are reporting rates well below that, and 23 recorded fertility rates below 1.5, so all are likely to contract significantly over coming decades. All but 3 of these nations are European, and we see historic lows in countries like Germany (1.3), Italy (1.2), and Spain (1.1). All the members of the former Soviet bloc are also in sharp decline: the Russian rate now stands around 1.2. In the Russian case, historically low birth rates are compounded by soaring death rates and the revival of infectious diseases. According to the Russian Ministry of Health, 12 percent of that nation's people might be infected with the HIV virus by 2015. The United Nations projects that the present-day Russian population of 145.6 million could fall to 121 million by 2050, but some pessimists imagine an even worse decline, to 80 million or so. If true, that would bring the Russian population back to where it stood before the revolution of 1917.[4]

The main non-European member of this declining cohort is Japan which, as a long-established industrial nation, shares many European social patterns. If present trends continue, the Japanese population that today amounts to 126 million will fall to 100 million by 2050, and to 67 million by 2100. By 2015, one-quarter of Japanese will be 65 or older. The demographic contraction in Europe and the advanced nations would be even more advanced if not for the fertility of recent immigrant groups, mainly from Africa or Asia. Conversely, the absence of mass immigration in Japan goes far toward explaining the perilous condition of that country.[5] Although debates over immigration policy are often framed in humanitarian or altruistic terms—"We should help poor people by letting them come here"—for many countries, mass immigration represents the only possible means of maintaining a viable society.

SOUTHERN BOOM

In stark contrast to Europe and Japan is the experience of sub-Saharan Africa. At the end of the twentieth century, the eight largest nations in this region (Nigeria, Ethiopia, Democratic Republic of Congo, South Africa, Sudan, Tanzania, Kenya, and Uganda) had a combined population of about 400 million: by 2050, that figure could well rise to over a billion, an increase of 150 percent. Obviously, AIDS has had a devastating effect in this region, and the eventual population totals may be somewhat less than this. AIDS-related deaths have dramatically slowed population growth in southern African nations like South Africa and Zimbabwe, and over the next decade or two, Central and Western African nations will suffer dreadfully from the epidemic, with the roster of deaths peaking between 2010 and 2020. But even taking this ongoing catastrophe into account, the estimates cited here all explicitly allow for the disease factor, and demographers still confidently predict very large population growth across the region.

Although projected growth rates for Latin America and Asia are somewhat slower, they still dwarf European figures. Between 2000 and 2050, population growth in the 8 largest nations in Latin America will be around 40 percent. The combined population for these countries, 429 million today, will rise to 600 million by 2050.

According to projections by the U.S. Census Bureau, several nations should double their population within just the next quarter-century, even after we have allowed for the effects of AIDS. These countries of super-rapid growth are all located in either sub-Saharan Africa (Uganda, Madagascar, the Democratic Republic of Congo) or Asia (Saudi Arabia, Yemen, Cambodia). The highest fertility rates in the world are found in Yemen, Uganda, Afghanistan, and Angola, all of which report astonishing fertility rates between 6.8 and 7.3. These are followed closely by nations like Chad, Iraq, and Bolivia. Certainly, not all African and Asian populations are exploding at anything like this rate, and growth rates have declined markedly in countries like China, Thailand, and Indonesia, but most Southern nations are still very fertile.[6]

The contrast between growth and stagnation can be seen from the respective age profiles of north and south. In a typical European country, the number of people age 65 or over normally runs at around one-sixth of the population: the figure is 16 or 17 percent in France, Britain, and Spain. Yet people over 65 make up only 3 or 4 percent of most Southern nations. At the other end of the age spectrum, the proportion of people age 14 or under normally runs at 16 to 20 percent or so of the population in European nations. Across the global South, in contrast, the figure is usually around

TABLE 5.1
The Most Populous Nations in the World, 2025 and 2050

Nation	1975*	2000	2025	2050
1. India	622	1,014	1,377	1,620
2. China	918	1,262	1,464	1,471
3. United States	216	276	338	404
4. Indonesia	138	225	301	338
5. Nigeria	59	123	205	304
6. Pakistan	75	142	213	268
7. Brazil	109	173	201	206
8. Bangladesh	76	129	178	205
9. Ethiopia	33	64	115	188
10. Democratic Republic of Congo	25	52	105	182
11. Philippines	44	81	122	154
12. Mexico	61	100	134	153
13. Vietnam	48	79	106	119
14. Russia*	134	146	136	118
15. Egypt	37	68	95	113
16. Japan	112	127	120	101
17. Iran	33	66	88	100
18. Saudi Arabia	7	22	48	91
19. Tanzania	16	35	60	88
20. Turkey	41	66	82	87
21. Sudan	16	35	61	84
22. Uganda	11	23	48	84
23. Germany	79	83	85	80
24. Yemen	7	17	40	71
25. Thailand	42	60	71	70

Note: Nations are listed in order of their projected rankings as of 2050. All figures are in millions.
*1975 figures for Russia refer to the Russian Socialist Federated Soviet Republic (RSFSR), and not to the Soviet Union, of which it then formed part.

one-third, and it rises much higher in some African countries. In Uganda, half the people are below this age, a figure also approached in neighboring countries like the Democratic Republic of the Congo. The world's youngest nations—Uganda, Niger, and the Congo—are African. In those countries the median age of the population is around 16. By the same measure, the oldest countries are all in Europe or Japan (40 is the median age of the people of Italy, Germany, Sweden, and Japan).

These trends can only lead to an ever-larger proportion of the Earth's people living in what have long been the economically less advanced regions, in Africa, Asia, and Latin America. Table 5.1 suggests the growing predominance of "Southern" nations over the next half-century or so.

By 2050, seven of the world's twenty-five most populous nations will be on the African continent. Among Northern nations, apart from the United States, only Russia and Japan will retain their positions among the world's largest nations, and neither of these is likely to remain on the list for much longer. Equally striking is the emergence of ever more nations with what presently seem inconceivably vast populations ranked in the hundreds of millions. In 1950, only four nations boasted populations of 100 million or more, namely the United States, the Soviet Union, China, and India. By 2025, at least fifteen will fall into this category, and these leading fifteen states will account for two-thirds of the human race. By the end of the present century, fourteen states could each have *200* million people or more, and of these, only the United States will represent what is presently the advanced Western world.

These projections are markedly different from the perceptions that prevail in the contemporary West. Asked to name the world's largest countries either now or in the near future, most Americans or Europeans would probably think of China, India, Pakistan, Nigeria, and some other obvious names on the list. But how many would include lands like Ethiopia, Uganda, Tanzania, or even Yemen? The rankings also include some extreme incongruities for anyone who grew up in the mid-twentieth century. For those of us who remember the Vietnam War era, it is inconceivable that "heroic little Vietnam" might soon outpace Russia in population.

DAMNED LIES AND STATISTICS

In addition to revolutionizing global power balances, these demographic changes will inevitably have their impact on the world's religious structures. The difficulty is, though, that religious patterns are far harder to quantify than those in other areas of life. We can be reasonably sure *where* the bulk of the world's people will be living in 2050, but do we dare make statements about what they will believe? When we collect statistics for birth or marriage, we are measuring specific and provable events, which are biological or legal in nature, and we have some grounds for making projections. Equally, we can at least attempt to predict changes in economics or environmental conditions, although in neither area can experts claim a terribly impressive record of accuracy. In the 1990s, everyone knew how swiftly the Pacific Rim was coming to dominate the world economy, under the leadership of the Tiger states like South Korea and Dragons like the Philippines and Indonesia. Many people kept on believing this right up until the Tiger and Dragon economies imploded messily in 1997–98. But religious matters are still more intractable. What, exactly, do we mean if we say that a given country has 10 million Christians, or even more questionable, that the number of Christians is likely to double over the next twenty or thirty years?

Since so much of this book concerns numbers and focuses on present and future religious statistics, it is important to say what can and cannot be done with the evidence that we have. As the saying goes, you can prove anything with statistics, even the truth. Most social statistics can be challenged or modified, depending on the definitions used and the means by which information is collected. These problems become acute when matters of religion are concerned, and even the definition of "Christian" can be controversial. Talking with an American Pentecostal in the 1980s, I mentioned the desperate state of the Christian community in Lebanon, only to be sternly corrected on the grounds that that country, in fact, had virtually no Christians. This was surprising because by most accounts, the population of Lebanon at that point was 40 or 50 percent Christian, in a line of tradition that dated back to Roman times. In my friend's view, though, the term "Christian" could only be used for someone who had experienced a personal born-again conversion, and basically applied to evangelicals in the North American mold. This is the same attitude that produced the notorious evangelical comment that the nation of Poland contained only 100,000 or so Christians, and the rest of the population were all Roman Catholics.

These restrictions can seem overly-narrow or bigoted, but the "Christian" title becomes more problematic in other cases. There are many denominations around the globe that have no doubt of their own claim to this status, yet which have been attacked for theological peculiarities that seem to put them beyond the Christian pale. Are Mormons Christian?[7] Latter Day Saints themselves are quite certain of the fact, yet conservative and evangelical believers reject them just as assuredly, since Mormons use additional scriptures over and above the Bible, and espouse doctrines substantially different from those of traditional Western Christianity. Similar caveats would remove from the Christian fold many of the African and Asian independent churches that are presently at the cutting edge of Christian expansion. Also problematic are the millions of Latin Americans who define themselves confidently as Catholic, yet who practice African-derived spiritualities like Santeria, Umbanda or Candomblé. Denying that Mormons are Christians does not raise too many statistical problems for overall numbers, but excluding these other groups could make an immense difference to our picture of religious loyalties.

But if some observers under-claim Christian numbers on grounds of theological strictness, others are just as likely to make exaggerated claims. The reasons are clear enough. Religious statistics often rely on overly-optimistic reports by church bodies themselves. Some churches have well-controlled mechanisms to measure types of involvement in a given community, and they carefully collect numbers for baptisms, confirmations, or marriages, but literally have no way of detecting when a church member leaves for any reason other than death. Missionaries place a high premium on recording conversions, which are the primary means of measuring success, but do not count converts who slip away or become indifferent or actively hostile.

Nor are problems of counting confined to the new Christian lands. In any country, when you have once been a member of a particular Roman Catholic parish, it is all but impossible to convince that church that you have resigned from it, even if you have demonstrated full commitment to another denomination. A Mother Church does not abandon her errant children. In various European countries, it is equally difficult to remove yourself from the official registers of the various state churches that act as if they still had the established official role they possessed centuries ago. Some churches count as members everyone baptized within that tradition, so that "Christian" becomes a default status in official surveys and virtually means "none of the above." "You're not a Catholic? Not a Muslim? Not a Jew? Fine, I'll put you down as a Lutheran"—or an Anglican, or some other group, depending on the country in question. This tactic accounts for the inflated numbers claimed by English Anglicans, German Evangelicals, or Italian Catholics. The Church of England claims the loyalty of 25 million baptized Anglicans, although under a million of those are ever seen within the precincts of a church.

Different churches measure membership in different ways. One church includes as a member every person baptized in infancy, while another confines the term to those who have made some kind of adult commitment. Some count active participants who share regularly in ritual life, for instance, by taking Communion every Easter or Christmas, so that anyone who fails to meet this standard is purged from the rolls. Others (like Catholics) simply never remove a supposed member. We could easily imagine two denominations with roughly the same number of "real" active members, although one less careful about record-keeping could report numbers ten times larger than the other. Most churches do not actively lie about their membership statistics, they genuinely do not know the figures. This helps explain why indigenous churches in Africa are so often credited with X million members: the number is not so much a real statistic as a symbolic way of saying "a great many people."

Problems of evidence become particularly tricky when international issues are involved. Generally, though, estimates of Christian populations are more likely to be accurate in countries that lack an official or established church. In the newer Christian cultures, practices like baptism do not yet have the same role as obligatory social rituals that they do in England or Spain, while church membership is likely to be more active and less formal. In this sense, church statistics for, say, Uganda or Nigeria are actually likely to be *more* reliable than those reported for Britain or France.[8]

With all these issues in mind, it is tempting to ask whether any religious statistics at all are worthwhile, but I believe that they are, provided certain commonsense guidelines are followed. First, for working purposes, we cannot be too precise about defining Christianity. Ever since the movement began two thousand years ago, the range of groups defining themselves as followers of Jesus has always been very diverse, and we should acknowledge and accept that broad range of self-conceptions. For the purposes of this book, a Christian is someone who describes himself or herself as Christian, who believes that Jesus is not merely a prophet or an exalted moral teacher, but in some unique sense the Son of God, and the messiah. Beyond that, we should not inquire into detailed doctrine, whether for instance a person adheres to the Bible alone, accepts the Trinity, or has a literal belief in Jesus' bodily resurrection. The vast majority of self-described Christians worldwide do in fact meet most of these criteria for membership in the faith, but for present purposes, we cannot label as heretics those who do not.

Equally, we have to pay attention to the sources of the numbers we are offered, whether, for instance, they represent official "none of the above" choices, or the more plausible estimates of actual religious involvement in given communities. Even so, with all due awareness of the problems involved, I will in many cases be using official definitions of religious loyalty, the admittedly exaggerated statements about numbers of adherents put out by various official and established bodies. With whatever qualms, this means accepting the official figures that suggest that for all its evident secularization, Europe is still overwhelmingly Christian, and appears to remain the world center of Christianity.

This approach acknowledges that people often do retain a lingering cultural loyalty to a church label, even when actual religious involvement is nonexistent. The fact of living under the hegemony of a particular tradition inevitably tends to shape one's consciousness, so that even a not very enthusiastic believer can appropriately be seen as a cultural Christian, or a cultural Muslim, or whatever the tradition in question. Even when someone claims to abandon religion, it is this predominant religion that she or he is rebelling against, and which largely shapes the form taken by that rebellion.

The usefulness of this idea of "cultural Christianity" can be seen from looking at Roman Catholics in a society like that of the United States. Surveys regularly indicate that millions of Americans describe themselves as Catholic even though they reject many or most of that Church's official positions, often on what most would consider essential doctrine. Are these people "really" Catholic? It all depends who you ask. For present purposes, my view is that if they consider themselves Catholic, then that is what they are.

As a final obstacle, religious trends simply do not develop as logically and predictably as demographic factors. To take what should be one of the world's pivotal nations in the near future, at least 40 percent of Nigerians are currently Christian, some 50 million people, but how will that number change in future decades? No church or religion has a guaranteed market share in any country. It is quite possible to imagine a scenario in which the proportion of Nigerian Christians could fall as low as 10 percent, in the event of persecutions or a successful jihad by the nation's Muslim majority. The figure could rise far higher if a sweeping Christian revival were to occur.

THE FUTURE DEMOGRAPHICS OF RELIGION

Although we might be tempted to despair about any attempt at prediction, we are still observing major trends in the development of Southern Christianity, and in every case, these suggest surging growth. In Africa especially, experience over the past half-century indicates that the Christian share of the population will rise substantially across most of the continent, making deep inroads in the center and east. This trend is so marked any projections offered here might be overly-conservative. The religious maps may change, the frontiers may shift, but Southern Christianity will be growing.

To illustrate this, let us visualize the shape of the Christian world in another twenty-five or fifty years. Where will the bulk of Christians live? What should be the largest Christian communities in the year 2025 or 2050? For present purposes, we will make the conservative assumption that Christian communities will remain relatively stable as a proportion of national populations (see table 5.2). One uncertainty about this table is the political integrity of the states named, and it is possible that countries like the Democratic Republic of Congo will no longer exist in that form or may have disintegrated into two or more smaller entities. Nevertheless, the regions in question will be major Christian territories, and this fact confirms a powerful southward shift. By 2050, six nations could each have 100 million Christians or more, and of these, only one represents what is presently the

TABLE 5.2
The Largest Christian Communities, 2025 and 2050

	Estimated Christian Population (in millions) Year		
Nation	2000	2025	2050
United States	225	270	330
Brazil	164	190	195
Mexico	95	127	145
Philippines	77	116	145
Nigeria	50	83	123
Zaire/D. R. Congo	34	70	121
Ethiopia	36	65	79
Russia	90?	85	80
China	50?	60	60
Germany	58	61	57

Note: Both in this table and throughout this chapter, information about religious affiliations is based on U.S. government statistics, found respectively in the *Annual Report on International Religious Freedom* (http://www.state.gov/www/global/human_rights/irf/irf_rpt/irf_index.html) and the *CIA World Fact Book* (http://www.odci.gov/cia/publications/factbook/).

advanced industrial world, namely the United States. Equally striking, perhaps, are the nations that are not found on this list, such traditional heartlands of Christian loyalty as Britain, France, and Italy.[9]

To put this another way, we can consider the most populous nations of sub-Saharan Africa mentioned earlier. Today, these eight states have around 200 million Christians, representing roughly half the total population. If we assume that the religious distribution of those populations will remain stable, then, by 2025, that number will have grown to 330 million. However, recent history suggests that these churches will expand by evangelization, so that we could be speaking of closer to 400 million believers in just these leading nations. Even in terms of formal adherence to Christianity, sub-Saharan Africa will already have displaced Europe as the chief Christian heartland within a mere quarter-century.

The example of a single country allows us to see such continental trends in better focus. Uganda is representative of the fast-growing tropical countries.[10] The country's population in 1950 was a mere 5.5 million people, in a land the size of Oregon, but the number of people was roughly doubling every quarter-century or so. To put this in context, this was the same stunning growth rate that North America experienced during the colonial and early national periods. There were 11 million Ugandans by 1975, 23 million by 2000. According to UN statistics, the total should grow to about 33 million by 2025, and to 65 million by 2050. The U.S. Census Bureau offers an even more remarkable projection, with the possibility of 84 million Ugandans by the mid-twenty-first century. The country currently records an annual growth rate of 2.7 percent, which sounds impressive enough until we recall that that is not the birth rate, but the actual rate of annual growth. The *birth* rate is four times that of most European nations. The rate of overall growth would be even higher if not for the effects of AIDS and civil violence.

In religious terms, Uganda represents one of the triumphs of the missionary movement, in a country where Christianity was newly planted in the mid-nineteenth century. Today, about 40 percent of the population is Protestant, 35 percent Catholic, and 10 percent Muslim, while the remainder follow traditional African religions. If we assume no further expansion by means of conversion, then the Ugandan Christian population should grow from around 17 million today, to 24 million in 2025, and to 43 million by mid-century (55 million if the higher projections are accurate). Perhaps, though, even these estimates of religious affiliation are too conservative, since the various churches will probably continue to make inroads among the traditional and animist believers. A mid-century total of around 50 million Ugandan Christians is possible. At that point, there will be more self-described Christians in Uganda than in nations like Germany or Britain. By some estimates, Uganda could by that point have more active church members than the four or five largest European nations combined.

For an Asian example, we can take the Philippines, which should by 2050 be home to the third or fourth largest number of Christians on the planet.[11] The current population of around 80 million will expand quickly due to a high rate of population growth, currently estimated at 2.1 percent each year. It is also, like Uganda, a very young country, in which 37 percent of the population is currently under the age of 15. By 2050, there could be over 150 million Filipinos. The city of Manila reports a population of around 1.8 million, but the larger metropolitan area contains perhaps 9 million. By 2050, the Manila metropolitan area could easily have 18 or 20 million inhabitants.

In religious terms, Christianity has deep roots in the Philippines, which was part of the Spanish colonial expansion of the sixteenth century. About 85 percent of the nation presently has some degree of identification with the Roman Catholic Church, while another 8 percent are associated with various Protestant groups (a further 4 or 5 percent are Muslims). If we assume that these proportions will remain constant, then by 2050, we will be speaking of roughly 143 million Filipino Christians. This growth will have major implications for the shape of global Catholicism. Today, the Catholic Church of the Philippines reports 61 million members, which represents a larger Catholic population than that found in any individual European state, and the number of Catholics is growing swiftly. At present, the Philippines reports 1.7 million Catholic baptisms each year, a number larger than the *combined* totals for the four leading Catholic nations of Europe, namely France, Spain, Italy, and Poland.[12] By 2025, the number of Filipino Catholics could grow to 90 million, and to 130 million by 2050.

That the Philippines will remain a major Catholic state is a reasonably safe bet, but we can be far less confident about another emerging superstate, namely Brazil. This country has also grown enormously, and this pattern will continue. There were 53 million Brazilians in 1950, there are around 170 million today, and by 2050, there should be around 207 million. An upsurge of AIDS-related deaths means the rate of increase is lower than it would have been otherwise, but even so, we are still dealing with a classic Third World population profile. Almost 30 percent of Brazilians are age 14 or less. But religious statistics are much more tenuous than secular demographics. Today, about 75 percent of Brazil's population is reported as Catholic, while a further 20 percent are Protestant or Pentecostal. If we extrapolate those figures into the mid-twenty-first century, then we see a society with over 150 million Catholics and 40 million Protestants. But can we make this projection with any confidence? The non-Catholic population has swelled so very quickly in recent years as to make any such predictions moot, and it would not be astonishing if Brazil by this stage was half-Protestant. That Brazil will be a key center of world Christianity is beyond doubt, but the precise contours of its religious life are unknowable.

THE UN-SECULAR CITY

None of the reasons why churches have been growing so astonishingly in the global South is likely to change in the near future. These emerging churches work so well because they appeal to the very different demographics of their communities, and do best among young and displaced migrants in mushrooming mega-cities. The most successful new denominations target their message very directly at the have-nots, or rather, the have-nothings. Again, demographic projections suggest that the environment in which they have flourished will continue to exist well into the new century. By 2050, there will be an ever-growing contrast between the age profiles of

TABLE 5.3
**The World's Largest Urban
Concentrations in 2015**

City	Population (in millions)
1. Tokyo	28.7
2. Bombay/Mumbai	27.4
3. Lagos	24.4
4. Shanghai	23.4
5. Jakarta	21.2
6. São Paulo	20.8
7. Karachi	20.6
8. Beijing	19.4
9. Dhaka	19.0
10. México	18.8

Source: United Nations projections (http://www.sru. edu/depts/artsci/ges/discover/d-6–9b.htm).

the global South and North, between the world of the young and very mobile and the world of the old and static.

Most of the global population growth in the coming decades will be urban. Today, around 45 percent of the world's people live in urban areas, but that proportion should rise to 60 percent by 2025, to over 66 percent by 2050. The result will be a steadily growing number of huge metropolitan complexes that could by 2050 or so be counting their populations in the tens of millions. We think of cities like Cairo, Mumbai (Bombay), Dhaka, Karachi, Jakarta, Lagos, and Mexico City, each with perhaps 30 or 40 million people, and next to nothing in working government services. Tens of millions of new urban dwellers will in effect be living and working totally outside the legal economy or any effective relationship with officialdom.[13] There will be other future colossi, giant cities with names hitherto unfamiliar to Westerners, centers like Kampala, Kinshasa, Dar-es-Salaam, and Sana'a.

In another epochal change, these urban centers will be overwhelmingly Southern. In 1900, all the world's largest cities were located in either Europe or North America. Today, only three of the world's ten largest urban areas can be found in traditionally advanced countries, namely Tokyo, New York City, and Los Angeles, and by 2015, the only one of these names left on the list will be Tokyo (see table 5.3). Currently, 80 percent of the world's largest urban conglomerations are located in either Asia or Latin America, but African cities will become much more significant by mid-century. The proportion of Africans living in urban areas will grow from around 40 percent today to almost 66 percent by 2050. Rich pickings await any religious groups who can meet these needs of these new urbanites, anyone who can at once feed the body and nourish the soul. Will the harvest fall to Christians or Muslims? And if to Christians, will the winners be Catholics or Pentecostals?

EUROPE

Demographics alone cannot tell the full story of the broadening gap between the numerical strength of Christians in the First and Third Worlds, since cultural shifts too will play their part. Not only are there going to be far more Christians in the global South than the North, but the Southerners are also likely to be much more committed in terms of belief and practice. The cultural change is evident from Europe, which notionally has a present-day Christian population of 560 million. To say the least, that number looks optimistic. Over the past century or so, massive secularization has seriously reduced the population of European Christians, whether we judge "Christianity" by general self-definition, or else demand evidence of practice and commitment. Rates of church membership and religious participation have been declining precipitously in a long-term trend that shows no signs of slowing.

Great Britain offers a model example of dechristianization. Of a population of around 60 million, the number adhering to non-Christian religions is still not large. Jews, Muslims, Sikhs, and Hindus combined represent no more than 5 percent of the British total, roughly the same non-Christian proportion as in the United States. But we cannot safely conclude that the remaining 95 percent of British people should be classified as Christian. According to a survey taken in 2000, 44 percent of the British claim no religious affiliation whatever, a number that has grown from 31 percent in 1983. More worrying still for the churches, two-thirds of those ages 18 to 24 now describe themselves as non-religious: almost half of young adults do not even believe that Jesus existed as a historical person, which is quite a radical stance.[14]

Only about 40 percent of British people identify themselves as Christians, and the degree of this identification is often slight. Based on baptismal records, Great Britain claims to have 25 million members of the Church of England, which has long enjoyed an established status. As we have seen, though, under a million of these supposed Anglicans can ever be found in church, even for Easter or Christmas. Between 1989 and 1998 alone, Sunday church attendance for all Christian denominations combined fell from 4.7 million to 3.7 million, a decline of 22 percent in just a decade. Extrapolating these figures would leave English churches literally abandoned within a generation or two. In a recent dispute over using faith-based charities to provide social welfare, prominent Labour Party politician Roy Hattersly protested that "This is an agnostic nation. People don't take [religion] seriously." It is difficult to argue with his assessment—and the fact that he could offer it so uncontroversially amply illustrates the gulf that separates religious practice in the United States and Europe.[15]

Britain offers a singularly clear example of an emerging post-Christian society. Since people have moved to religious indifference rather than active participation in some other faith, the abandonment of Christianity is difficult to measure accurately. Still, useful indicators are provided by the growing popularity of practices once condemned by the church, including cremation of the dead, which accounts for about 70 percent of all British funerals in a given year. Over half of the weddings in Britain in a typical year are civil, with no religious element whatever.

Similar situations can be found in most other west European nations, and in the former communist countries of eastern Europe. In Germany, the situation of the Evangelical Church is comparable to that of British Anglicans. In theory, the church claims the loyalty of most German Protestants, around one-third of the population, but out of 28 million notional members, only a million or so demonstrate any regular religious participation. Activity is apparently higher among German Catholics, but still represents only a small share of reported members. About a quarter of the population claim no religious affiliation, not even a residual Christianity.[16]

Declining religious identification is just as obvious in the historically Catholic nations. In France, as in Britain, a substantial majority of the people has some notional degree of identification with Christianity, but only 8 percent, or some 5 million, emerge as practicing Catholics. Italy offers a similar story. Because of the church's long-standing hegemony, it is still customary for most Italians to acknowledge some vestigial Catholic identity, and most Italians are baptized as Catholics. According to church statistics, some 97 percent of Italians count as Catholics, or some 55 million adherents. Based on this figure, Italy is now the only European country listed among the world's five most populous Catholic nations. However, religious practice in Italy has declined steeply in recent years, and a more reasonable estimate of belief and loyalty would suggest an active Catholic population only one-tenth of this level.[17]

Because both Anglicanism and Roman Catholicism are global communions, declining loyalties in Europe should be more than compensated by gains elsewhere in the world, but that pattern will not hold true for all denominations. The Eastern Orthodox churches will suffer acutely from demographic changes, given that the church's numbers are so heavily concentrated in declining Europe. Presently, the Orthodox Church worldwide claims about 214 million followers, almost all in countries of eastern and southeastern Europe that are likely to be losing population steadily over the next fifty years. Although post-communist Russia has experienced a substantial Orthodox revival, demographic trends mean that the long-term future of that church must be in doubt. Falling birth rates will ultimately be more destructive to Orthodox fortunes than Muslim or communist persecutions ever were. Taking an optimistic population projection, Orthodox believers will by 2050 have shrunk to less than 3 percent of the world's population, pathetically smaller than the early-twentieth-century figure. In the worst-case scenario, the total number of Orthodox believers in the world by 2050 might actually be less than the Christian population of a single nation like Mexico or Brazil.[18]

THE NEW EUROPEANS

A largely secularized First World confronts a rapidly growing "South" in which religion thrives and expands. We can illustrate this by comparing Uganda, say, with Britain, or Brazil with Spain. But this contrast does not just involve societies separated by oceans, since the interaction of North and South will be reproduced within the individual countries of North America and Europe themselves. This will occur as a consequence of mass migrations.

The far-reaching ethnic transformation of Europe was largely an accidental by-product of the Cold War. As western European industries boomed during the 1950s and 1960s, the natural source for cheap labor would have been the poorer (White) countries of southern and eastern Europe, but the rigid nature of Cold War boundaries forced employers to turn elsewhere. Industrial states recruited in Asia and Africa, often in former colonial territories: the British drew labor from Jamaica and Pakistan, the French from Algeria and West Africa. The significance of these immigrant populations has grown steadily, since these groups have experienced far higher birth rates than the older populations of the metropolitan countries. People of African and Asian stock now play a crucial part in European societies, especially in the major cities. About half of London's people are now non-White, and by the end of the twenty-first century, Whites will form a minority within Great Britain as a whole. The empires have struck back.[19]

Across Europe, mass immigration has been deeply controversial for decades, but it is difficult to see how else European nations could cope with what otherwise would be sharply declining (and aging) domestic populations. If Germany, for instance, ceased to accept immigration, then its current population of 80 million would shrink by about one-quarter by 2050: in the same years, the working population would fall from around 41 million to only 26 million. Yet the problems would become acute long before this. Europe's baby boom generation will begin to retire in 2010, and by 2020, the vast demands on social security could well crash fiscal systems across the Continent. A report recently issued by the French government argued that Europe would have no alternative but to admit 75 million immigrants over the coming half-century, with the frank admission that this would mean becoming a racially hybrid society and accepting "cross-fertilization." The U.S. intelligence community sees the demographic decline as a serious potential brake on global economic progress: "European and Japanese populations are aging rapidly, requiring more than 110 million new workers by 2015 to maintain current dependency ratios between the working population and retirees." In the long term, by 2050, say, the numbers needed will be correspondingly greater.[20]

Looking at the supply side of the equation, Southern peoples will face continuing pressures to move northward en masse, due to poverty and environmental catastrophe. Presently, western Europe alone has between 10 million and 20 million illegal immigrants from Africa and Asia, over and above the legally settled communities. One enormous and continuing incentive will be water resources, since the regions of fastest population growth are often those in most acute danger of drought and drought-related famines. By 2015 nearly half the world's population—more than 3 billion people—will live in countries that are "water-stressed."[21]

Demographic changes naturally have their religious consequences, since the new immigrant groups follow cultural patterns more akin to their home societies than to the host nations. The most visible aspect of religious change has been the upsurge of mosques and Muslim community centers across most western European nations, so that there are now 3 million Muslims in Germany, 2 million in France, at least a million in Britain, and perhaps 750,000 in Italy. The most thorough transformation has been in French cities like Marseille, which have acquired a strongly North African flavor. In Frankfurt, immigrant groups make up some 30 percent of the population, and about one person in 8 is of Turkish Muslim origin: the city has

27 mosques. Muslims make up around one-fifth of the population of Vienna, a figure that has more than doubled just since the late 1980s. Europe as a whole has some 15 million Muslims, many of whom are of ancient stock, particularly in southeastern parts of the Continent.[22]

Looking at the spread of mosques across urban Europe, it would be easy to believe that Islam might indeed be Europe's future religion. Yet a great many other European immigrants are Christian, and they raise the prospect of a revitalized Christian presence on European soil. This was symbolized for me by an encounter while researching this book, as I was visiting Amsterdam, which is at the heart of one of the world's most secular societies. Being there on a Sunday morning, one becomes aware of how little religious activity, Christian or otherwise, takes place in or near the center city. It was all the more interesting, then, to venture into a working-class quarter to see a swelling stream of individuals all clearly bound for the same destination. Each was an African, clearly not terribly well-off, but each was in his or her Sunday best, and everyone clutched a well-thumbed bible. Some families were in evidence, but most of the passers-by, en route to an African church, were single men, presumably immigrants separated from homes and families. That one congregation probably represents, in miniature, the future face of Christianity in Western Europe.

The effects of immigration can be seen across the denominational spectrum. People of African and Caribbean stock have revived Catholic communities in the metropolitan countries. Other churches are of a type quite different from local traditions, including Pentecostals, Baptists, and independents. Even in Germany and Switzerland, there are enough independent African churches to form their own separate federation or Conference.[23]

Great Britain is now home to a substantial network of African and Caribbean churches, heavily Pentecostal in worship style. Currently, about half of all churchgoers in London are Black. Often, outsiders only get a sense of the scale of this activity when a scandal erupts, for instance, during the recent Anna Climbie affair, which drew attention to the popularity of exorcism in some Black churches. Such incidents are wildly untypical, but the reporting does suggest just how "Southern" is some of the religion in what was once the capital of the British Empire. Much more representative of the new churches would be London's Kingsway International Christian Centre (KICC), founded by Pastor Matthew Ashimolowo, who came from Nigeria as a missionary. Although he began in 1992 with only 300 members, the KICC now seats 5,000 worshipers at its main facility, the Miracle Centre, as well as several satellite churches. The KICC is claimed to be the largest church created in Britain since 1861, and the Miracle Centre's auditorium offers double the capacity of Westminster Abbey or St. Paul's Cathedral. The pastor uses cable television and radio to speak to a wider audience in the United Kingdom, and beyond, in Nigeria, Ghana, and Europe. He has attracted controversy by urging, logically enough, that the Anglican Church should just "die gracefully" in the United Kingdom and hand its buildings over to newer groups like his own.[24]

In Canada as in Europe, immigrant groups have slowed the general decline in churchgoing.[25] Between 1988 and 1998, the number of Canadians attending a religious service at least monthly fell from 41 percent to 34 percent. The most serious slippage occurred in the once solidly Catholic province of Quebec, where churchgoing declined in the same decade from 48 percent to 29 percent of the population. Also as in Europe, though, the figures would have been still more depressing for churches of all denominations if not for the vigorous religious life of Caribbean and Asian immigrants. Montreal's Catholic churches would be poorly attended if not for the enthusiasm of new Canadians of Vietnamese and Haitian stock.

It is hard to predict how the newer ethnic communities will continue to affect the religious life of the host societies. Aside from the usual difficulties in assessing religious loyalties, there is also the issue of harmonization, of judging how far the children of immigrants will adopt the laxer and more "modern" thought-ways of Europe. Based on the American experience, sociologists of religion argue that new immigrants are commonly more religiously active than their forebears at home, and this pattern may well be followed in Europe. On the other hand, we see some evidence that the children of British Muslims see their family religion mainly as a matter of ethnic and cultural pride, rather than a powerful motivating ideology. Girls, in particular, chafe at traditional restraints. The next generation might conceivably be as religiously lukewarm as their White neighbors. Yet having said this, the process of secularization is not yet that advanced, and for the next few decades, the face of religious practice across Europe should be painted in Brown and Black. When we measure the declining strength of Christianity in Europe, we must remember how much leaner the statistics would be if not for the recent immigrants and their children, the new Europeans.

THE UNITED STATES

The contrast between population trends in Europe and the global South could hardly be more marked. The United States, though, offers a more complex picture. Although in most senses the heart of the West, demographically the United States has less in common with Japan or western Europe than with the developing nations. Critically, the U.S. population will continue to grow in the new century, if not at Ugandan rates, then far more impressively than any European nation. Today, there are about 280 million Americans. That figure should grow to 400 million by 2050, to 570 million by 2100.

As the nation grows, its ethnic character will also become less European and less White, with all that implies for religious and cultural patterns. For most of American history, the racial question essentially concerned two groups, Black and White, people of African and European descent. In 1930, the nation was comprised of 110 million Whites, 12 million Blacks, and just 600,000 "Others," meaning Native Americans and Asians. From the 1960s on, the Otherness of America developed apace, largely due to a relaxation of immigration controls. As we gain greater distance from the event, the passage of the Immigration Reform Act in 1965 increasingly looks like the most significant single event of that much-ballyhooed decade. By 2000, the United States was home to 30 million immigrants, about 11 percent of the population. Over 13 million migrants arrived in the 1990s alone. Almost 5 percent of Americans have been in the country for a decade or less.

American society is steadily moving from a Black and White affair to a multicolored reality. In 2000, 35 million Americans were counted as Hispanic, almost 60 percent of them of Mexican ancestry. Nearly 12 million more Americans were Asian, of Chinese, Japanese, Filipino, Vietnamese, and Korean stock. Asians and Hispanics combined make up 15 percent of the population today, but this share is projected to grow to almost 25 percent by 2025, and to 33 percent by 2050. As recently as 1970, Asian and Hispanic Americans accounted for only 8 percent of total births in the United States, but today, that figure has increased to more than 25 percent. One reason for this transformation is that Latinos are generally much younger than longer-established populations. The national census of 2000 showed that the median age for Hispanics was about 26, younger than that of any other ethnic group, and far lower than the media age for Anglo-Whites, which stood at a venerable 38.5.[26] By mid-century, 100 million Americans will claim Hispanic origin. They will then constitute one of the world's largest Latino societies, more populous than any actual Hispanic nation with the exception of Mexico or Brazil. By that point, 50 or 60 million Americans will claim Mexican descent.

Although the ethnic change will ultimately affect all parts of the country, it is already evident in some regions. In the late 1990s, California became the nation's first "majority-minority" state, in which non-Latino Whites ceased to form an absolute majority of the population. Within a decade, Latinos alone will constitute a majority of California's people. Latinos also make up one-third of the population of Texas, the second largest state, which could achieve majority-minority status as early as 2005. While the proportion of foreign-born people in Houston was less than 3 percent in 1960, today it is about 25 percent.[27] Looking at these changes should make us reconsider our whole view of American history. In the nineteenth century, Manifest Destiny led Anglos to overwhelm the whole continent, leaving the older Hispanic cultures as shrinking islands of language and faith within the new U.S. borders. At best, they were treated as quaint tourist attractions. In retrospect, those islands look more like bridgeheads from which new advances would someday occur.

Far from what anyone foresaw at the time, the 1965 Immigration Act had vast consequences for American religion. As in Europe, it is the newer "Southern" populations who will account for much of what denominational growth will occur in coming decades. Just to take an East Coast example, around half the congregations active today in the Boston–Cambridge area worship in languages other than English. Since immigrant congregations are often small, this does not imply that anything like half of all believers are non-Anglophone, but it does suggest a vigorous growth. When the Greater Boston Baptist Association used posters on subway trains to spread its evangelistic message, the languages used included English, French, Spanish, Portuguese, and Korean. Today, around a third of the Black population of Massachusetts is foreign-born, with roots in the Caribbean or Africa itself, and this influx is suggested by a new wave of Black churches. The whole concept of "African-American" identity is in urgent need of redefinition.[28]

Latinos represent the most obvious aspect of religious change, and the Hispanic presence has radically altered the nature of U.S. Catholicism. In the mid-1990s, Mass was celebrated in Spanish in some 3,500 parishes.[29] A century ago, an upsurge in the American Latino population would have been seen as part of a general Catholic menace, since Hispanics were assumed to be automatically, and blindly, members of the Roman Catholic Church. Yet the overall picture is much more complex. Only about 70 percent of U.S. Latinos are Catholic, while 20 percent more are evangelical Protestants. The remainder divides its loyalties among a number of smaller faiths. How this distribution will change in coming decades is far from clear, although some observers believe that the evangelical share will expand significantly. Among first-generation Latinos in the United States, Catholics massively outnumber Protestants, by 74 to 18 percent, but among the third generation, the Catholic share has shrunk to a 59–32 majority. To try and reduce the continuing hemorrhage of believers, Latino Catholics in the United States have tried very much the same solutions as their counterparts in the Philippines or South America, importing Pentecostal customs like traditional music and instruments during services, and encouraging emotional expressions of spontaneous praise and thanksgiving. These tactics may or may not succeed, but in any case the Latino religious scene has been so volatile in recent decades that detailed predictions of any kind are rash. But whatever the exact denominational balance may be, the changing racial picture is only going to strengthen overall Christian numbers.[30]

Predicting the religious loyalties of Asian-Americans poses similar problems. Some follow traditional Asian religions such as Buddhism, but many others are Christian. In some cases, immigrant communities derive from strongly Christian homelands, like the Philippines, or from countries with large Christian minorities, like Vietnam or South Korea. Other Asian migrants are recent converts. In this sense, the Asian-American communities of Los Angeles or San Francisco can usefully be seen in the same religious context as other Pacific Rim cities like Manila, Seoul, or Jakarta. In addition to strengthening Christian numbers in the United States, such migrant communities transmit American ideas to home countries, because of the constant interchange between Asian-American communities and their ancestral nations. Family and social links thus help promote Pentecostalism in Korea or the Philippines. As in Europe, the presence of migrant churches is likely to introduce the practices of the newer churches into the religious mainstream of the host nation. Transnational groups like El Shaddai have a solid presence in the United States. For all the writing over the past decade or so on the enormous cultural and economic significance of the Pacific Rim region, few observers have noted that this region would increasingly become a Christian Arc.[31]

The Christian presence is powerfully evident in any Asian community in North America. Vancouver, for example, has such a sizable Asian presence that it sometimes seems like a thriving Chinese city accidentally misplaced on the wrong side of the Pacific. Inevitably, the city has its quota of Asian temples and holy places, including sumptuous Buddhist and Hindu temples, and some evocative Taoist sites. These are the places that tourists visit when they want to seek out characteristically "ethnic" religion. Yet the greater Vancouver area also has around fifty Christian congregations labeled with some Asian ethnic title, such as "Chinese Pentecostal" or "Korean Baptist," and that figure does not count distinct services in ethnic languages offered by mainstream Catholic or Protestant churches. Roughly half of these Christian congregations and special services cater to the Chinese community, while the remainder are directed toward Koreans, Japanese, and Filipinos. In addition, thousands of Vancouver residents of Asian descent attend mainstream Christian services in the English language. A similar picture can be found in Chinatowns and Little Saigons across the United States.

The experience of Korean Americans illustrates the dimensions of Asian American Christianity.[32] Although Korean immigration to the United States began in the late nineteenth century, virtually all the million or so Americans who today claim Korean ancestry trace their roots in the new land to the past thirty years or so. The Korean community in the United States is deeply imbued with Christian teaching: Christians outnumber Buddhists by ten or twenty to one. In many cases, immigrants were already Christian upon their arrival, so that a sizable majority of first-generation Korean Americans is Christian, and these are usually enthusiastic church members. In addition to mainstream churches—Presbyterian, Methodist, and Catholic—there is also a large para-church network of small group and Bible study activity, and many of these cells will evolve over time into full-scale churches that will draw ever closer to the cultural mainstream. The example of European ethnic churches on American soil suggests that Korean Christian communities will become progressively less ethnically centered as time goes by. Already in the 1990s, many Korean churches realized that they would have to make greater use of English in order to retain the loyalty of younger members.

CHRISTIAN AMERICA?

The strength of American Christianity, present and future, contradicts much received wisdom. Americans like to think of their land as one of diversity, perhaps a diversity unparalleled anywhere on the globe, but in religious matters at least, such a view is strikingly far from the truth. America remains today substantially what it has always been, namely a Christian country. That observation can sound aggressively partisan or intolerant, since some believe that Americans are a Christian people who require a Christian government, with all that implies about religious exercises in schools and public displays. I am making no such assertion, since I personally believe that religion flourishes best when it is kept farthest away from any form of government intervention, even the best-intentioned.[33] I just observe that while the United States is home to a remarkable number of religious denominations, overwhelmingly, these are traditions within the broader stream of Christianity.

The number of adherents of non-Christian religions in the United States is strikingly small. If we combine the plausible estimates for the numbers of American Jews, Buddhists, Muslims, and Hindus, then we are speaking about 4 or 5 percent of the total population. Even if we take the controversial step of excluding Mormons from the Christian community, this only raises the non-Christian total to around 7 percent. According to the *World Christian Encyclopedia,* even by 2025, the combined strength of the non-Christian religions will only be about 7 percent, not counting Mormons. This makes the United States about as religiously diverse as most European nations, and less so than some. Adherents of non-Christian religions presently make up 10 percent of the population of France, 4 percent for Great Britain, 5 percent for Germany and the Netherlands.

The degree of religious diversity in the United States is very limited compared to what we find in many African and Asian nations, where religious minorities commonly make up 10 or 20 percent of the people, or often more. Ironically, in terms of American perceptions, some of the most diverse lands are to be found in the Middle East, which Westerners often imagine in terms of Muslim homogeneity. In fact, countries like Egypt and Syria are more diverse than the United States. So, of course, is Israel, which is avowedly a Jewish state. Nevertheless, the population of the core pre-1967 state of Israel is only 80 percent Jewish, and this proportion falls steeply when we take account of the occupied territories.

Political factors help explain why Americans tend to misunderstand the religious complexion of their society. Projections about the possible future of American religion have become an important weapon in debates concerning the separation of church and state. When conservatives demand school prayer, for instance, liberals object that the present Christian predominance will not last much longer, and that demographic trends might well lead to Islam or Buddhism growing quickly in the United States. To quote the subtitle of a recent book by Diana Eck, we are witnessing the story of *How a "Christian Country" Has Become the World's Most Religiously Diverse Nation.*[34] The political implications are clear. Would those Christians who want school prayer or public displays of religion really make the same demands if they were forced to listen to Muslim prayers, to see Asian Buddhist shrines on public grounds? Do conservative Christians want to see tax moneys flowing to faith-based charitable organizations if the faiths in question are Muslim or Buddhist? Partly because of this political agenda, liberals offer unrealistically high projections of Muslim or Buddhist numbers in the United States, and these optimistic figures are echoed by activists from those religions.

In reality, the number of new immigrants who practice non-Christian religions is far less than is often supposed. The powerful Christian presence among East Asians means that Buddhist or Taoist numbers are smaller than they might appear, and the numbers commonly given for American Muslims are likewise exaggerated. Although we read suggestions that the United States is home to as many as 8 million Muslims, actual numbers remain a good deal smaller than this, probably 4 million or so, or 1.5 percent of the population. Though Americans tend to assume that all Middle Eastern immigrants must be Muslim, many Arab-Americans are in fact Christian. The United States has been a popular destination for better-off Arab Christians from Palestine, Lebanon, and Syria.[35] Any likely Muslim growth through immigration will be far exceeded by the continuing Christian influx from Africa, Asia, and, above all, Latin America. To adapt Professor Eck's title, what we are rather seeing is *How Mass Immigration Ensured that a Christian Country Has Become an Even More Christian Country.*

For better or worse, in numerical terms at least, the United States is substantially a Christian country now, and Christian predominance is likely to be still more marked in decades to come. Out of all the leading Christian nations of the past two hundred years, the United States will be the last to occupy this role in the twenty-first century.

Coming to Terms

Cristianizar no puede ser equivalente de occidentalizar
To Christianize cannot be the same as to Westernize.
—*Vitalino Simalox (Maya)*

Ecclesia semper reformanda
—*Martin Luther*

I f demographic change just meant that Christianity would continue to be practiced in more or less its present form, but by people of a different ethnic background, that would of itself be a fact of some historical moment. But the changes of the coming decades promise to be much more sweeping than that. The types of Christianity that have thrived most successfully in the global South have been very different from what many Europeans and North Americans consider mainstream. These models have been far more enthusiastic, much more centrally concerned with the immediate workings of the supernatural, through prophecy, visions, ecstatic utterances, and healing. In fact, they have differed so widely from the cooler Northern norms as to arouse suspicion that these enthusiastic Africans (for instance) are essentially reviving the pagan practices of traditional society. This view frankly challenges the authenticity of African Christianity, just as, in other settings, critics point to pagan or non-Christian parallels for practices in new Korean and Latin American churches.

Nor is this question of authenticity just a matter of academic interest. If in fact the bulk of the Christian population is going to be living in Africa, Asia, or Latin America, then practices that now prevail in those areas will become ever more common across the globe. This is especially likely when those distinctive religious patterns are transplanted northward, either by migration, or by actual missions to the old imperial powers, to what were once the core nations of world Christianity. If we are to live in a world where only one Christian in five is a non-Hispanic White, then the views of that small minority are ever less likely to claim mainstream status, however desperately the Old World Order clings to its hegemony over the control of information and opinion. When we look at the Pentecostal enthusiasm of present-day Brazil, or the indigenous churches of Africa, then quite possibly, we are getting a foretaste of the Christianity of the next generation. Or—as some worry—might it be less than a pure Christianity? Just how much have the newer churches done to fit in with the cultures in which they find themselves?

Claims that the Southern churches have strayed from older definitions of Christianity are seriously exaggerated. However greatly Southern types of Christianity have diverged from older orthodoxies, they have in almost all cases remained within very recognizable Christian traditions. Far from inventing some new African or Korean religions that derive from local cultures, the rising churches usually preach a strong and even pristine Christian message. This approach has implications for future missionary efforts. While we can scarcely imagine a church having a global appeal if its faith was cloaked purely in (say) an African ethnic form, it is possible to see some of the newer bodies exercising an appeal across racial and national boundaries. Another new "missionary century" may dawn, although next time, the missionaries would be traveling northward.

WHOSE CULTURE?

In modern Christian writings, we often encounter the word "inculturation," which means interpreting the Christian proclamation in a form appropriate for particular cultures, usually with the implication of non-Western cultures.[1] The idea of adapting religious practice to local conditions sounds at worst harmless and, at best, essential for any evangelistic endeavor. People differ in their cultural expression, and what works in one cultural setting won't in another. To take an obvious example, northern Europeans tend to view dancing or swaying as inappropriate for a solemn or religious setting, while Africans regard such physical movement as perfectly normal. Also, this dancing is not simply a display by a soloist or troupe, it is a truly communal activity that involves the whole congregation.[2] This attitude is evident from religious groups across the lands of the African diaspora, in Brazil, Cuba, and the United States. Churches that try to enforce practices from "back home" on unwilling locals are going to be displaced by more flexible groups. Adaptation as such is essential, and attracts little criticism, so long as the fundamental truths of a faith are not compromised.

The issue then becomes determining just what are the core beliefs of Christianity, and what are cultural accidents. To take an obvious example from the modern West, is the ancient prohibition against women clergy a core belief or a cultural prejudice? What about ordaining homosexual clergy? The debate over substance and accidents goes back to the very origins of Christianity. The biblical book of Acts records the furious debate over whether Gentile converts were required to accept the rules of Judaism, complete with circumcision and dietary laws. Ultimately, the church, or at least the majority party, concluded that these practices were not essential to the faith. In varying forms, these issues have echoed through the history of Christianity, and have surfaced on virtually every occasion when churches have come into contact with some hitherto unfamiliar society. We recall the Chinese Rites controversy of the seventeenth century. In Victorian southern Africa, the missionary bishop J. W. Colenso refused to order his Christian converts to renounce polygamy, since it was so obviously an integral part of their African culture (and the practice deterred adultery). Naturally, Colenso's attitude was furiously denounced, but the controversies remain unresolved.[3] As Andrew Walls has remarked, "This question is alive for Africans just as it was for Greek converts in the ancient Hellenistic world. Do we have to reject our entire history and culture when we become Christians?"[4]

Because of the long Western dominance of Christianity, debates over faith and culture often focus on attitudes toward specifically European matters. When a Christian group acclimatizes to a new society, the common assumption holds that what is traditionally done in Europe or North America is correct and authentic, and provides the reliable standard by which to assess local adaptations. The more we look at the Christian faith in its European guise, though, the more we can see this too represents a kind of inculturation, albeit an old-established example. This is not to say that there is no such thing as an unchanging "historic Christian faith," but we must be careful to distinguish the core idea from the incidentals.[5]

The cultural assumptions of European missionaries and empire-builders become obvious when we see a great church in one of the old British or French colonies in the tropics. The visitor leaves the bright sunshine to enter into a dark Gothic chamber, which seems quite inappropriate for the local climate and environment. Still, Victorian builders knew in their hearts that a "religious" building had to follow certain cultural norms, and that meant using the Gothic styles that mimicked the brooding forests of medieval northern Europe. Its enthusiasts described the Gothic style simply as "Christian architecture." Presumably if the course of Christian history had run differently, then other societies would have succeeded in spreading their distinctive cultural visions across the world, with equal confidence that these too were the only fit vessels for conveying Christian truth. To take an outlandish example, if Central America had become an early Christian heartland, then our religious literature and architecture would be full of imagery that used jaguars rather than lions. And who knows but that, in another century or two, the jaguar will indeed become a primary Christian symbol for millions of believers?

Most observers today would agree that Gothic architecture was just a cultural manifestation, rather than a core element of Christianity, but other parts of so-called traditional Christianity can perhaps be treated just as flexibly. Western Christianity itself has changed greatly over the centuries, and grown and flourished precisely by incorporating ideas from various cultures. Walls aptly describes Christianity as "infinitely translatable." Christianity became inculturated in different societies, and each in turn contributed to the larger package of Christian beliefs. Within the first few centuries of Christianity's existence, its adherents in Egypt used figures of the goddess Isis with her child Horus as the model for devotional imagery of Mary and the infant Jesus. Across the Mediterranean, the functions of numerous local deities were transferred to Christian saints. Borrowings from paganism are well known, to the extent that the pope himself takes his title of *pontifex* from one of the chief priests of pagan Rome. Christianity has been highly flexible about these adaptations, and there is no obvious reason why the age of absorption should have ceased in the fifth or tenth centuries, or indeed will in the twenty-fifth.[6]

Historically, one of the greatest examples of accommodation to native religions occurred when the Mediterranean-based religion of Christianity expanded into the realms of the northern barbarians in the dark centuries following the fall of Rome.[7] The Mediterranean Christians who converted northern Europe overtly tried to ensure that the new converts would see the continuities from their old religion. Writing to the missionaries to England about 600, Pope Gregory the Great ordered that "the temples of the idols should on no account be destroyed. The idols are to be destroyed, but the temples themselves are to be aspersed with holy water, altars set up in them, and relics deposited there . . . and since they have a habit of sacrificing many oxen to demons, let some other solemnity be substituted in its place, such as a day of dedication, or the festivals of the holy martyrs whose relics are enshrined there."[8] Those converted temples became the sites of what would later become great Christian churches, although these origins were long forgotten: London's St. Paul's Cathedral almost certainly stands on the site of an ancient pagan structure. By the nineteenth century, perhaps some of these ancient temples were the spiritual homes of the Christian missionaries who set off to convert Africa and Asia. In their turn, these men and women worried about just how many of the pagan practices they found could possibly be reconciled with the new faith.

Reusing buildings is one thing, but Pope Gregory's letter suggests that the missionaries were also compromising with the older religion to the extent of absorbing older ritual calendars. In the English language, even the greatest Christian festival, Easter, bears the name of a pagan goddess. This kind of adaptation explains why the ancient pagan seasonal festivals are so often blessed with the names of the greatest Christian saints: across Europe, Midsummer Day is associated with St. John the Baptist. Almost certainly, the newly venerated saints acquired some of the characteristics of the gods they were replacing.

The European Christianity that was exported from the sixteenth century on was already a magnificent example of successful inculturation, and the process continued in the lands encountered beyond the oceans. One of the best-known stories in New World Christianity concerns the Mexican-Indian Juan Diego, who in 1531 reported a vision of a divine Lady whom the Spaniards believed to be Our Lady of Guadalupe. The Lady, the dark one (*la Morena*), soon attracted the passionate devotion of the Indian people, and was recognized as patron of Mexico. In explaining her phenomenal popularity, scholars believe that she was initially identified not as the Virgin worshiped at the Spanish shrine of Guadalupe, but rather as *Coatlaxopeuh*, "she who crushes the serpent." This was a title of the pre-Christian Aztec goddess Tonantzín, who was appearing on ground that had been sacred to her long before the coming of Christianity. Elsewhere in Latin America, too, the cult of the Virgin carries pagan associations. Cubans devote themselves to *La Caridad, La Virgen de la Caridad del Cobre*, who was viewed as a goddess by the many West African slaves imported into that land, and today her cult is part of Afro-Cuban Santeria.

We might take these stories to indicate that Catholicism had only a tenuous hold on the native and African peoples, who carried on their ancient religions under a thin disguise. This may have been the case at first, but the cult of the Virgin helped native people to accept the full panoply of Catholic belief and ritual, and also served to Christianize the new slave populations. Ethnically as much as spiritually, she is *their* Virgin. Just as Guadalupe is usually seen in the company of the Indian Juan Diego, so images of *La Caridad* show her appearing to rescue Black and *mestizo* sailors. In Ecuador, the equivalent of Guadelupe is the Virgin of El Quinche, who is so popular because her skin color is that of the local *mestizos*. In Central America, meanwhile, ancient Mayan priestly dynasties maintained their spiritual power in the guise of Catholic confraternities. The Church made large compromises with pre-Christian practices to accomplish its goals, but no more than it had done in northern Europe a millennium before. And as in those earlier lands, the Latin American church soon occupied a place as the authentic religious voice of the people.[9]

LITURGY AND LANGUAGE

As Christianity becomes increasingly Southern, it cannot fail to absorb the habits and thought-worlds of the regions in which it is strongest. Much of that adaptation will be unconscious, as it was during the historic Christianization of Europe. Latin Christians did not hold learned theological debates over whether Gothic architecture should become a favored style for building churches, they just did what seemed natural given their physical and cultural environment. Much of what we think of as "normal" Western Christianity reflects the same type of unconscious absorption.

There is nothing deliberately racist or exclusive about the process that traditionally made White Northern Europeans portray Jesus as one of themselves, just as Africans and Asians use their own familiar imagery in their religious art. The process of absorption goes back at least as far as the ancient Ethiopian church, which naturally depicted Jesus in local guise. Kongolese metalworkers of the seventeenth century similarly produced very African-looking crucifixes. Over the past century, the gallery of Christian imagery from Africa and Asia has expanded exponentially, and an image of Christ as an African or Asian scarcely causes any surprise for most observers.[10]

Perhaps the most important acts of assimilation occur in the area of language, as believers absorb the faith by translating its ideas into intelligible terms. We Westerners can easily see the need for such a quest, since the Bible is so foreign to us culturally. The New Testament emerged from a specific eastern Mediterranean society, and used language and metaphors that made excellent sense for the kind of societies and economic communities that prevailed across the Roman Empire. Suitably modified for different environments, the ideas also work well in most agricultural communities, but for modern urban or suburban dwellers, the language has lost its meaning. With the aid of a learned commentary, a modern reader can understand concepts like separating wheat and chaff, grafting vines, new wine and old wineskins, but in becoming so remote, the metaphors have lost their relevance. We respond to their obsolescence by generating new figures and analogies that speak to us.

In the same way, the newer Christian societies have been creative in adapting religious language to local settings. Lamin Sanneh argues that the simple decision to translate the scriptures into local languages was in itself a key concession to native cultures, and one made by even the most obtuse Northern missionaries. The mere act of translation proved that no single language was privileged as a vehicle of salvation. This is important in light of modern postcolonial critiques of the tyranny of the European languages. According to this view, forcing subject peoples to speak English or French also requires them to internalize colonial worldviews, to accept their own submission with every word they utter. Yet this problem does not apply to religious matters, at least to anything like the same degree. Sanneh writes that "Much of the heat with which mission has been attacked as Western cultural imperialism begins to dissipate when we apply the vernacular principle."[11]

Through the act of translation, too, and the use of familiar local terms and concepts, the scriptures are forced to become relevant to each individual culture. To take an obvious problem, there is no point in using the phrase "as white as snow" for people who have never seen snow. Better to speak of "as white as a strand of cotton." Such minor changes can have complex effects. While the Bible has Jesus declare, "I am the true Vine," some African translators prefer to replace vine with fig. This botanical change introduces a whole new theological meaning, since "this African tree represents the ancestors, and is sometimes planted on tombs." Jesus now speaks as the voice of death and resurrection.[12]

However unconsciously, translation transforms Jesus and his followers into Africans for African hearers, makes them Chinese for a Chinese audience. In a book of African "prayers and praises," the Ghanaian writer Madam Afua Kuma offers this version of the feeding of the 5,000:

> He is the one
> Who cooks his food in huge palm-oil pots.
> Thousands of people have eaten
> Yet the remnants fill twelve baskets[13]

The collection from which this passage comes is aptly entitled *Jesus of the Deep Forest*. Another of her prayers proclaims

> He is the great Grass Hut, the Shed which shelters mice
> The 'Thump thump' of the pestle, he beats down our hunger
> Hard wood hoe-handle, which brings us our food
> *Onyankopon Amponyinam;* God the provider.

Vernacular prayers and liturgies come to be associated with new holy places, with shrines or martyrdom sites drawing purely on local traditions. The independent churches of southern Africa have been very active in spiritualizing the landscape through vast ritual gatherings and pilgrimages. One of the great shrines is Ekuphakameni, in South Africa, the "high and elevated place" chosen by prophet Isaiah Shembe. The site has acquired all the cultural resonance of the biblical Zion, and it features in the hymns of the group's Nazarite Baptist Church:

> I remember Ekuphakameni
> Where the springs are
> Springs of living water
> Lasting for ever.[14]

Although the language is biblical, its associations are purely African. In time, Ekuphakameni may become as great a Christian shrine as Lourdes or Walsingham.

Once naturalized in a culture, such local imagery comes to be expected, while a conspicuously foreign Jesus arouses suspicion. Earlier, we looked at the phenomenal success of the independent African church founded by Alice Lenshina in the 1950s. Many of her followers were attracted by the many hymns she composed, which used local languages far more fluently and eloquently than the mission churches had ever attempted.

Where the Bible is concerned, freedom of translation is restrained by some sense of obligation to the sacred text, but liturgical texts and practices can be handled with greater freedom. Particularly since the 1960s, there has been an upsurge of locally oriented liturgies that use culturally relevant terms and practices. At their worst, these innovations have been forced and unconvincing, but some have been impressive. The much-admired New Zealand liturgy was developed to reflect both the local physical environment and the racial balance between native Maoris and white *pakeha:*[15]

Dolphins and kahawai, sealion and crag,
coral, anemone, pipi and shrimp:
give to our God your thanks and praise.

You Maori and Pakeha, women and men,
all who inhabit the long white cloud:
give to our God your thanks and praise.

Liturgical innovation became widespread in the Roman Catholic Church
after the Second Vatican Council of the 1960s encouraging the use of vernacular language and practice. Some of the innovations were quite creative,
and fit well with local tradition. In Zaire/Congo, ancient custom held that
distinguished visitors were to be greeted by spear-bearers, and accordingly,
spears were added to the liturgical procession as a means of acknowledging
the presence of God. Some Catholic churches have tried to use local foodstuffs in the Eucharist, to make the communion meal a genuine banquet
held by a powerful chief, rather than an imported symbolic affair. Millet
and corn replace wheat in the host, while wine is made from palm or banana.
In Brazil too, progressive Catholic clergy import African customs like drum-
ming and dancing in order try to make the Mass relevant to the poorest
believers, who are usually of African descent.[16]

THE LAW OF BELIEVING

An ancient Church maxim declares, *lex orandi, lex credendi,* that the law
of prayer is the law of belief, that how we worship shows what we believe.
As worship patterns change so do the underlying beliefs, and changes in
practice in the global South will inevitably have their consequences in terms
of belief and theology. As one Catholic archbishop has remarked, "Our
Namibian African people have accepted Christ. But this Christ walks too
much among them in a European garment." Inculturation "must be carried
deeper than just music, drums and clapping of hands."[17] In recent years, we
can trace the emergence of innovative Southern theologies.

Steeped as they were in Jewish tradition, Jesus' first Palestinian followers
portrayed him as the great High Priest. Modern Africans, in contrast, find
more power and relevance in the vision of Jesus as great Ancestor, an idea
that also resonates in East Asia. This Jesus exercises for all people the
same care and love that the ancestor of a specific tribe would for his or her
descendants. Integrating the idea of ancestors into the liturgy has been a

primary goal of the newer African Catholic rites. In contemporary Eucharistic prayers, God the Father is firmly placed in this "ancestral" context:

O Father, Great Ancestor, we lack adequate words to thank you. . . .
O Great Ancestor, who lives on the brilliant mountains . . .
Our Father, father of our ancestors, we are gathered to praise you and to thank
   you with our sacrifice.

Independent churches also stress Jesus' role as prophet and healer, as Great Physician. Although this approach is not so familiar in the modern West, this is one of many areas in which the independents are very much in tune with the Mediterranean Christianity of the earliest centuries.[18] The idea of the Holy Spirit has also gone through subtle changes. An intriguing trend in African churches has been to name this figure "the Earth-keeping Spirit," a term with vast implications for ecological aspects of religion. The notion also has a wider appeal, for instance, in Native American Christian thought.[19]

Latin American churches have been creative in evolving new theologies based on the distinctive experience of those cultures.[20] Given the historic social inequalities of the Latin countries, Hispanic theology is acutely concerned with issues of liberation, suffering, and social justice, while matters of race are also paramount. Some of the most active thinkers have been Latinos based in North America, and a key concept in these circles is that of *mestizaje*, "mixedness," the status of being *mestizo* or mixed blood. In contemporary theology, *mestizaje* is so critical because it transcends traditional racial hierarchies. It thus comes closer to the New Testament goal of a society without racial privilege or domination, in which there is neither Jew nor Greek, Latino nor Anglo. And while mixed race people were traditionally marginalized and despised, newer theologians see this status as uniquely privileged.

Mestizaje allows a society to draw equally on its diverse cultural inheritances. "The mestizo affirms both the identities received while offering something new to both." *Mestizos* are uniquely qualified to question the arrogant claims to purity made by given races or states. Since they have no abiding city on earth, *mestizo* loyalty is to neither race nor nation, but to Christendom, the pilgrim church. To quote the title of a book by Mexican-American theologian Virgilio Elizondo, *The Future is Mestizo*. These ideas are important for other societies in various stages of racial mingling, notably in Europe, and are likely to gain in importance in coming decades. It is a potent theology for a world of deracinated migrants and wanderers, those who (in Paul Gilroy's phrase) define their identities in terms not of roots but of routes.[21]

This approach profoundly affects readings of the Bible. Elizondo memorably presents Jesus as a *mestizo* son of Galilee's mixed and marginalized society, who enters the great city of Jerusalem in order to challenge its wealth, to confront the racial arrogance of the pure-blooded elite. For Elizondo, the world's poor and marginalized have a distinctive role in the divine plan. His Galilee Principle asserts that "what human beings reject, God chooses as his very own." This idea has much in common with the Christian theologies of rejection formulated by other once despised groups, such as India's Dalits or untouchables.[22]

THE QUEEN OF THE SOUTH WILL RISE UP

Contemporary Hispanic theology raises challenging questions about the whole area of popular religious practices, the world of devotions, processions, and pilgrimages often dismissed by a term like "folk Catholicism." In the context of Latin American history, though, these practices are quite central to popular religious identity, and it is no longer acceptable to regard them simply as a dilution of the superior European reality. "Popular religious expressions of the people" thus become "the living creed and primary sources of theology."[23] By European standards, these practices may be flawed or suspect, but whoever said that European criteria were absolutely valid for all times and places? Europe created its own religious identity through a lengthy process of mingling and adaptation.

This emphasis on popular belief and tradition has major implications for the veneration of the Virgin Mary and, consequently, for the whole approach to the divine. In Latin Catholicism, Mary is often portrayed as something like a feminine face of God. For Mexicans, the Virgin of Guadelupe is an absolutely central symbol, just as *La Caridad* is for Cubans. Modern theologians like Elizondo proudly defend this veneration, citing the exalted biblical image of the woman clothed with the Sun in the book of Revelation. In his view, Guadelupe becomes a messianic symbol for the resurrection of the world's oppressed races, the "Galileans." "In the person of Juan Diego was represented the Indian nations defeated and slaughtered, but now brought to life." In every sense, she is the mother of all border-crossers.[24] Repeatedly, Mexican popular and revolutionary movements have claimed to be directly serving *La Morena,* the weak woman who conquers the conquerors. But modern writers go well beyond just defending this devotion, and ask moreover why Northerners seem so appalled by it. Roberto Goizueta argues that simple racism causes Northerners to reject "the racial, cultural and religious *mestizaje* of the Guadalupan symbol. . . . And like Jesus, *la Morenita* continues to ask us today, 'Why be frightened'?"[25]

In this specific area of theology, a southward shift may already be having a global impact. In modern Catholicism, the figure of the Virgin has usually been associated with more conservative and traditional forms of religious practice, so the veneration of Mary has played a significantly smaller role in devotion in liberal Northern countries. This tendency has been reversed somewhat under the conservative papacy of John Paul II, and at the start of the new millennium, remarkable attention is being paid to Marian shrines and visions. On his 1998 visit to Cuba, the pope made a special trip to the shrine of El Cobre to crown the statue of *La Caridad,* and proclaim her queen and patron of the island. There is now talk that the Virgin might be proclaimed a mediator and co-Savior figure, comparable to Jesus himself, even a fourth member of the Trinity. Such ambitious schemes remain controversial, but demographic trends within the Church make it highly likely that they will be implemented in the coming decades. Exalting the Virgin to the highest possible degree fits very well with the Catholic traditions of Latin America, the Philippines, and other regions that are steadily assuming a more central position within the church. As we will see, the College of Cardinals is becoming steadily more Latin in complexion.

These Marian trends will be reflected within the United States itself. In a potent acknowledgment of the shifting ethnic foundations of world Christianity, the Church has proclaimed the Virgin of Guadelupe as patron of all the Americas. In 1988, the liturgical celebration of the Mother of the Americas, *la Morena,* was raised to the status of a feast in all dioceses in the United States.[26] Although I have made no attempts to predict exact dates for the changes described in this book, there is one key date that can be cited with confidence, namely December 12, 2031. This is the feast day of Our Lady of Guadelupe in the year that marks the 500th anniversary of the original apparition to Juan Diego. The event will unquestionably be commemorated with a vast celebration of Mexican and Chicano Catholic identity, both north and south of the Rio Grande. This year might in fact come to be seen as America's true and proper Quincentennial, in contrast to all the ambiguities associated with the celebration of Columbus' landing in 1992.

Recently, I was able to observe firsthand the role of "the Queen of the South" in drawing together the various currents within American Catholicism. I was watching a Peruvian procession of the sort that occurs many times each year in the villages of the Andes. The centerpiece of the event was the ornately decorated figure of the Virgin, richly dressed and surrounded with flowers, and borne on a bier by the distinguished men of the vicinity.

They were heralded by women in traditional gowns, who strewed the way with flowers. Behind the figure of the Virgin came the band, enthusiastic and cheerfully discordant, and behind them ambled several hundred Peruvians, their faces proclaiming an ethnic identity that can be traced long before the Inca empire was born. The unusual thing about this celebration was its location, since the hilly path through which they marched was found not in the Andes, but in the gentler slopes of western Maryland, and the pilgrims were en route to the national shrine of the Virgin at Emmitsburg. Emmitsburg has an excellent claim to be one of the birthplaces of U.S. Catholicism, as a missionary center that in the early nineteenth century was home to Elizabeth Seton, the first American-born saint. Watching this Peruvian pilgrimage in the summer of 2001, one could see the oldest and newest faces of Catholic North America confronting each other quite amiably.

A revived cult of Mary would have an appeal far beyond the Americas. Marian devotion is a powerful force in African Catholicism, and has been since the time of the earliest native converts. One of the first Catholic martyrs of sub-Saharan Africa was Isidore Bakanja, who was converted in the Belgian Congo in 1906, and whose fervent Marian piety led to his murder at the hands of secular-minded White colonists. In the 1980s, mystical visions of the Virgin were reported in Rwanda, Kenya, and Cameroon. Amazing reports of Marian apparitions have also occurred within the Coptic Church. In Egypt, spectacular Marian visions and miracles were recorded at Zaytoun, near Cairo, in 1967 and 1968. The events at Zaytoun galvanized the Egyptian people during the grim period following the disastrous 1967 war, and the shrine attracted millions of seekers, Muslim as well as Christian (the Virgin Mary is a prominent and beloved figure in the *Quran*).[27] A Catholic Church dominated by Latin Americans and Africans would prove highly receptive to new concepts of Marian devotion, which might serve as a bridge to other ancient Christian communities, and even to other faiths. A Black or Brown Mary would be a powerfully appropriate symbol for the emerging Southern Christendom. Although these new theologies might disturb or repel some North Americans or Europeans, Northern views on religious matters should become less and less significant as the new century develops.

BEYOND CHRISTIANITY?

So far, we have been looking at forms of adaptation that clearly build on familiar Christian traditions, but some patterns in the emerging churches raise searching questions about the acceptable limits of accommodation. At what point does inculturation end, to be replaced by the submergence of Christianity into some other religion? When cultural assimilation reaches a certain point, Western observers complain that what is being transformed is not merely the trappings but the core of the faith. What is being practiced, it appears, is not inculturation but syncretism, the blatant adulteration of Christianity by elements of other religions.

In recent years, charges of syncretism have been directed against a number of Third World churches and theologians. In 1991, the annual meeting of the World Council of Churches experienced a fierce controversy following a liturgical presentation by Korean theologian Hyun Kyung Chung, who freely integrated practices from Confucian and Asian shamanistic religions. For Chung, "God speaks through Buddha, through shamans and through Christ in my culture." She has said that "My bowel is Buddhist bowel, my heart is Buddhist heart, my right brain is Confucian brain, and my left brain is Christian brain." Although she has been denounced as a syncretist and pagan, she argues that all religions, including Christianity, are built upon a series of cultural compromises, and she is different only because "I'm admitting it."[28]

Intellectuals like Chung might have an impact in the academic or media worlds, but do not generally influence large numbers of believers. Far more significant is the retention of older religious practices by emerging churches which command the loyalties of millions, and which can be expected to expand in coming decades. Across southern Africa, some independent churches have retained a wide range of traditional practices, including polygamy, divination, animal sacrifices, initiation rites, circumcision, and the veneration of ancestors. By no means all the independent congregations accept the full range of older practices, but most African churches accept prophetic and visionary ideas that have long since fallen out of fashion in the West. Ideas of healing and prophecy have permeated the far more numerous mainstream denominations, such as Catholics, Anglicans, and Lutherans.

Sometimes, pagan parallels seem quite strong. The Zulu Zionist churches, for instance, are headed by charismatic prophets who lead the church, pray for the sick, determine the causes of disease, and specify remedies. Even for the most sympathetic Western observers, these prophets should properly be seen as a later manifestation of the tribal diviners who played such a key role in pagan times.[29] The new Christian prophets, like the pagan diviners before them, are healer figures who possess supernatural gifts and act as channels to the ancestors. In some cases, they seem to be superhuman, and become messiah figures. Some of Simon Kimbangu's followers saw him in this role, while Isaiah Shembe's disciples presented him as a new incarnate God on Earth, who appeared to them after his death.[30] Such extreme doctrines come close to elevating prophets to Christ-like status.

It is tempting for Western commentators discussing Southern Christianity to focus on such seemingly odd features, partly to make their presentation more picturesque. In 2001, a major *Newsweek* account of "The Changing Face of the Church" accurately charted the southward shift of Christianity, but implied that the rising churches were recklessly syncretistic. Author Kenneth Woodward argued that "As in the past, today's new Christians tend to take from the Bible whatever fits their needs—and ignore whatever fails to resonate with their own native religious traditions. . . . On the Chinese New Year, says Catholic Bishop Chen Shih-kwang of Taichung, Taiwan, 'we do mass, then we venerate the ancestors'—a notion that is totally foreign to Western Christianity. In India, where sin is identified with bad karma in this and previous lives, many converts interpret the cross to mean that Jesus' self-sacrifice removes their own karmic deficiencies, thus liberating their souls from future rebirths." In this view at least, Christianity remains little more than a cultural veneer.[31]

Sometimes, too, rejecting the authenticity of Southern churches has a polemical purpose. One example of this occurred at the 1998 Lambeth Conference of the world's Anglican bishops, who were considering a liberal statement concerning homosexuality. The statement was heavily defeated due to the votes of Asian and particularly African bishops, to the fury of American liberals. One of these was Bishop John Spong of Newark, who declared that the African bishops had "moved out of animism into a very superstitious kind of Christianity," and this explained their failure to understand the issues at hand. Spong professed himself appalled by the whole tone of Third World spirituality, with its "religious extremism": "I never expected to see the Anglican Communion, which prides itself on the place of reason in faith, descend to this level of irrational Pentecostal hysteria." Spong was in effect suggesting that "Pentecostal" fervor was a thinly disguised continuation of ancient paganism, with all its unenlightened moral trappings.[32]

PREPARING THE GOSPEL

The indictment is clear. Many Southern churches are syncretistic, they represent a thinly disguised paganism, and all in all they make for "a very superstitious kind of Christianity," even "post-Christianity."[33] Certainly there are parallels between the new Christianity and the older religious world, but these can be explained in different ways. While a puritanically inclined critic might believe that the Southern churches had simply sold out to the old pagan religions, a more benevolent interpretation is possible. Since the older traditions already included many elements that fit well with the faith that the missionaries were preaching, it was natural to draw upon them.

Christians have long practice at explaining their use of traditional (and even "pagan") ways of thought. When early Christians saw the many parallels between their own new religion and the ancient practices of Mediterranean paganism, they argued that God had already sowed the older cultures with ideas and themes that would grow to fruition once they were interpreted in a fully Christian context. The traditional religions should be seen as a *preparatio evangelica,* a preparation for the gospel. Since potentially Christian themes were so abundant in older African cultures, it is scarcely surprising that the newer churches of the past century have so enthusiastically absorbed so many of the old ideas. Where such ideas went flagrantly beyond the pale of Christian doctrine—as in the apotheosis of the prophets—the independent churches themselves usually tried to restrain or suppress these ideas.[34]

In sub-Saharan Africa, European missionaries were excited to find how many of their ideas resonated with native cultures. There was little need to explain the idea of monotheism to societies that already venerated a high God, a being far more exalted than the common run of spirits and deities. As veteran missionary Diedrich Westermann wrote in 1926, "The African, apart from his magical practices, believes in God. He is not a tribal God, but Lord of the universe, and the Christian missionary can in most cases introduce himself as ambassador of the God the African knows."[35] The problem in this passage concerns the "magical practices," which are presented almost as an incidental irritant, which would fade away quickly. In practice, they certainly did not. The main problem the missionaries faced in Africa and much of Asia was not that they were trying to explain a bafflingly alien worldview, but that their message almost rang too true with local cultures. In the realm of spiritual and magical beliefs, Christian/pagan parallels opened the door for evangelism, but on the negative side, they also attracted charges that converts were just recycling the traditional outlook on this world and the next.

Unlike in modern Europe or North America, Christian preachers did not have to convince Third World audiences of the reality of the supernatural, of spirits and spiritual powers. In much of Africa or East Asia, older cultures had a powerful interest in spirits, particularly the souls of ancestors, and the real effects that these could cause in the human realm. Ancestors who were offended or neglected could cause problems for their living heirs. Misfortune, sickness, and death were attributed to the workings of mischievous spirits, commonly directed by ill-meaning neighbors. In the early twentieth century, American missionaries in Korea noted that "Many of the religious characteristics of the Korean people mark them for discipleship in the Christian faith. Believing as they do in the universal presence of spirits, it is not difficult for them to accept the doctrines of the spiritual nature of God."[36] While these ideas seemed superstitious to the early missionaries, they could easily find a fit with older Christian ideas, and with the thought-world of the Bible itself.

If there is a single key area of faith and practice that divides Northern and Southern Christians, it is this matter of spiritual forces and their effects on the everyday human world. The issue goes to the heart of cultural definition and worldviews. In traditional African society, various forms of divination were used to seek out the cause of evil, and to identify the wrongdoer as an essential first step toward neutralizing his or her evil powers. At every stage, this scheme of explanations offended the sensibilities of European missionaries, who saw themselves in a heroic struggle against the evils of superstition, fatalism, and witchcraft. How could churches possibly accept such ideas?

As in the earlier Chinese debates, the issue of ancestors generated fierce argument and much mutual misunderstanding. While missionaries denounced what they thought was ancestor worship, native peoples in Africa and much of Asia believed they were only showing due veneration to past generations, who survived as a spiritual presence essential to the well-being of family and community. For decades, the White-dominated churches were simply baffled at the resilience of the older ideas. As Andrew Walls has remarked, "The role of ancestors and witchcraft are two important issues. Academic theologians in the West may not put witchcraft high on the agenda, but it's the issue that hits ordinary African Christians full in the face." Far from declining as society modernized, witchcraft accusations actually flourished in the booming cities, and became rife during times of economic slump and political crisis. Even today, a single outbreak of witch-panic can lead to hundreds of murders in a period of weeks or months. Moreover, one of the main centers of modern witch-hunting activity has been South Africa, the most developed state on the whole continent. What White missionaries failed to realize was that they were in reality at war with the whole foundations of a society, the most basic means of understanding the world. Conflicts between European and African ways were also inevitable when the missionaries challenged the ceremonies, initiations, and rites of passage that were so crucial to the cycle of life in traditional society.[37]

The dilemma faced by the European churches is illustrated by a parable told by John Mbiti, who imagines a brilliant African student going off to a European seminary. Here, he "learned German, French, Greek, Latin, Hebrew, in addition to English, church history, systematics, homiletics, exegesis and pastoralia." He reads all the great European Bible critics, such as Rudolf Bultmann. Returning home to his native village, the student is welcomed joyfully by his extended family but, suddenly, his sister falls dangerously ill. With his Western training, he knows that her illness requires scientific medicine, but everyone present knows with equal certainty that the girl is troubled by the spirit of her dead great-aunt. Since this fine student has so much theological training, the family knows that it is obviously up to him to cure her. The debate between the student and his family rages until "the people shout 'Help your sister, she is possessed.' He shouts back, 'But Bultmann has demythologized demon possession!'" The family is not impressed.[38]

Most churches eventually acknowledged that the older beliefs were too deeply embedded to be removed, and either made their peace with tradition or else made it an integral part of their own system. The influential African prophets won followers by acknowledging the older spiritual powers and absorbing them within a new Christian synthesis. Their examples have been followed enthusiastically by the African indigenous churches, with their beliefs in spirits and exorcism: "their very life and worship revolves around healing, visions, dreams, the overcoming of evil forces." The ZCC believes that ancestors intercede on the behalf of the living. A belief in spirits is also fundamental to the Aladura churches of West Africa. The Cherubim and Seraphim movement "claims to have conscious knowledge of the evil spirits which sow the seeds of discomfort, set afloat ill-luck, diseases, induce barrenness, sterility and the like." Exorcism is the common response. The group also has its prophets, who receive visions in trances and offer dream interpretations.[39]

HEALINGS

In practical terms, the belief in spiritual powers has its most direct impact in terms of healing through spiritual means. The practice of healing is one of the strongest themes unifying the newer Southern churches, both mainstream and independent, and perhaps their strongest selling point for their congregations. Yet this emphasis should certainly not be seen as a compromise with paganism, since it is so thoroughly integrated into Christian practice as well as with local cultures. As Walls describes the African experience, "Healing is being addressed to the person, as the center of a complex of influences. It is addressed to the person as target of outside attack, as sufferer from unwanted legacies, as carrier of the sense of failure and unfulfilled duty. It is the long established African understanding of the nature and purpose of healing that is at work. What distinguishes its Christian phase is that the central Christian symbol of Christ is identified as the source of healing."[40]

From the earliest days of the European missions, the promise of healing was at the heart of Christian successes. Prospective converts were excited by biblical accounts of healing miracles, stories that the missionaries themselves were already treating with some embarrassment. Fundamentally minded Europeans had no doubts about the reality of biblically recorded cures in apostolic times, but questioned whether miracles continued into the modern age. Their converts, though, were quite willing to accept modern miracles. In nineteenth-century China, an enthusiastic convert called Xi Liaochi began his own highly successful mission focused on exorcism and the spiritual treatment of opium addiction. His career led to bitter controversies with the Europeans, who saw him as little more than a witch-doctor on the farthest fringes of the faith. The affair ignited a lasting feud within the missionary establishment.[41]

Yet there can be no doubt of the appeal of such healing activities. In Africa, the explosion of healing movements and new prophets in the first quarter of the twentieth century coincided with a dreadful series of epidemics, and the religious upsurge of those years was in part a quest for bodily health. Today, rising African churches stand or fall by their success in healing, and elaborate rituals have formed around healing practices. Typically, in the Church of the Lord (Aladura), a healing ritual involves confession, "followed by the exorcising or expulsion of evil spirits, priestly blessings, and administration of holy words." Many congregations use material symbols like holy water and sanctified healing oils. The Aladura churches have debated for years whether believers should use any modern or Western medicine, or else rely entirely on spiritual assistance. The same customs are found in what were the mission churches. In Tanzania, some of the most active healing work in recent years has occurred within the Lutheran Church, under the auspices of a bishop who himself claimed prophetic powers.[42]

Healing is equally central in many of the new churches of Latin America.

When Andrew Chesnut tried to explain the upsurge of Pentecostalism in the Brazilian city of Belém, he placed health and sickness at center stage, since these issues so often occur in the conversion narratives told by believers. Addiction problems are usually to the fore: Chesnut argues that "More than any other reason, it is the desire to be cured of alcoholism that impels Brazilian men to convert to Pentecostalism." Issues of healing, whether of mind or body, dominate the everyday life of the churches of the poor. Accordingly, "in some churches, faith-healing so dominates the liturgy that the sanctuary resembles a hospital."[43] Nowhere in the global South do the various spiritual healers find serious competition from modern scientific medicine, since this is so far beyond the reach of most of the poorest. For most ordinary people, Western medicine implies the assembly-line treatment of public hospitals, where any chance of receiving adequate treatment is outweighed by the dangers of catching new infections.

Healing is the key element that has allowed Christianity to compete so successfully with its rivals outside the Christian tradition, with traditional religion in Africa, with various animist and spiritist movements of African origin in Brazil, with shamanism in Korea. To some extent, the churches are forced to share the same intellectual universe as their competitors. In Brazil, the Pentecostal churches that recruit poor urban dwellers find their most intense competition from African-derived spiritist movements like Umbanda, which promises cures and exorcism. Edir Macedo, founder of the IURD, is a former disciple of Umbanda, and the two groups recruit from much the same populations. The Korean Pentecostal churches that have flourished in recent years offer spiritual healing, especially the mega-churches with tens or hundreds of thousands of members. Here too, the newer congregations face charges that they are only dressing up older local traditions, in this case shamanism. To quote Harvey Cox, a sympathetic observer: "There can be little doubt that what one finds in the Yoido Full Gospel church of Seoul involves a massive importation of shamanic practice into a Christian ritual."[44] Although conditions in China are more difficult to observe, healing-oriented groups provide the key competitors for Christian growth. One fast-growing religious movement of recent years has been the Falun Gong sect, which owes its appeal to claims of miraculous healing.

Given the central emphasis on physical health, we have to ask how the rising churches have been affected by the AIDS crisis that has so devastated Africa, as well as other Third World nations like Brazil. Sub-Saharan Africa presently accounts for over two-thirds of known cases of HIV infection. In some regions of the continent, perhaps 40 percent of inhabitants carry the AIDS virus, and by 2015, Africa may be home to 16 million orphans. Since the late 1970s, 17 million Africans have probably died of AIDS. In Kenya alone, perhaps a million have already died from AIDS-related illnesses, and 2 million more carry the HIV virus.[45]

The chief centers of Southern Christianity are also the regions hardest hit by AIDS, in African nations like the Democratic Republic of the Congo, Uganda, and South Africa, as well as in Brazil. A Western audience might think that AIDS would be a powerful deterrent to religion, in showing the futility of prayer or spiritual healing. In reality, the epidemic has had no such effect, largely because no other form of treatment has proved any more effective. Western medicine has not acquitted itself any better than prayer, because the treatments that have proved effective in North America are just not accessible to poor Africans or Asians. No church can credibly claim to be offering a cure for AIDS, although some Pentecostal congregations have significantly reduced the kind of risky sexual behavior that spreads the disease. On the other hand, other churches have arguably made the situation even worse by fighting the promotion of condoms. On balance, the churches have not contributed greatly to stemming the disease, though this does not mean they have ignored the crisis. Many congregations have exercised different kinds of ministry in the worst affected areas. In Uganda, for instance, churches focus on comforting the dying and offering help to bereaved families.[46]

THE OLDEST CHRISTIANITY

Considering the central role of healing and exorcism in Southern churches, it is tempting to look for older pagan roots, and to ask how the emerging congregations justify their ideas. Of course, Southern churches thrive because of their appeal to distinctively African or Latin American ideas, their ability to work within traditional culture, but these examples of accommodation do not amount to a betrayal of the faith, still less to syncretism. The rising churches can plausibly claim to be following abundantly documented precedents from the founding ages of Christianity. The Bible itself so readily supports a worldview based on spirits, healing, and exorcism.[47] When Jesus was asked if he was the Messiah, he did not give an abstruse theological lecture, but pointed at the tangible signs and wonders that were being done in his name. "Go back and report to John what you hear and see: The blind receive sight, the lame walk, those who have leprosy are cured, the deaf hear, the dead are raised, and the good news is preached to the poor."[48] When Paul took the Christian faith to Macedonia, the first known mission into Europe, he was responding to a vision received in a dream.[49]

In understanding what can look like the oddities of Third World churches, it is helpful to recall one basic and astonishing fact, which is that they take the Bible very seriously indeed. To quote Richard Shaull, "In Pentecostalism, poor and broken people discover that what they read in the Gospels is happening now in their midst." For Southern Christians, and not only for Pentecostals, the apostolic world as described in the New Testament is not just a historical account of the ancient Levant, but an ever-present reality open to any modern believer, and that includes the whole culture of signs and wonders. Passages that seem mildly embarrassing for a Western audience read completely differently, and relevantly, in the new churches of Africa or Latin America. As David Martin remarks of another region in which this type of faith has spread in recent years, "The Pentecostal emphasis in Korea is really to see 'The Kingdom' both future *and* present in the signs of the Kingdom, especially healing and the 'baptism of the Spirit.'"[50]

Against this background, we need to think exactly what we mean when we say that a given person "believes in" the Bible and its stories. It is possible to believe in the stories recorded as if they are literally correct narratives of events that really occurred, but this is quite different from seeing them as applicable to present-day conditions. In Southern Pentecostal and independent churches, though, belief goes much further, to the stage of participation in a present event. It has been said of Prophet William Wadé Harris that, after his conversion, "it was no longer a question of what Moses did, or what Elijah did, or the words and works of Jesus as reported in the Bible. It became a question of involvement—as with the ancestors, the living dead—with Moses, with Elijah, with the archangel Gabriel, and supremely with Jesus Christ."[51]

For many new believers, stories of miracles and healing are so self-evidently crucial to the early Christian message that some suspicion must attach to any church that lacked these signs of power. As one Old Testament passage laments, "In those days the word of the Lord was rare; there were not many visions." To quote a modern follower of the Shona prophet Johane Masowe, "When we were in these synagogues [the European churches] we used to read about the works of Jesus Christ . . . cripples were made to walk and the dead were brought to life . . . evil spirits driven out. . . . That was what was being done in Jerusalem. We Africans, however, who were being instructed by white people, never did anything like that. . . . We were taught to read the Bible, but we ourselves never did what the people of the Bible used to do."[52]

Parallels with ancient Christianity are just as clear when we consider prophetic leadership. In most Western cultures, the word "prophecy" is much debased from its original meaning. Today, a prophet is basically a fortune-teller, whose reputation stands or falls by the accuracy of his or her predictions. For the world of the first century, though, a prophet was someone who spoke the inspired word of God, which might or might not be relevant to current worldly concerns. Often, then and now, the prophetic inspiration was conveyed by means of material symbols. Isaiah Shembe received his divine call when he was burned by lightning, leaving a scar on his thigh.[53] The vitality of prophecy in the contemporary South means that the rising churches can read biblical accounts with far more understanding and sensitivity than Northern Christians can. In the book of Acts, prophecy was a sign of the true church. If that was true 2,000 years ago, why should it not be true of a man or woman today, a Kimbangu or a Shembe? Prophetic powers are exactly what Jesus promised his disciples, without any caveat that these gifts might expire with the end of the first century.

SPIRITUAL WARFARE

These signs of power usually imply the concept of spiritual warfare, of confronting and defeating evil demonic forces. For African Christians, one of the most potent passages of the New Testament is found in the letter to the Ephesians, in which Paul declares that "Our struggle is not against enemies of blood and flesh but against the rulers, against the authorities, against the cosmic powers of this present darkness, against the spiritual forces of evil in the heavenly places."[54] However superstitious and irrelevant it appears to mainstream Northern Christians, the passage makes wonderful sense in most of Africa, as it does for believers in Latin America or East Asia. Once again, we can draw parallels between the modern expansion of Christianity and the growth of the religion in ancient times. Writing of the Roman world, Peter Brown comments that "However many sound social and cultural reasons the historian may find for the expansion of the Christian Church, the fact remains that in all Christian literature from the New Testament onwards, the Christian missionaries advanced principally by revealing the bankruptcy of men's invisible enemies, the demons, through exorcisms and miracles of healing."[55]

The cultural conflict over literal interpretations of exorcism and spiritual healing has in modern times found a face in Roman Catholic Archbishop Emmanuel Milingo. In 2001, Milingo won notoriety in the West when he not only violated his oath of celibacy by marrying a woman, but doing so in a service held under the auspices of the notorious Rev. Sun M. Moon. Yet it would be unfortunate if the archbishop was to be remembered only for this bizarre event, since for many years, he has epitomized African concerns within the Catholic Church. In 1969, he became archbishop of Lusaka, Zambia, and increasingly, he saw his religious vocation in terms of combating the all too real forces of evil. As he declared, "In my tradition, the society knew that these spirits could cause spiritual disorder in the community, even before the Christian period. They knew there was something in the community that could disturb." He placed spiritual healing and exorcism at the center of his ministry, combining traditional beliefs with the language of the charismatic revival. He was duly attacked for charges of heresy and witchcraft, all the more ferociously because his stern condemnations of political corruption had made him many enemies. The Vatican removed him from his see in 1982, but he was subsequently vindicated of most charges, and he gained the favor of Pope John Paul II. He later acquired an international reputation as an exorcist, whose powers are as much in demand in Europe as in Africa. Although his views stand far outside the conventional spectrum of Western religious thought, Milingo has no doubts about his biblical roots. Speaking of the many possessed individuals who seek his help, he has remarked that "I found it a shame for us as Christians that we were not able to help them. Jesus Christ has given us authority and power to take care of these problems. Luke nine recalls Jesus giving his apostles authority over all demons and at the same time over all sorts of diseases."[56]

Also illustrating the cultural gulf that separates Northern and Southern churches is Moses Tay, the Anglican archbishop of Southeast Asia, whose see is based in Singapore. In the early 1990s, Archbishop Tay traveled to the Canadian city of Vancouver. When he visited that city's Stanley Park, he encountered the totem poles that represent an important element of the local tourist trade, and he was deeply troubled. The archbishop concluded that as artifacts of an alien religion, these were idols possessed by evil spirits, and they required handling by prayer and exorcism. This behavior horrified the local Anglican church, which was committed to building good relationships with local native communities, and which regarded exorcism as absurd superstition. Considering his own standards, though, it is difficult not to feel some sympathy for the archbishop. He was quite correct to see the totems as authentic religious symbols, rather than merely tourist kitsch. Considering the long span of Christian writings on exorcism and possession, he could also summon many literary witnesses to support his position, far more than the Canadian church could produce in favor of tolerant multiculturalism.[57]

OLD AND NEW TESTAMENTS

When Southern churches read the Bible as a document of immediate relevance, they are accepting not just the New Testament, but also the Old. This often gives rise to beliefs and practices that look Jewish rather than Christian: we recall the distinctive features of the Ethiopian church. The taste for the Hebrew Bible is not hard to understand, since the patriarchal world looks so very familiar to many new Christian societies, above all in Africa. The first books of the Bible show us a world based on patriarchal clans that practice polygamy and circumcision, and which regularly honor God through blood sacrifice. African Christians also find it difficult to understand just why there are some parts of the Bible they are expected to believe with absolute literalism—for instance, the resurrection—while stories about Moses and Solomon must be treated as no more than instructive fables. Who made that capricious decision?

When a modern church follows ancient Hebrew ways, we must ask whether it is subtly reviving paganism, or just trying to observe the Old Testament in all its details. One active community in West Africa is the Musama Disco Christo Church (MDCC), founded in the 1920s by the inspired prophet Joseph Appiah. Following the Genesis story of Jacob, the group has erected a sacred pillar; it has an Ark of the Covenant and a Holy of Holies that may only be entered once each year by a high priest. The MDCC also practices animal sacrifice, and sacrificial blood is used in an annual ceremony modeled on Passover.[58] Other churches ordain a Saturday Sabbath, some prefer to call God by the name "Jehovah," and some, including the ZCC, ban the eating of pork. Even the ancient and thoroughly orthodox Ethiopian church has absorbed some aspects of biblical Judaism.

The question arises of how much further the new churches might go in absorbing pre-Christian traditions, if they found warrant in the Old Testament. In 2000, the Roman Catholic archbishop of Bloemfontein, South Africa, not only suggested that Christians might be permitted to honor their ancestors through blood libations, but that a ritual sacrifice of sheep or cows might be incorporated into the Mass. The archbishop, Buti Tlhagale, saw his proposal "as a step towards meaningful inculturation." Critics reacted with horror, as much because the suggestion violated animal rights as on grounds of heresy. Animal sacrifice had explicitly been condemned by some of the most venerated leaders of African Christianity, including the Ugandan martyr Janani Luwum. Still, Archbishop Tlhagale's opinion was far from isolated, since blood is used in some of the liturgical practices that have developed across Africa since the 1960s. In keeping with traditional ideas of consecration, the Congolese church uses a profession rite in which a drop of the candidate's blood is placed on the altar cloth. Such practices make great sense in African terms, and it would be easy to justify the practice by an arsenal of biblical texts. The whole New Testament notion of atonement is presented in the language of ritual blood sacrifice, which is precisely why it has become ever more distant (and even repulsive) for many modern Christians. Bizarre though it might seem, the whole idea of sheep having their throats cut during a Christian service raises to an acute degree the whole question of the limits of inculturation.[59]

THE ONCE AND FUTURE CHURCH

It is easy enough to find behaviors or rituals that seem to place the new churches beyond what Westerners see as the legitimate bounds of Christianity, but in so many critical ways, the independent congregations undeniably lie within the great tradition. Even in some of the areas in which they might seem odd or deviant, they are not so much departing from the Christian mainstream as emphasizing some aspects that have become unfamiliar—for example, in their Hebraism.

Perhaps the best way of refuting charges that emerging churches are anything less than fully Christian is to cite the example of a movement that genuinely is syncretistic, and that has, by any imaginable standard, moved far outside Christianity. Northern Mexico is home to a native people called the Tarahumara, who have adapted elements of Christianity to a traditional mythology. They believe in God and his wife, the Virgin Mary, who correspond to the Sun and Moon, together with their son Jesus. The divine family created all Indians, while non-Indians are the offspring of the Devil and his wife. Holy Week is the centerpiece of the ritual year, since that is the one time of year at which the Devil can defeat God. The Devil gets God drunk and seduces God's wife by his splendid guitar playing. Throughout Holy Week, the Tarahumara flock to the churches to defend the dangerously weakened divine couple, and they demonstrate their strength through elaborate processions of Soldiers and Pharisees. The Tarahumara consider themselves the "saviors of God in the Sierra Madre."[60]

I am not citing this example to mock or criticize the beliefs of the Tarahumara people, but rather to provide a point of reference in the debate over what is or is not Christian, as against what has been appropriated from pre-Christian ideas. In the case of the Tarahumara, the Christian veneer is slight, and mainly involves borrowing sacred names, together with some aspects of Catholic ritual. The contrasts with the vast majority of independent churches are obvious. These latter preserve all the fundamental beliefs that would be recognizable from any stage of Christian development, including strict monotheism, a recognition of Christ's unique role, and a firm sense of the division between divine and human realms.

Members of the independent churches themselves have no doubts whatever about their claims to authentic Christian status. This assertion is proudly proclaimed in denominational titles: the Zion Christian Church of the Star, Mount Ararat Apostolic Church, or the Eleven Apostles Spirit Healing Church. Many churches include the word "Apostolic" in their title, indicating a sense of direct continuity with the believers of the New Testament era and with the powers manifested by the Christians of that age. Among the Aladura churches of West Africa, typical denominations take their names from both apostles (Christ Apostolic Church) and angels (The Cherubim and Seraphim Society). These churches believe staunchly in the divinity of Christ, his miracles, and his resurrection. The belief statements of the different churches are classic statements of Christian doctrine. Botswana's St. Michael's Apostolic Church proclaims that "The *ecclesia* is a congregation of faithful men in which the pure word of God is preached and the sacraments are daily administered according to Christ's ordinances."[61]

In many ways, the Christian texts and creeds make far more sense for the independent churches than they do in the West. Western churches might teach the doctrine of the communion of saints, and imagine the supernatural church as a union of living believers with those past souls who have already died. For the African churches, the notion of continuity with the world of the ancestors is not only credible, it is a fundamental component of the belief system. And while many Western Christians have difficulty in accepting notions of the afterlife or resurrection as literally rather than symbolically true, these theories find a powerful resonance in African or Asian independent churches. The fact that believers regularly see their dead ancestors in dreams and visions is taken as proof that the deceased are still alive in God. Closeness to native traditions gives a powerful relevance to corporate and communal visions of the church, the *ecclesia*.[62]

These beliefs have implications for liturgy and worship. Even African Catholic churches struggle to find ways of honoring these ancestors without straying into actual worship. In one rite, a priest presents a consecrated host to a vase symbolizing the presence of the bygone generations, proclaiming the coming of Christ, and saying, "We join with you [ancestors] so that you also may attain the fullness of life in the new heaven." Burial rites have also been restructured to take more account of the continuity with the ancestors. To the casual observer, other rituals seem to come close to the idea of postmortem baptism for departed ancestors.[63]

INITIATES

Practical necessity has forced some newer churches to revive ancient customs long dormant in the older Christendom. One striking example is the catechumenate, the probationary stage through which new Christians were required to pass before earning full membership in the church. In the ancient church, this was a significant institution, associated with rigorous training and gradual revelation of the mysteries of the faith. The catechumenate largely died out in the Middle Ages when it was assumed that all church members were born and brought up in a Christian community, but in modern times, the institution has enjoyed a resurgence. In many African and Asian societies, new Christians can reasonably be assumed to be coming from a pagan background, or else from entirely different religions, so they require intense training and preparation as catechumens. In the late nineteenth century, Cardinal Lavigerie and his White Fathers demanded that converts go through a probationary period of four years, and this rigorous approach influenced Protestant counterparts. A catechumen was not automatically qualified to graduate to full membership in the congregation, and a moral or disciplinary lapse could mean that the person was forced to begin the process anew.[64]

In some Congolese dioceses, the transition from catechumen to baptized Christian has taken on many of the features of traditional initiation rites. Candidates may spend time away from their communities, learning both religious knowledge and new worldly skills, and the Easter baptism ceremonies may involve an exchange of masks, signifying the shedding of old pagan identities. The baptism is accompanied by an exorcism, which is given far more weight than the symbolic vestige that this rite occupies in the West. In twenty-first century Africa, as in second-century Rome, baptism is an awe-inspiring symbol of the believer's separation from a failing pagan world, an act of divine rescue.[65]

The point about the catechumenate reminds us that, in many ways, Southern Christianity today stands in much the same relationship to the wider society that the church did in the Roman Empire, before and during the great age of conversions. The new churches rise and fall for many of the same reasons as their ancient predecessors, and the enemies they face are much the same. Observers of contemporary Southern conditions often draw such ancient parallels. Andrew Walls notes that "Our knowledge of the early church prior to the Council of Nicaea in 325 is fragmentary, but the fragments reveal many of the concerns African churches have today, from distinguishing between true and false prophets to deciding what should happen to church members who behave badly. Even the literary forms are often similar. . . . Reading the pre-Nicene literature and the literature of the European conversion period in the light of modern African experience cast floods of light. African and Asian Christians can vastly illuminate 'our' church history." Walls has even said that he is "everlastingly grateful that . . . that second-century Christianity (and third-century, and even first-century) can still be witnessed and shared in," namely in contemporary Africa.[66]

CHURCHES AND SECTS

The idea that Southern churches are living in something like a renewed apostolic age inspires nothing short of awe, and it would be easy to write of all these developments in a thoroughly supernatural, even credulous, way. (Not for a second am I suggesting that critical scholars like Walls fall into this trap.) A religious believer might accept that God really is inaugurating a new era of signs and wonders, to give Christianity a kind of rebirth. Such a revival would be all the more miraculous because it so directly contradicts every secular assumption, and undermines the values of the world's dominant social order. I am in no position to affirm or deny that miraculous quality, but solid secular reasons also go far in explaining the character of the rising churches. Placing the churches in a social context does not make them any less impressive, but it does help to explain why they have the beliefs and practices they do. Even more usefully, looking at Southern churches in this way might help us understand how they are going to evolve in coming decades. Just because these churches look and act a certain way now does not mean that this is how they will be for centuries to come.

Much of the success of the newer churches unquestionably reflects their adaptation to local traditions and thought-patterns, so that African Christianity has become quintessentially African, Korean Christianity thoroughly Korean, and so on. But accommodation with local ways is not the sole explanation why the rising churches possess such a vital sense of the divine presence in everyday life. In fact, many of what initially seem to be characteristically African or Latin American ways of worship also appear regularly in Northern cultures, and these commonalities cannot simply be explained in terms of Africanness or Koreanness. If we find that Africa's flourishing indigenous churches place a far greater weight on healing than do their Northern neighbors, we might be tempted to explain this in terms of the functions expected of religion in traditional African society. On the other hand, spiritual healing has frequently characterized new and fringe religious movements in Europe and North America over the centuries, and the theme might be seen as a universal element in popular religion. Just as African churches often look to charismatic leaders and prophets, so do sects and new religious movements in any part of the world.

Even some of the allegedly "primitive" attitudes toward the spiritual world found in Africa or Asia would in the late twentieth century acquire steadily growing credence among White Western evangelicals and Pentecostals, with their belief in spiritual warfare. One aspect of this is spiritual mapping, identifying localities in which evil forces are believed to lurk, so that they can be confronted by prayer and exorcism.[67] It is not just in the global South that people read Paul's letter to the Ephesians, and believe that they too are warring against vast powers of spiritual evil. A phrase from this very passage inspired the title of Frank Peretti's *This Present Darkness,* one of the best-selling American books of recent years. Even exorcism, the centerpiece of the spiritual warfare idea, has enjoyed a massive revival in the contemporary West, usually among people of European descent.[68] Looking at the widespread impact of such ideas, it becomes harder to draw a strict geographical or cultural boundary between "Northern" and "Southern" patterns of religious experience.

When we see such broadly similar churches growing in so many diverse regions, then the parallels cannot simply be explained in just cultural or racial terms. Rather, some of these practices reflect the *newness* of the rising churches. In understanding the character of the new Christianity, it is helpful to use the division between "churches" and sects" that is so basic to the academic study of religion.[69] A century ago, sociological pioneer Max Weber tried to define the differences between Europe's religious organizations, in passages that sound as if he is analyzing the present-day religious realities of global North and South. *Churches,* in Weber's view, are formal bodies that intellectualize religious teachings and restrain emotionalism in their services. They offer believers a formal liturgy and set prayers, in ways that portray the divine as remote from daily life. *Sects,* by contrast, are overtly emotional and spontaneous, and encourage individual mystical experience;

they tend toward fundamentalism, while shunning the intellect as a possible source of danger. The prayers of the sects indicate a firm belief that the divine is ever-present, ever-ready to act in everyday life.

Sociologist Ernst Troeltsch further developed this theoretical division, and he contrasted the upstart quality of the sects with the deeper roots of the churches. The matter of recruitment was critical. Most sect members are voluntary converts, whose lives are largely controlled by the organization, so that the sect becomes a small, exclusive fellowship of people seeking spiritual perfection. Churches, in contrast, are larger and better-established bodies, whose members are customarily born into the organization. Churches also attract members of higher social status and educational level than do the sects. Additionally, the two types of structure differ widely in terms of their leadership. Sects demand that leaders demonstrate spiritual and charismatic gifts; churches are run by formally trained ministers, who operate within a bureaucratic framework.

What most strikingly unites the otherwise diverse Southern churches is that in most cases, Christianity as a mass popular movement is a relatively new creation, so that first- and second-generation converts are well represented in the various congregations. They simply cannot assume that members are likely to be born into the group, hence the importance of the catechumenate. In terms of the sociology of religion, this means that these communities are classic sects, with all that implies for leadership, worship style, and degree of commitment. They are fundamentalist and charismatic by nature and theologically conservative, with a powerful belief in the spiritual dimension, in visions, and in spiritual healing. With their claims to prophetic status, figures like Simon Kimbangu or Isaiah Shembe exactly fit the classic profile of sect leaders. Leadership roles in Pentecostal and independent churches are open to anyone who is accepted as having spiritual gifts, regardless of any formal education or theological training.

The sociological model of the sect offers a useful means of understanding both independent and Pentecostal churches across the South. When we see independent churches in South Africa or Nigeria, some of what initially appear to be their odd and African features are in reality no such thing. Yes, they are indeed distinctive when measured against the "mainline" churches of Europe or North America, but not when compared with countless smaller and fringe movements that largely attract White believers.

The literature on new religious movements not only provides good models for understanding the distinctive beliefs of such groups, but it may also predict their future development. As time passes, successful sects become more churchlike in their own right, more formal and bureaucratic. Crucially, they might insist that clergy acquire formal academic training, rather than merely being "called by the Spirit." The history of Methodism from the eighteenth century on provides a classic model of such a process. As sects drift away from their origins, they in turn spawn a new generation of enthusiasts who seek to recapture the charisma and spiritual power that they believe to be integral to religious experience. Churches beget sects, which in turn become churches, until they in turn beget new and still fiercer sects. The cycle has recurred many times, and will continue ad infinitum.

As Southern churches grow and mature, they will assuredly lose something of their sectarian character and become more like the major churches, with all that implies for the nature of leadership, worship style, and so on. They will move toward the mainstream, just like Methodists and Quakers did in their day. One symbolic example of such a change occurred in 1969, when the Kimbanguist church, one of the largest indigenous churches, actually joined the World Council of Churches, then as now dominated by liberal and mainstream Protestants. The Church of the Lord (Aladura) took the same step in 1975, the Harrists and several other independents in 1998. If past precedents are anything to go by, Southern religious organizations will become more formal and churchlike, and just possibly more skeptical toward claims about healings and prophetic visions.

A change from sects to churches could accelerate as their host societies modernize, as Western medicine becomes more affordable and gains more credibility. African and Asian societies might undergo the same kind of secularization that Europe experienced in the eighteenth century, when concepts like witchcraft and prophecy gradually fell out of favor.[70] Conceivably, the new churches themselves could become key agents of modernization. Studies of Latin American Pentecostalism note how believers gain a new sense of individual respect and responsibility, together with habits of thrift, sobriety, and literacy, and similar observations can be made of their African counterparts. A growing Pentecostal community tends to create a larger public base for the growth of democratic capitalism and, in the long term, perhaps for greater secularism.[71] At the same time though, as churches become part of the establishment, newer and more radical bodies will spin off from them. In the coming decades, the newer Christian communities will develop at least as much diversity as those of the old Europe did in the Middle Ages, or the early modern period.

Yet all these changes are likely to occur over generations, and the transformation described here will not be anything like complete until well into the present century. For the foreseeable future, then, Southern churches should continue to offer a powerful and attractive package for potential converts, both North and South. They can plausibly present themselves as modern-day bearers of an apostolic message that is not limited by geography, race, or culture, and claims of signs and wonders will serve as their credentials. If and when the rising churches turn their attentions northward, they might well find a deeply interested audience willing to listen to these very old messages repackaged in such unexpected forms.

God and the World

Do not be afraid. I see God's hand in this.
—*Archbishop Janani Luwum of Uganda*

In the name of God, in the name of this suffering
people whose cries rise to heaven more loudly
each day, I implore you, I beg you, I order you,
in the name of God: stop the repression.
—*Archbishop Oscar Romero of San Salvador*

We can predict something of the beliefs and practices of the emerging Southern Christianity, but what of the future relationship between God and the world? The greatest change is likely to involve our Enlightenment-derived assumption that religion should be segregated into a separate sphere of life, distinct from everyday reality. In the Western view, religion may influence behavior in what is often, revealingly, termed the real world, and faith might even play a significant political role, but spiritual life is primarily a private inward activity, a matter for the individual mind. For Americans particularly, the common assumption holds that church and state, sacred and profane, are wholly separate enterprises, and should be kept as separate as oil and water. In most historical periods, though, such a distinction does not apply, and is even incomprehensible. Scholars studying medieval Europe are scathing about any attempt to draw lines between "religion" and ordinary life, and doubt whether anyone living in those times could actually have understood the modern distinction between church and state.

In this sense, many societies of the global South live in an intellectual world far closer to the medieval world than to Western modernity. In recent decades, the politics of much of Africa, Latin America, and Asia have been profoundly affected by religious allegiances and activism, as clergy have repeatedly occupied center stage in political life. This phenomenon is not unknown in the modern West, which so esteems clerical activists like Martin Luther King Jr. and Dietrich Bonhoeffer, but it happens much more systematically in the South. In Southern Christian communities, cardinals and bishops have emerged as national moral leaders in a way that really has not happened in the West since the seventeenth century. Also, as in the European Middle Ages, political interventions by the clergy have been explicitly religious in nature, drawing on ancient prophetic traditions, and on a powerful and innovative kind of biblical exegesis.[1] It is not just in the Muslim world that religious ideologies tend to trump political and national loyalties.

However unimaginable it may have appeared fifty years ago, not only is Christianity flourishing in the Third World, but so are distinctively Christian politics. If in fact Christianity is going to be growing so sharply in numbers and cultural influence in coming decades, we can reasonably ask whether the faith will also provide the guiding political ideology of much of the world. We might even imagine a new wave of Christian states, in which political life is inextricably bound up with religious belief. If so, then the South will soon be dealing with some debates that have a very long pedigree in the traditional centers of Christianity, issues of the proper relationship between church and state, and between rival churches under the law. Other questions that inevitably arise in such settings involve tolerance and diversity, the relationship between majority and minority communities, and the extent to which religious-inspired laws can (or should) regulate private morality and behavior. However these issues are resolved, this political dimension will further intensify the enormous cultural gap between North and South, between secular and religious societies.

OUT OF COLONIALISM

The association between church and state has a very long history in the global South. Under colonial regimes, Christian churches enjoyed state support, which they reciprocated by their strongly conservative political stances. The church was in effect an arm of government. In Latin America, the preferential position enjoyed by the Catholic Church continued long after independence, and in some countries survives today. In Chile, only in 2000 did a new law end the church's legal hegemony over education and cultural life, and that in a country with one of the largest Protestant minorities in the region. Prior to this, only Catholics could appoint chaplains to the armed forces, only Catholic organizations obtained tax exemptions on property and donations, and religious education in schools was purely Catholic. In the early twentieth century, Catholic thinkers were entranced by the theory of integralism, a neo-medieval notion that Catholic social doctrine should pervade every aspect of social, economic, and political life, with the clergy exercising broad influence over secular matters. Although the theory was discredited by its association with ultra-Right views and fanatical anti-communism, it maintains a subterranean existence.[2]

During political conflicts in Latin America, Catholicism was dependably on the side of the traditional ruling orders, often to the point of approving repression. During the Argentine crisis of the 1970s and 1980s, Catholic Church authorities were notorious for their acquiescence in official violence and the brutal proceedings of the dirty war.[3] Radicals on the other side of the conflict were often strongly anti-Catholic and anti-clerical. In Mexico, the church suffered violent persecutions at the hands of radical regimes through the first half of the twentieth century. In Africa too, the mission churches supported by the colonial powers were sporadically attacked during insurrections.

Increasingly during the twentieth century, Third World churches came to be identified with the cause of reform or, frequently, revolution. Although the ideological bent of the churches changed massively, we still find the idea that they should be thoroughly involved in politics, and even to lead the nation. In the early twentieth century, exponents of radical political Christianity were chiefly to be found on the fringes of the mission churches. The most visible leaders were African prophets like John Chilembwe or William Wadé Harris, or radicalized Catholic priests like Brazil's legendary Father Cicero. From the 1950s on, however, such ideas penetrated the mainstream churches, in Europe and North America and across the Third World. Protestants were deeply affected by memories of the churches' failure to confront Nazi Germany, and were radicalized by campaigns against racism and against the apartheid regime of South Africa. These ideas gained a stronghold in the World Council of Churches, which since the late 1960s has often espoused radical and left-wing political causes. The organization faced serious controversies over precisely how far to go in its opposition to unjust states. Resentment became highly public in the 1970s, when the WCC's Special Fund regularly gave money to guerrilla fighters opposing the White Rhodesian regime. For critics, this funding uncomfortably crossed the boundary dividing the Church Militant from the Church Militarist.[4]

In the Roman Catholic Church, theologies of liberation spread widely following the Second Vatican Council of 1963–65. At least for a while, the Vatican not only permitted but endorsed radical political action. In 1967, the papal encyclical *Populorum Progressio* called for "bold transformations" to redistribute wealth globally. Both Catholics and mainstream Protestants shared similar ideas about the right and obligation to oppose oppressive regimes, and to combat the structural racial and economic injustices found across the global South. Both also found rich precedents in Christian history for such activism. They looked to the Exodus story of liberation from slavery, as well as to Old Testament prophets of justice like Amos. In the New Testament, too, liberationist readers found much ammunition for a radical social critique. One potent idea was that of *Kairos*, the "Hour" of God's judgment on human injustice, and on exploitative social structures.[5]

In its various forms, liberation theology motivated individual believers to participate in political struggles, and made it clear that the churches were no longer on the side of oppressive regimes. This movement had real political consequences in repressive states, since clergy were allowed a much greater latitude of speech and action than ordinary citizens, and so could serve as symbolic centers of resistance and activism. If an ordinary union member spoke out against torture and repression, then he or she was likely to be jailed or killed forthwith, but a government had to be more circumspect when a priest or bishop uttered the same words. Jailing a priest, particularly a Catholic priest, invited the condemnation of the Western media and a probable confrontation with the Vatican. Clergy became valued spokesmen for opposition movements. Similar constraints on official behavior applied when protests or organizational meetings were held under church auspices. At least when under the eyes of Western media, repressive regimes had qualms about storming churches or firing on religious processions that they would not have if protesters were waving red flags. Churches offered a kind of safe zone, as radical clergy effectively reinvented the medieval Christian notion of sanctuary. In the bloody aftermath of the 1973 coup d'état in Chile, the families of the persecuted had nowhere to turn, with the conspicuous exception of the *Vicaría de la Solidaridad,* a mission under the protection of the nation's Catholic Church. In the repressive Brazil of the 1970s, by far the most effective source of opposition was the Catholic Church under the leadership of São Paulo's Cardinal Paolo Arns, who freely exploited the fact that the military dictatorship would never dare touch a religious figure of his stature.

Of course, the church's immunity was strictly limited, and only applied when governments cared about world opinion. The "sanctuary" principle worked in authoritarian South Korea, tied as it was to the Western world system, but not in isolated and paranoid North Korea, in which the churches were ruthlessly destroyed.[6] Even in the Western Hemisphere, governments under threat of collapse might strike at the church. A decent respect for the opinions of mankind did not save the life of Archbishop Oscar Romero, when in 1980 he issued his frontal challenge to the far-Right regime of El Salvador. In 1989, six Jesuit priests were murdered as further victims in the ongoing savagery in that nation. In Guatemala too, murderous state violence has reached even into the episcopal ranks, with the 1998 slaying of the auxiliary bishop who served as head of the archdiocese's human rights office.[7] In practice, such violence has actually reinforced the church's reputation as defender of the exploited. In many countries, churches would in the last quarter of the twentieth century acquire an enviable reputation for courageous and effective opposition to repressive regimes.

LATIN AMERICA AND LIBERATION

Liberation theologies took very different courses depending on the politics of the region where they took root. It was in Latin America that liberationist ideas achieved their earliest successes, although in some ways, the movement had less long-term effect here than elsewhere. The story of Catholic radicalism is so central to Latin American history from the 1960s to the 1980s that it is scarcely possible to discuss it in any detail here.[8]

Catholic activism received a kind of official charter in 1968, during the conference of the Latin American bishops at Medellín, Colombia, an event that has been described as a virtual declaration of independence. Borrowing extensively from Marxist terminology, the assembled bishops condemned neo-colonialism, exploitation, and the institutionalized violence of capitalist society, and demanded fundamental economic and social reforms.[9] In 1971, the Peruvian theologian (and Catholic priest) Gustavo Gutiérrez published what was perhaps the best-known work of the new movement in his *Teologia de la Liberación.*[10] Over the next twenty years, many church leaders took very seriously the call for a "preferential option for the poor." Radicalism was personified by activist bishops like Helder Cámara, who from 1964 to 1985 served as archbishop of the Brazilian province of Recife and Olinda, where he was known as the "Bishop of the *Favelas.*" Dom Helder himself grew out of an integralist background, suggesting how naturally the new left-wing synthesis could be reconciled with older theocratic notions. Catholic radicals developed a popular constituency through the base communities, which some visionaries saw as the nuclei of a future church of the people. In what was loosely a Leninist model, the base communities were to be the seeds of the new society emerging within the shell of the old, until they eventually became strong enough to discard the old husk. By the late 1970s, there were said to be 80,000 such communities in Brazil alone.[11]

Catholic radicals remained in lively dialogue with Marxist groups, and Christians participated in some of the revolutionary movements of these years. Already in the mid-1960s, some priests working with the poor were becoming heavily politicized, and some wholeheartedly adopted a revolutionary agenda. The patron saint of this movement was Colombian priest Camilo Torres, who fought with a leftist guerrilla group until he was killed in battle with the armed forces in 1966: he became an international martyr for the far Left. He was not concerned about allying with the Left, since "Even though the Communists themselves may not know it, you have many among them who are authentic Christians." For Torres, "The revolution is the way to obtain a government which will feed the hungry, clothe the naked, teach the ignorant, fulfill the works of charity, of love of neighbor. . . . Therefore, the revolution is not only permitted but is obligatory for Christians who must see in it the only effective and complete way to achieve love for all."[12] Although he stood at a far extreme of Catholic politics, Torres was representative in his belief that the church and clergy needed to reshape government for the good of the poor.

Liberationist hopes reached a new height in the late 1970s. When the Sandinista revolution triumphed in Nicaragua in 1979, several current and former priests served in the radical government. The following year, the assassination of Archbishop Romero created a genuinely popular martyr, as Central America became the focus for the Christian Left worldwide.[13] These events, though, proved the high-water mark for the movement. In 1978, the election of John Paul II brought to the Vatican a conservative pope whose experiences in Poland had given him a deep distrust of Marxism in any form. Through the 1980s, the new regime in the Vatican systematically silenced radical theologians, like Brazil's Leonardo Boff. Meanwhile, revolutionary hopes in Central America were dashed by global conditions, in the form of U.S. intervention and the collapse of the Soviet bloc. The Sandinista regime lost power in 1990.[14]

Over the next twenty years, a series of new episcopal appointments brought the Latin American church into a much more conservative line. The new pattern was exemplified by Peruvian Juan Luis Cipriani, a member of the highly conservative Opus Dei organization and bishop of the diocese of Ayacucho. This position was so sensitive because Ayacucho was the storm center of the fierce guerrilla war waged by the nation's Maoist guerrillas, the Shining Path, who were suppressed by bloody military campaigns in the 1990s. Cipriani hewed closely to the government line, which was also that of the Vatican, namely that the regime was fighting for Christianity and civilization. He consistently defended the armed forces against charges of atrocities, and argued that "Most human rights organizations are just covering the tails of political movements, almost all of them Marxist and Maoist." In 2001, nevertheless, Cipriani was raised to the rank of cardinal.[15]

Under such leadership, the popular organizations that had sprung up over the previous generation now entered a political ice age. Though some survived and flourished, many base communities withered, and failed to become the nuclei of a radical Catholic reformation. Much of the impulse that originally inspired the communities has been diverted into Pentecostalism, which appeals to similar constituencies among the urban poor. In part, Pentecostal growth can be seen as a response to the failed revolutionary expectations of earlier years, and in several countries, the newer sects expanded most rapidly during the political repression of the 1980s.

Contrary to the extravagant hopes of the 1970s, Latin America would not become subject to a kind of left-wing theocracy, but it would be wrong to see recent changes exclusively in terms of a withdrawal from idealism. Nor have church leaders renounced a political voice, and they remain active in secular politics to a degree that would be unthinkable in the global North. Despite the rightward shift of the church in that region, Latin American clergy remain major political players, who often do intervene on the side of democracy and human rights. As a counterpoint to Peru's Cipriani, we can cite Oscar Andrés Rodriguez Maradiaga, archbishop of Tegucigalpa, Honduras, and another of the new group of cardinals chosen in 2001. Although obviously approved by the Vatican, Cardinal Rodriguez speaks freely on issues of social justice, and has emerged as a leading spokesman in the campaign to cancel the crushing debts owed by Third World nations. Within Honduras, his work for political democracy resulted in an overenthusiastic parliament electing him as the nation's new chief of police. Although he declined the honor, the incident speaks volumes for continued assumptions about the moral ascendancy of the Church and its proper role in secular life.[16]

AFRICA'S REVOLUTIONS

Elsewhere in the world, too, the link between Christianity and popular politics is stronger than ever. In Africa, religion has been tied to liberation struggles since the 1960s. Most of the first generation of independent Africa's political leadership was Christian, commonly the products of mission schools, and these pioneers were often active church members in their own right. Zambian president Kenneth Kaunda was the son of a Presbyterian minister, while Senegal's leader Leopold Senghor had trained for the priesthood. Tanzanian Prime Minister Julius Nyerere and Ghanaian leader Kwame Nkrumah had both taught in mission schools. Nyerere was a Catholic who worked closely with the churches, and for all his radical nationalism, he praised the missionaries who, he felt, "had brought the best they knew to Africa, their church and way of life." He drew heavily on Christian thought and language in formulating his radical variant of African socialism, which he traced back to the early Christian communism described in the book of Acts.[17]

The linkage between Christianity and insurgent nationalism was enhanced over the next thirty years as church leaders of many denominations became prominent in the struggle against the entrenched White South African regime. In the process, the churches enthusiastically adopted the messages of liberation theology, and tried to present a prophetic witness against secular evils. In 1985, Catholic and Protestant leaders agreed on the *Kairos* statement, a sophisticated application of radical theology to modern politics. The statement was called forth by the bizarre and shocking situation in which Blacks and Whites "sit in the same Church, while outside, Christian policemen and soldiers are beating up and killing Christian children, or torturing Christian prisoners to death, while yet other Christians stand by and weakly plead for peace." The document declared that "When we search the Bible for a message about oppression we discover, as others throughout the world are discovering, that oppression is a central theme that runs right through the Old and New Testaments." In the South African case, repression was an apocalyptic sign: "The god of the South African state is not merely an idol or a false god, it is the devil disguised as almighty God—the Antichrist." Having committed themselves so wholeheartedly to the idea of resistance, the churches enjoyed great prestige by the time of the fall of the White regime in 1994, when Anglican Archbishop Desmond Tutu emerged as an unquestioned moral leader. It was Tutu who tried to reconcile the nation's old rivals through a Truth and Reconciliation Commission, an innovative attempt to apply Christian ideas of repentance and forgiveness to national secular politics, rather than just individual relationships.[18]

Christian involvement in the South African conflict is well known in the West, but far less celebrated is the key role that churches and clergy have taken in what has been called the second African revolution. Many of the new independent regimes that took power in the 1960s themselves became corrupt and oppressive, and these governments in their turn came under pressure to reform. In the worst cases, the independent governments became monstrous tyrannies, like those that successively ruled Uganda in the 1970s and 1980s. In the Ugandan case, the resulting struggle against oppression claimed the lives of many Christian protesters. Archbishop Luwum was murdered on the orders of Idi Amin in 1977. The same year, political strife in the Republic of Congo (Congo-Brazzaville) led to the murder of a Catholic archbishop, Cardinal Biayenda.[19]

Contrary to Western impressions, the leadership exercised by Archbishop Tutu was not unique in Africa, or even exceptional. In some cases, bishops and clergy led national movements against dictatorship, as in the attacks on Malawi's Hastings Banda or Kenya's Daniel Arap Moi. In Benin, Togo, and Congo-Brazzaville, senior clergy supervised transitions from dictatorship to democracy. The Roman Catholic Church was in demand as an honest broker even in countries that did not have a Christian majority. Unlike in Latin America, Catholic activism in Africa did not run afoul of the Vatican, since local churches were evidently pushing for democratic constitutional reforms, rather than sweeping revolutionary change on a Marxist blueprint. Studying worldwide trends toward democratization in the 1980s, Samuel Huntington identified the Catholic Church as one of the principal engines for progress.[20]

Across Africa, senior clergy have become the focus of popular hopes and loyalties in a way in which the fragile nation-states of the continent cannot. We can see powerful analogies to the experience of European churches in the Middle Ages, and in both eras, prelates are expected to run serious risks as a normal part of the job. To take an English example, between 1000 and 1650, no less than five archbishops of Canterbury died violently, whether by execution or assassination. European examples have been rarer in modern times, although the struggles between Christianity and communism produced some modern-day martyrs, like the priest Jerzy Popieluszko, murdered by the Polish military regime in 1984.

In terms of the scale of violence, though, there are few modern parallels to the dangers faced by African clergy, for whom cases of martyred prelates like Thomas Beckett are not just matters of remote historical interest. To take an example that received next to no coverage in Western media, in 1996, Catholic Archbishop Christophe Munzihirwa was murdered by Rwandan troops surging over his province in what was then eastern Zaire, and his body was left in the street. Over the previous years, the archbishop had acquired a reputation for his impartial condemnation of violence and abuse in the region, no matter who the perpetrators were. He had repeatedly opposed and embarrassed the regime of dictator Mobutu Sese Seko, behavior that posed a grave threat to life and limb. When the Mobutu government collapsed,

Archbishop Munzihirwa stood as the last hope that the hundreds of thousands of Rwandan refugees in his province might escape massacre. Reading the accounts of his last days, we recall the stories of bishops during the collapse of the Roman Empire, trying to lead their flocks to safety from invading barbarians.[21] Then as now, the question was simple: if not the church, who else could the people turn to?

Heroic careers like those of Archbishops Munzihirwa or Romero have consequences that long outlast even the memories of those living individuals whom they have helped and defended. Deeply established in the Christian tradition is the powerful sense of martyrdom and heroic sanctity, and it would be astonishing if these deaths were not soon commemorated through cults and shrines. Already, there is a powerful movement for the canonization of Romero, but popular devotion has a habit of running far ahead of what the Vatican may decide. In future generations, the church will gain vastly enhanced strength from devotion to these new saints. In life, Romero, Luwum, Munzihirwa, and their like were powerful nuisances to secular authority. In death, they become indomitable foes.

Reinforcing the medieval analogy has been the response of the embattled dictators. When a medieval king was denounced as an enemy of the church, he would commonly try to prove himself a paladin of piety, perhaps by launching a crusade or making a pilgrimage. In modern Africa, the situation is comparable. When Kenyan President Arap Moi came under attack from mainstream churches (Catholic, Anglican, and Presbyterian), his response was not to denounce the churches or to condemn religious intervention in politics, but rather to prove himself a fervently pious supporter of independent and Pentecostal churches. His behavior illustrates the deeply religious and ecclesiastical nature of contemporary politics in Christian Africa. When Zairean Catholics criticized the abuses of the Mobutu government, the dictator launched an anti-Christian reaction, demanding that people abandon their Christian baptismal names. (He himself had been formerly Joseph Mobutu.) Even so, Mobutu also favored rival Christian groups whom he saw as more docile and nationalist-minded than the Catholics, namely Protestants and Kimbanguists.[22]

ASIAN REGIMES

Clerical activism for human rights can give an enormous boost to church prestige, which in turn increases the church's political weight, and this cycle has occurred in Asia as well as in Africa and Latin America. The Catholic

Church in the Philippines has a distinguished record of activism on social justice issues. Priests were prominent in anti-colonial struggles in the early twentieth century, and later in the revolutionary movement that led to the overthrow of dictator Ferdinand Marcos in 1986. Most visible was Cardinal Jaime Sin, who served as the symbolic focus of national resistance against Marcos. More recently, Cardinal Sin played a similar role in the movement to impeach a subsequent Philippine leader, President Joseph Estrada, who was accused of receiving massive bribes. As the anti-Estrada campaign reached its climax in 2000, protests had a frankly ecclesiastical tone that would have been instantly understandable in medieval or early modern Europe. Services described as "protest Eucharists" were attended by members of Catholic social and labor groups, and the Catholic universities, and were led by Sin and other bishops. The Catholic Church was by no means alone in its campaign, which was strongly supported by newer Protestant and Pentecostal groups, but there was no doubt about the potent religious content of the popular upsurge. As in the Kenyan conflict, the embattled president responded not by attacking religion as such, but by invoking his support in religious groups outside the mainstream. Through the controversy, one of his strongest supporters was Mike Velarde of the Catholic charismatic group El Shaddai.[23]

Korea has been a remarkable success story for the churches. Christian numbers have swelled since the 1970s, and the church's growing prestige and popularity has partly resulted from its willingness to stand up and suffer for democratic rights and for nationalist causes. Christian successes also owe much to repeated official efforts to suppress the faith, a fact that would have been instantly understandable to the Christians of ancient times. If bishops are not actually executed, then jailing them can be almost as effective in promoting Christian solidarity and in attracting recruits. The history of Korean Christianity since the seventeenth century has been a turbulent one. Under native Korean rule, massacres and persecutions were repeatedly provoked by the Christian rejection of ancestor cults. Persecutions continued sporadically through the twentieth century, but in a dramatically different political context. More recent actions were launched by the occupying forces of imperial Japan, which were trying to destroy Korean cultural identity. This put Christians in the position of patriotic martyrs. For ordinary Koreans, joining a Christian church was an effective symbolic means of declaring pride in Korea and opposition to the invaders. When Korean nationalists issued a symbolic Declaration of Independence in 1919, almost half the signatories were Christian, although Christians represented only one percent of the population at that time.[24]

Although persecutions in recent years have not been as violent as those launched by the Japanese, we can see a continuation of older patterns. As popular opposition to South Korea's successive military regimes grew from the mid-1970s on, the churches emerged as forceful voices for reform. Protestants and Catholics allied to launch national protests, and bishops and laypeople became prominent as political prisoners. Korean churches evolved their *Minjung* theology, a local variant of liberationist thought. Dissident leader Kim Dae Jung has described his own Roman Catholic Church as "the centrifocal point of the spiritual struggle against the Park dictatorship." The opposition triumphed in 1992, when the country held free elections, and in 1997, Kim was elected president of the Republic of Korea. Vastly increasing Christian numbers reflect the prestige acquired by the churches through their sufferings.[25]

CHRISTIAN NATIONS

The modern story of Christian political activism is often an inspiring one, but history suggests that there are potentially disturbing sides of the story. To take an obvious problem, when a church helps establish a new government, religious leaders often expect some kind of recognition of their authority, perhaps even a share in government. In the Philippines, for instance, the president who replaced the controversial Estrada was mocked for her ostentatious displays of respect for the Catholic hierarchy. According to a journalistic attack, Gloria Macapagal-Arroyo has "been busy polishing her Catholic credentials by adopting the bishops' line that cults are bad, and by handing down all sorts of pious edicts."[26] Such rhetorical displays may not pose any great threats to a nation's freedom, but far worse can occur in other settings.

It is not a vast leap from churches exercising political power to demanding an exclusive right to that power, perhaps within the confines of a theocratic Christian state. That assertion can offer a real provocation to non-Christian groups, to Muslims, traditional believers, and secularists, as well as to denominations that feel they are excluded from the new established order. Sometimes, the provocation is deliberate. In the Pacific nation of Fiji, native Fijians represent a razor-thin majority of the population, closely followed by ethnic Indians, and for years, the two communities have been in bitter conflict over political and cultural dominance. Since the native community is heavily Christian, Fijian self-assertion takes the form of repeated attempts to declare the nation a Christian state, as a snub to the Hindu minority.[27]

The complex religious makeup of most African nations ensures that political regimes have been cautious about speaking of themselves explicitly as Christian societies, but there are some exceptions. Zambia declared itself a Christian nation in 1991, and the nation's vice president has said that this aspiration needs to be taken very seriously, urging citizens to "have a Christian orientation in all fields, at all levels." In the Ivory Coast too, recent regimes have been criticized for financially sponsoring Christian churches, organizations, and activities in a land in which Muslims actually outnumber Christians. The trend finds its most excessive manifestation in the astonishing basilica church of "Our Lady of Peace," begun in the 1980s by then-President Felix Hophuet-Boigny in his hometown of Yamoussoukro. If completed, this would be the world's largest Catholic church, larger than St. Peter's in Rome.[28]

Such grandiloquent ambitions seem so inappropriate to economic realities as to be mildly comic, but they do raise serious questions about the religious nature of Southern states. As we will see, one of the most divisive issues in modern Africa is the adoption of Islamic law in states like Sudan and Nigeria, and predominantly Christian nations might retaliate by asserting their own religious beliefs through legislation. The separation of church and state is a wholly foreign idea in African nations, which follow the quite different models offered by former colonial powers like Britain, France, or Portugal. In these older views, church establishment was a perfectly familiar idea. We may yet see many more "Christian states," perhaps in which one denomination occupies the dominant role—what European scholars term a *Staatskirche*.

These newly defined Christian regimes would not necessarily share the passionate concern for democracy and constitutionalism that has so distinguished Southern churches in the age of Desmond Tutu and Kim Dae Jung. Long before the recent rediscovery of the fiery prophetic tradition associated with liberation theology, church-state relations were commonly defined by doctrines of Christian acquiescence to political power. Christian political thought has often been influenced by submissive ideas represented in the thirteenth chapter of Paul's letter to the Romans ("Let every soul be subject to the governing authorities. For there is no authority except from God, and the authorities that exist are appointed by God"). Ideas like these are generally held by independent and Pentecostal churches, who also have a devotion to the Old Testament, with all its accounts of kingdoms pledged to serving God's will. (The idea of integralism is by no means confined to Catholics.) We can imagine a future in which cooperative churches are enlisted into the service of government under the rhetoric of creating a

Christian society, complete with appropriate moral legislation. Repressive regimes could benefit enormously from the support of these churches, which would provide a widespread propaganda network preaching the message of non-resistance to government, in exchange for their privileged status.[29]

Submission to a "Christian state" can easily turn into a willful refusal to acknowledge the flaws of that regime, and to connive at official corruption and violence. One of the rare independent African states to declare its Christian status from the outset was Liberia, in which religion was used to justify the gross corruption of the nation's political elite and the oppression of the native country people. More recently, the Zambian president who proclaimed the nation's official Christianity, Frederick Chiluba, developed worrying tendencies to act illegally, and by 2000 he was seeking an unconstitutional third term in office. In the controversies that followed, he could count on docile support from the Pentecostal churches that he ostentatiously favored. R. Drew Smith writes that "When opponents of the Chiluba government staged an unsuccessful coup in October 1997, for example, the general secretary of the Pentecostal Assemblies of God stated that 'God cannot allow Zambia to be disturbed by selfish individuals because he is in total control of the Christian nation.' He went on to say that 'thanks and praise should be given to God for enabling Zambian soldiers to crush the coup attempt.' " If there is one thing that struggling Third World states do not need, it is additional justifications to keep dictators in power.[30]

In addition, there is a real temptation for churches that have led or participated in revolutions to provide uncritical support for the new regimes, and to judge them by different standards from those applied to the old order. Acknowledging this temptation in the newly democratized South Africa, Archbishop Tutu shrewdly observed that "It is easy to be against. It is not nearly so easy to be clear about what we are *for*."[31] South African churches could easily have become pliant tools of the new government, the African National Congress at prayer. Accordingly, Tutu's Truth and Reconciliation effort examined the sins of the revolutionaries as searchingly as those of the government, and recognized both sides as requiring forgiveness. Other ecclesiastical revolutionaries are not so perceptive.

CHRISTIAN FIGHTS CHRISTIAN

In other ways too, Christian growth raises potential political difficulties, and can on occasion lead to violence. We have already seen how commonplace messianic, prophetic, and apocalyptic groups have been in the Christianizing world. Usually, such groups tend to be peaceful, confining their threats of divine judgment to the other world; but a few movements, singularly fanatical, carry out actual violence in the present life. One notorious example occurred in 2000, when a Ugandan church with Catholic roots apparently launched a mass suicide that claimed the lives of over a thousand believers. Reportedly, the Movement for the Restoration of the Ten Commandments of God gathered at Kanungu to await a mystical vision of the Virgin Mary. Followers then immolated themselves by fire, in what was described as an African Jonestown. Subsequent reporting raised serious doubts about this interpretation, and the believers are more likely to have been murdered in what was in reality an act of organized crime or terrorism. Still, the Kanungu disaster focused attention on other fringe African movements that indisputably have been involved in grossly violent acts.[32]

Often, such millenarian and messianic movements grow out of the many civil wars that have rent the continent in recent decades, producing social collapse and general despair. During the civil conflicts in Uganda over the past twenty years, one of the most ruthless guerrilla groups has been the Lord's Resistance Army, which became notorious for its mass abductions of children. The Army grew out of a classic messianic anti-witchcraft movement called the Holy Spirit Mobile Force, founded by the prophet Alice Lakwena. Thousands of this group's followers perished when they went into battle believing that the magic oils smeared on their bodies would protect them from bullets. As so often in European history, it is the leaders most convinced of their divine inspiration who carry out the most bloodthirsty actions.[33]

Religious rivalries are also problematic. Often, relations between expanding denominations are cordial or at least non-confrontational, on the grounds that each church has plenty of room to grow, with ample likely converts. In much of Africa, different denominations have evolved good working relations in the form of conferences or federations of Christian churches. Serious conflicts appear, though, when a new denomination makes inroads into areas that another faith has traditionally regarded as its own distinctive territory. This kind of rivalry can be all the more deadly when religious loyalties coincide with national or tribal frontiers, so that religion can provide yet another incentive for violence. Many of southern Africa's independent churches are closely linked to existing tribal leaderships, so that a religious challenge automatically becomes a political threat, demanding a forcible response.

A linkage between tribalism and religious zealotry has been alleged in several recent conflicts in Africa. One of the most alarming involved the

genocidal violence in Rwanda in 1994, one of the worst single acts of carnage in the world since the end of the Second World War. The violence was
overwhelmingly tribal in nature, with Hutus murdering members of the
minority Tutsi tribe. Some of the activists in the slaughter were themselves
Hutu Christian clergy, including both Catholic and Anglican bishops and
clergy, and even nuns (although some Hutu clergy risked their lives to prevent murders). At the least, clerical involvement in mass murder raises
alarming questions about the nature of Christian conversion in a region that
had been held up as a model of successful evangelization. More serious,
although still unresolved, is the issue of whether denominational loyalties
might actually have encouraged the violence. Reportedly, Hutus in the
Catholic hierarchy used the massacres as an opportunity to purge Tutsi
priests and laity.[34]

In some circumstances, surging religious zeal can lead to instability and
bloodshed, and often in countries that already have more than enough difficulties standing in the way of their development. In Europe, modernization and state-building could only advance once the wars of religion had been
fought to a standstill and the would-be messiahs were driven out of mainstream political life. This was a piecemeal process taking centuries, and it is
unlikely that a parallel change in Africa or Asia would be much more rapid.

BETTER THAN GUNSHIPS?

Latin America provides many cases in which religious change has led to
political instability. As Protestant and Pentecostal numbers have boomed
over the past thirty years, Catholic authorities have become increasingly
resentful. Backed by the Vatican, local bishops regularly condemn the growth
of "sects," a term that in Romance languages usually signifies a dangerous
fringe movement, rather like what the U.S. media would term a cult. In
1992, Pope John Paul II warned the Latin American bishops' conference
about these "ravenous wolves." He has also said that evangelicals are
spreading "like an oil stain" in the region, where they "threaten to pull
down the structures of faith in numerous countries." Ironically, this may be
one of the few issues on which Catholic radicals see eye to eye with the
conservative hierarchy, since liberationists are also very suspicious of Protestant advances. From their perspective, though, the chief sin of the *evangélicos*
is that they preach political quietism and damp down the flames of revolution. As Andrew Chesnut remarks, "the Catholic Church has chosen the
poor, but the poor chose the Pentecostals," and the choice rankles.[35]

Some of the weightiest charges about religious rivalries derive from Central America, which in the early 1980s seemed to be on the verge of a general popular revolution. In countries like Guatemala and El Salvador, insurgencies were suppressed by extreme official violence, accompanied by massacre and torture, and it was in the midst of these dirty wars that Protestant and Pentecostal churches made their greatest advances. According to common allegations made at the time, military authorities were exasperated with the radical nature of the Catholic Church in the area, and explicitly decided to foster more amenable Pentecostal churches, who would preach unquestioning obedience to government. Pentecostal preachers were "better than gunships," not to mention cheaper.[36] Local governments were supposedly aided in this effort by U.S. agencies, funded by conservative evangelical groups. From this perspective, the Protestant/Pentecostal expansion of the 1980s was (at least in this region) little more than a cynical counterinsurgency tool, virtually a CIA plot to divide and rule. This opinion is summarized by Virginia Garrard-Burnett, one of the best-informed observers of the region, "To many, the proliferation of Protestantism in Latin America is proof of the complete U.S. cultural conquest of the region, a conquest bought—not won—by money, political influence and consumer goods." The recent conversion represented globalization at its worst, the forcible destruction of local communities and traditions. The linkage between Protestantism and repression was symbolized by Guatemala's born-again Protestant dictator Efraín Ríos Montt, who directed the armed forces during the most vicious anti-guerrilla actions of the early 1980s. Many of those murdered as dissident leaders were Catholic lay activists and catechists. In terms of interdenominational bloodshed, Guatemala in the 1980s looked a little like France or Germany in the 1580s.[37]

Many Westerners, somewhat simplistically, see Latin American Protestantism as no more than a conservative Trojan Horse, although of course it is far more than that. There is now a huge literature on the Pentecostal churches of the region, especially in Central America, and these studies show convincingly that *evangélicos* come in all political shades, including a minority of radicals, and even Sandinistas. Brazil in particular has a significant evangelical Left. Even when not politically radical, Pentecostals are often heavily involved in community organizing and social action, and it is misleading to see them as necessarily quietist or submissive. Chile offers an interesting example of this process. Pentecostal numbers boomed during the iron-heeled repression of the 1980s, when any secular political movement for the poor was crushed without mercy, and it would be easy to see the churches as a refuge from real-life struggles, a "haven of the masses." Yet

Chilean Pentecostals offer believers far more than pie in the sky, and work enthusiastically for social improvement. Although the armed forces might in some nations have supported Pentecostals as a way of undermining radical Catholics, that strategy rarely proved useful, since the new converts so enthusiastically adapted the faith to their own needs and interests. Far from manifesting globalization at its most stereotypical and demonic, the new Pentecostalism has flourished by channeling local interests and responding to local grievances.[38]

Whatever its origins, Protestantism has indeed emerged as a distinctive force in mass politics across Latin America, and has destabilized long-familiar social arrangements. Protestant and Pentecostal voting blocs have emerged in several nations, with the churches serving as efficient electoral machines and propaganda outlets. Often, believers are sincerely concerned to elect leaders who will effect social improvements, but also at work is the cozy principle of "brother votes for brother." In Peru, an *evangélico* bloc emerged quite suddenly in the 1990 contest that elected President Alberto Fujimori: a number of Pentecostal legislators were elected on his coattails. Some months later, Jorge Serrano of Guatemala became the first Protestant to be democratically elected president of a Latin American nation. In coming years, Protestant and Catholic parties will probably struggle for power across the continent, an additional source of conflict in what is already a very divided region.[39]

Religious conflicts would be all the more dangerous if election battles were to be accompanied by literal fights in the streets and villages, and something like this has occurred in some areas. One uniquely troubled area is the Mexican province of Chiapas, where tens of thousands of *evangélicos* and their families have been expelled by Catholic neighbors over the past thirty years, and many within the past two or three years. Pentecostals, in turn, have been among the government's most enthusiastic supporters in campaigns against local *Zapatista* rebels. Although the ongoing religious war in Chiapas is untypical in its length and brutality, this is not the only area where religious conflicts are fought out through night-riding and vigilantism.[40]

As in the time of the European Reformation, sectarian violence is often provoked by symbolic acts that seem petty to outsiders, like insults to figures of the Virgin or saints. In a Latin context, such iconoclasm is a frontal assault not just on religion but on national and racial pride. In one incendiary incident, the head of the Universal Church of the Kingdom of God (IURD) in São Paulo was seen on television kicking an image of *Nossa Senhora Aparecida*, Brazil's patron saint: this desecration led to attacks on the church's buildings and bomb threats. In Ecuador, when Pentecostals taunted pilgrims visiting the Marian shrine of El Quinche, Catholics retaliated by burning down a local Protestant chapel. Isolated actions against Protestant churches are not new, but what has changed is that increasingly, Protestants are strong enough to defend themselves, and to counterattack.[41]

Projecting the future of these partisan feuds is all but impossible, but Great Britain might provide one useful historical analogy for understanding how religious rivalries evolve over time. After hopes for political revolution collapsed during the early nineteenth century, Britain's urban and industrial masses converted to rising sects like Methodism, which is sometimes credited for saving Britain from anything like the recurrent revolutions of contemporary France. Yet by the end of the nineteenth century, these disciplined and motivated Methodist faithful were often the shock troops for effective trade unionism. This might conceivably serve as a blueprint for future Pentecostal progress in the Americas. Also, political clashes between Protestants and Catholics in modern Latin America recall the battles in nineteenth-century England between the established church and the rising Protestant sects. That conflict eventually turned into the familiar duel between constitutional parliamentary parties, the Conservatives representing the church, while the sects dominated the Liberals, and later the Labour Party. It would be wonderful if Latin American struggles could have such a bloodless and well-organized outcome, but few expect this in the near future.

UNDER WESTERN EYES

If we look at the role of religion in politics worldwide, we can already see a clear hemispheric division. The politics of religion are very much alive in the South, as they are not, generally, in the North, and the difference is likely to continue and increase in the new century. Religious issues will form political loyalties, and churches and clergy will play a key role as political leaders. Across much of the South, politics will be Christian politics. (In this matter as in so much else, the United States occupies a role somewhere between Southern fervor and European torpor.) As self-described Christian states face both internal crises and external conflicts with Christian neighbors, they might look to co-religionists to settle disputes. We may be entering the great age of Vatican diplomacy.

As we will see in the following chapter, the international politics of the coming decades are likely to revolve around interfaith conflict, above all, the clash between Christianity and Islam. These divisions will be increasingly incomprehensible to the North, which in this sense could be confined to the sidelines of history. Northerners are going to find themselves ever more out of touch with the religious dimensions that shape the new world, and literally unable to communicate with the new people of faith.

As I have already disclaimed any aspirations to prophecy, I can make no worthwhile guess about the power balances or issues of thirty or forty years hence. But the dual religious and demographic trends we have been observing are difficult to ignore. We will be looking at a world with an ever-greater imbalance between where the people are and where the wealth is. It would not take a great speculative leap to see the North–South economic divide as the key issue of the new century, and also (given the demographics) to see the conflict being defined in religious terms. Even in the past few years, the global campaign to forgive Third World debt has been led by Southern religious figures, by Cardinal Rodriguez of Honduras, by South African Anglican Primate Njongonkulu Ndungane, Desmond Tutu's successor in the see of Cape Town. These moderate clerics might look very benevolent indeed when compared with the more fiery religious leaders who could easily emerge in another decade or two. Just to take the Roman Catholic Church, the militant political conservatism of Pope John Paul II might represent a passing phase in the long history of the papacy, and we may yet live to see a revival of the radicalization of the 1970s.

At the same time, the lack of global ideological conflict that we have witnessed since the fall of Soviet communism could represent only a temporary respite, and it may not be long before revolutionary forces revive in the global South. When the U.S. intelligence community was projecting likely changes in the world political scene by 2015, religious activism occupied a prominent place, and not just the familiar bogey of radical Islam. The report suggests that "Christianity and Islam, the two largest religious groupings, will have grown significantly. Both are widely dispersed in several continents, already use information technologies to spread the faith, and draw on adherents to fund numerous nonprofit groups and political causes. Activist components of these and other religious groupings will emerge to contest such issues as genetic manipulation, women's rights, and the income gap between rich and poor." By far the most significant of these would of course be the income gap, and calls for a global redistribution of wealth.[42]

In one possible scenario of the world to come, an incredibly wealthy although numerically shrinking Northern population espouses the values of humanism, ornamented with the vestiges of liberal Christianity and Judaism.

(And although the United States remains a far more religious nation than Europe, North American elites are quite as secular as their European counterparts.) Meanwhile, this future North confronts the poorer and vastly more numerous global masses who wave the flags not of red revolution, but of ascendant Christianity and Islam. Although this sounds not unlike the racial nightmares of the Cold War years, one crucial difference is that the have-nots will be inspired by the scriptures and the language of apocalyptic, rather than by the texts of Marx and Mao. In this world, we, the West, will be the final Babylon.

This vision may simply be too far-reaching, but a secularized North could well be forced to deal with religious conflicts that it genuinely does not understand. One augur of this cultural divide is the dismal record of the United States and its allies in dealing with the new Islamic fundamentalism of the late twentieth century. We recall the policy disasters that resulted in Iran, Lebanon, and elsewhere from a basic failure to take seriously the concept of religious motivation. By common consent, Western policy makers have never excelled at understanding Islam, but perhaps the great political unknown of the new century, the most powerful international wild card, will be that mysterious non-Western ideology called Christianity.

As Northern media come to recognize the growing importance of Southern states, and seek to explain their values, it is all too likely that Southern Christianity will be interpreted through the same kind of racial and cultural stereotypes that have so often been applied to fundamentalist or enthusiastic religion. Two related processes will interact here, namely a familiar kind of Orientalism and a racially based concept of Third World primitivism. As Southern Christianity becomes ever stranger to Northern eyes, it will acquire the same kind of bleak stereotypes that were in bygone years applied to Muslims. In the 1980s, these labels particularly adhered to Shi'ites, whom Western media transformed into legendary monsters. The Christian faith of the rising states, we will probably hear, is fanatical, superstitious, demagogic: it is politically reactionary and sexually repressive.

Even today, on the rare occasions that the media report a religion-related story from the Third World, it is generally associated with images of death and fanaticism, such as the Ugandan mass suicides of 2000.[43] In this episode, the media uncritically accepted the bizarre and ill-substantiated theory of mass suicide, because it so exactly fit stereotypes of primitive Africa. As Christianity becomes ever more distinctively associated with Africa and the African diaspora, the religion as a whole may come to be dismissed as only what we might expect from the Heart of Darkness. (Although this term was originally applied to Central Africa, the experiences of the twentieth century suggest that the label more justly belongs to Europe, to regions somewhere between Berlin and Moscow.)

Modern Western media generally do an awful job of reporting on religious realities, even within their own societies. Despite its immense popularity in North America, evangelical and fundamentalist religion often tends to be dismissed as merely a kind of reactionary ignorance. Not long ago, the media mounted a furious campaign to prevent John Ashcroft being appointed the U.S. attorney general. Reasonable people can hold different views about the issues raised against Ashcroft, but it was striking how many critics illustrated his unsuitability by citing his supernatural beliefs, and specifically his Pentecostalism. Exhibit A against him was his membership in the Assemblies of God Church, which is already such a mass presence in Latin America and Africa.

It would be singularly dangerous if such uncomprehending attitudes were applied on a global scale and then aggravated by racial stereotyping. As Christianity comes to be seen as, in effect, jungle religion, the faith of one-third of the human race would increasingly be seen as alien and dangerous, even a pressing social problem. The North, in turn, would define itself against this unfortunate presence: the North would be secular, rational, and tolerant, the South primitive and fundamentalist. The North would define itself against Christianity.

The Next Crusade

Narrated Abu Huraira: Allah's Apostle said
"How will you be when the son of Mary
descends amongst you, and he will judge
people by the Law of the *Quran* and not by
the law of Gospel?"
—The Hadith of the Prophet Muhammad

At the turn of the third millennium, religious loyalties are at the root of many of the world's ongoing civil wars and political violence, and in most cases, the critical division is the age-old battle between Christianity and Islam. However much this would have surprised political analysts a generation or two ago, the critical political frontiers around the world are not decided by attitudes toward class or dialectical materialism, but by rival concepts of God.[1] Across the regions that will be the most populous in the new century, vast religious conflicts and contests are already in progress, although these impinge little on Western opinion makers. Over the past twenty years, bloodshed in the Sudan or Indonesia has received nothing like the coverage accorded to conditions in Tibet or Myanmar/ Burma; nor have the persecutions of Christians attracted any great attention on college campuses. Since the late 1990s, the U.S. government has been paying closer attention to religious freedom issues around the world, but persecutions still register little in the mass media.[2]

The parochialism of Western public opinion is striking. When a single racial or religious-motivated murder takes place in Europe or North America, the event occasions widespread soul-searching, but when thousands are massacred on the grounds of their faith in Nigeria, Indonesia, or the Sudan, the story rarely registers. Some lives are worth more than others. In addition, a kind of religious prejudice helps to explain the silence about nations like the Sudan. Liberal Westerners are reluctant to appear anti-Muslim or anti-Arab, and doubly dubious about taking up the course of Third World Christians.

Demographic projections suggest that religious feuds will not only continue but will also become worse. The future centers of global population are chiefly in countries that are already divided between the two great religions, and where divisions are likely to intensify. Often, conflicts become peculiarly intense when one religious tradition seeks to declare that nation X is or should be a Muslim (or Christian) society, enforcing the appropriate legal and cultural values, with all the problems that implies for the minority faith. In present-day battles in Africa and Asia, we may today be seeing the political outlines of the new century, and probably, the roots of future great power alliances.

UNDERSTANDING NUMBERS

In trying to understand the religious balance of the new century, we have to decide just what can and cannot be known with any accuracy. Projecting religious futures is difficult, whether we are dealing with Christians or non-Christian communities. Just as Western societies with established or official churches tend to claim every citizen as a church member, so states in which Islam is the official state religion often exaggerate Muslim loyalties in their society.

Other factors can come into play in such a process of official definition. Let us, for instance, take the nation of Indonesia, purportedly the world's most populous Muslim country. While most people would agree that Islam is very strong in Indonesia, it was primarily political factors that explained the enormous growth of self-described Muslims in that nation from the mid-1960s on. At a time of homicidal official anti-communism, failure to acknowledge any religion on official identity papers immediately raised suspicions about a person's possible seditious attitudes, and as a result, millions were now inspired to declare themselves Muslim. Memories of this era may explain why Indonesia appears to have such a vast Muslim population, 85 percent of the whole, or some 180 million strong. Similar patterns apply with other religions also. In India, religious loyalties are defined by a "none of the above" test. Under Indian law, all citizens are formally presumed to be Hindus unless they are specifically identified as either Christian, Muslim, Parsi, or Jew. According to some interpretations, this definition explicitly includes as Hindu all Sikhs, Buddhists, and Jains, who are otherwise regarded as members of separate religions.[3]

Also, not all countries are as impartial as the United States or Europe in undertaking a census. Whenever we read religious estimates for a particular African or Asian nation, we should recall that minority citizens of that society are often scornful of any official figures, and ask, suspiciously, what else would one expect a Muslim (or Christian) regime to say. Rightly or wrongly, the expectation is that governments massage figures to make their own side look more powerful, especially in regions with deep political and cultural divisions. The widespread assumption is that Muslim governments like Chad and Sudan vastly undercount the number of Christians, just as Christian-dominated states like Kenya or the Philippines simply make false statements about Muslim strength in those societies. Egyptian governments have long been accused of understating the numbers of Coptic Christians, partly to ensure the country's international status as a leader in the Muslim world. In a classic piece of statistical chicanery, the Indian national census only acknowledges that untouchables (Dalits) might belong to the Hindu, Sikh, or Buddhist faiths. In practice, this means ignoring the religious beliefs of some 14 million Dalit Christians, and tens of millions of Muslims.[4] Sometimes, too, mistakes can be made honestly, when minorities are concentrated in inaccessible or out of the way regions that represent difficult territory for census takers. However impressive the official statistics look, they can only be as accurate as the bureaucracies involved wish to make them.

With all these caveats, Muslims stand to benefit from exactly the same global demographic trends that are producing the unimaginably rich harvest for Christians. In Africa, the twentieth century witnessed an upsurge of Islam similar to that of Christianity, and both religions should continue to grow apace.[5] If we look at the countries that presently have the highest birth rates in the world, they are neatly divided between mainly Christian states, like Uganda and Bolivia, and mainly Muslim nations, like Yemen and Afghanistan. Muslims will thrive from the explosive growth of nations like Bangla Desh, Indonesia, Pakistan, and Iran, and from the population boom across North Africa and the Near East. There are 240 million Arabs today, and this people will be over half a billion strong by 2050. Islam is now booming across Central Asia, in young and growing countries that have classic Third World demographic profiles: Uzbekistan has 25 million people today, but this figure should double by 2050. Finally, the faith of Muhammad faces uncertain but intriguing prospects in China. Just as Chinese Christians are believed to be very numerous, so Muslims may run into the tens of millions across that vast country.

Growth in the Middle East and Central Asia is all the more significant politically because of the continuing connection between Islam and oil wealth. The key factor is not so much where oil resources are located today, but rather where they will continue to be found in fifty or a hundred years, the areas with the richest reserves and the deepest pockets. By this standard, Islam will have an enduring material foundation for its power, since the areas of key population growth are also those that will still be producing at a time when other historic oil-nations will be exhausting their reserves. This trend bodes very well for the nations of the Arabian peninsula as well as for nearby countries like Iraq and Iran. Possibly, too, this is bad news for global Christianity. When Muslims and Christians fight in a Third World nation, the United States and Europe might well find that helping the Muslim cause promotes good relations with Middle Eastern oil producers, and that helps keep the oil flowing to Western ports. Intervening on behalf of Christians, though, offers no advantage beyond the sentimental, and even that element will shrink as the West distances itself ever more from Christianity.[6]

DIVIDED GIANTS

An earlier chapter projected the twenty-five most populous countries by the mid-twenty-first century. If we look again at the same countries in terms of their religious loyalties, then we see some striking, and perhaps alarming, facts (see table 8.1). Of the world's twenty-five largest nations by the mid-twenty-first century, twenty will be predominantly or entirely either Christian or Muslim. If we imagine that the current religious balance will still continue at that point, then there should be a remarkably even balance between Muslim and Christian forces. Nine will be wholly or mainly Muslim, eight wholly or mainly Christian, and three deeply divided between the two faiths.

In terms of the potential for conflict, we note the number of countries with divided populations, and thus a narrow gap between the two faiths in terms of numbers and power. Relatively homogeneous states are not likely to produce religious conflict. While there might be controversy about the practice of minority faiths in Muslim states like Saudi Arabia, dissidents are just not going to pose a threat to the state. Christians will never threaten Saudi society, any more than Muslims will become a significant force in Mexico. The potential flash points are those states with minorities representing 10 or 20 percent of the population, amply sufficient to resist efforts at religious harmonization, and quite enough to sustain military struggles

TABLE 8.1
**The Religious Balance of Power among the Largest Nations
of the Twenty-first Century**

---

1. *Overwhelmingly Muslim*
   Pakistan   Bangladesh   Saudi Arabia   Turkey   Iran   Yemen

2. *Mainly Muslim with significant Christian minorities*
   Indonesia   Egypt   Sudan

3. *Overwhelmingly Christian*
   United States   Brazil   Mexico   Russia

4. *Mainly Christian with significant Muslim minorities*
   Philippines   Zaire/Democratic Republic of Congo   Germany   Uganda

5. *Christian and Muslim, with neither a strong majority*
   Nigeria   Ethiopia   Tanzania

6. *Other nations, dominated by neither Christianity nor Islam*
   India   China   Vietnam   Thailand   Japan

---

against an unpopular government. Of the divided states listed in table 8.1, several have already experienced prolonged religious violence, with heavy loss of life. No less than ten of the world's twenty-five largest states in 2050 could be profoundly divided between Islam and Christianity, and judging by present trends, any or all of them could be the scene of serious interfaith conflict.

Two factors threaten to create religious instability, and perhaps violence. One is that population growth does not observe national or religious boundaries. Matters would be less complicated in a fictitious world where countries were entirely made up of a given ethnic or religious group, so that it would matter little whether the country's population grew or shrank. In the real world, though, there are precious few such countries, since most nations have minorities of varying sizes, and population change aggravates existing tensions. Since poorer or immigrant groups have higher birth rates than the better-off, their religious and cultural traditions become more influential over time, a trend that in the worst case could lead to instability. An example of this process in miniature occurred in Lebanon, where a Shi'ite Muslim minority made up the traditional underclass. Over time, their very high rate of population growth made Shi'ites a very potent force indeed, and much of that nation's fifteen-year (1975–90) civil war revolved around the issue of accommodating the poor masses. A number of European nations face huge disparities between very fertile immigrant groups and relatively static old-stock populations, and religious instability could easily result.

Also threatening to incite conflict is the issue of conversions. All the projections quoted here are based on the idea that Islam and Christianity will maintain roughly their present share of population in the respective countries, but that is a bold assumption. Both are successful missionary religions, and neither makes a secret of its aspiration to convert the entire globe. Both, too, have been advancing in very much the same parts of the world. Competition for converts is already acute in those regions of Africa that are currently blessed (or cursed) with the world's fastest rates of population growth. Rivalry is troublesome enough when both sides are competing for converts among followers of traditional indigenous religions, but in some situations, Christians are seeking to convert Muslims, and vice versa. Buoyed by successes across the globe, Western evangelicals are talking seriously about spreading their faith within the "10–40 window," the heartlands of Islam. To appreciate the sensitivity of such a movement, we have to remember that for a Muslim to abandon his or her faith is apostasy, an act punishable by death under Islamic law. As the maxim holds, "Islam is a one way door. You can enter through it, but you cannot leave."

CROSS AND CRESCENT

The fundamental question here is whether Islam and Christianity can coexist. The question may seem idle, since for centuries, the two faiths have existed side by side, often for long periods. Islam is after all the only one of the major religions that enshrines in its scriptures a demand to tolerate other religions, other "peoples of the book." Muslims and Christians have so very much in common. Scarcely known to most Christians, the Muslim scriptures are almost entirely focused on the same characters who feature in the Christian Bible. The Quran has much more to say about the Virgin Mary than does the New Testament, and Jesus is, apart from Muhammad, the greatest prophet of Islam. It is Jesus, not Muhammad, whose appearance will usher in the Day of Judgment. Moreover, Jesus was the primary inspiration for Islamic mysticism, the beloved model and mentor of the Sufis. When in the 1980s, the controversial film *The Last Temptation of Christ* was felt to portray Jesus in an unflattering light, Western Christians organized public protests, but it was only Muslim states that actually banned the work.[7]

In practice, both Christians and Muslims have often enjoyed good relations. For most of the Middle Ages, Muslim states were usually superior in terms of tolerance, although not all societies were as decent and civilized as the kingdoms of Moorish Spain. Jews and Christians survived in Muslim states, at a time when Muslims or Jews were massacred or expelled by their Christian neighbors. Even today, with all the well-publicized horrors of inter-religious violence in the Middle East, there are powerful demonstrations of harmony. Most Muslim states tolerate Christian worship, even Gulf nations like Oman and the United Arab Emirates, provided there are no attempts to convert Muslims. Ironically, in view of other religious divisions, modern Palestine has been a model of Muslim-Christian coexistence. When the pope visited Egypt and Syria in 2000 and 2001, he was greeted enthusiastically by crowds of ordinary Muslims, as well as by senior Muslim clerics. Strangely, even the worst recent instances of violence can produce expressions of good feeling between the religions. During the Algerian civil war of the 1990s, Muslim ultras targeted for assassination the few remnants of the one-mighty Catholic Church in the nation, and over twenty priests and religious perished. One victim, in 1996, was the bishop of Oran, whose funeral turned into a moving commemoration of a beloved man that the many Muslim mourners called "the Bishop of the Muslims." In most of Africa, too, Muslim-Christian relations at local level have often (at least until recently) been characterized by a live-and-let-live attitude. Partly, this reflects the strong affinity between the daily practice of the two great African religions, both of which have drawn enthusiastically on older animist traditions.[8]

Having said all this, the long-term prognosis for interfaith relations is not good. This does not mean that either religion is of itself violent or intolerant, but both have potent traditions of seeking to implement their views through political action: the two sisters are simply too much alike to live side by side. Both Christian and Muslim states can exist for decades or centuries without seeking to persecute minorities. All too often, though, persecution erupts, perhaps in response to some natural cataclysm, or to the rise of a particularly zealous regime. The minority community is reduced or scattered, and even after the hard times end, matters can never be quite the same again. Peace then resumes until the next cycle of intolerance begins, but the ratchet turns yet another notch, and life becomes correspondingly more difficult for the survivors of the shrinking minority. It is almost exactly the same story as that of the Jews in medieval or early modern Europe.[9]

Even if the dominant religion is generally tolerant, it only takes an outbreak of fanaticism every half-century or so to devastate or uproot a minority, and that has been the fate of religious minorities across the Middle East in recent years. Although Christian communities survive across the region, their numbers are a pathetic shadow of what they were even in 1850, and whole peoples have been obliterated since that time. The Armenian genocide of 1915 is well known, but quite as devastating were the massacres of tens of thousands of Lebanese and Syrian Christians in 1860, by both Muslims and Druzes.[10] In 1915, the Turks slaughtered or expelled hundreds of thousands of Christians of all sects, not just Armenians. A famine deliberately induced by the Turkish military claimed the lives of 100,000 Lebanese Maronite Christians. Across the Middle East, it was above all the bloodshed of 1915 that destroyed ancient Christian cultures that had lasted successfully since Roman times, groups like the Jacobites, Nestorians, and Chaldaeans. And the carnage continued after the war ended. Between 1919 and 1925, Greek Christians were expelled en masse from the new Kemalist state of Turkey. As late as 1955, Istanbul's Christians suffered "the worst race riot in Europe since *Kristallnacht*." In 1923, Istanbul's Greek Christian population was around 400,000; today, it may be only 4,000.[11]

These experiences remind us of the sad historical lesson that persecution can indeed be very effective, if carried out with enough ruthlessness. Perhaps one cannot kill an idea, but it is not that difficult to massacre or convert everyone who holds or expresses it. Once, the Nestorian church was one of the largest and most widespread institutions in the world: by 1500, it had almost ceased to exist. Once, Turkey had large Christian minorities, but these were squeezed out of existence in a decade or two. These events provide a bleak precedent for modern minority populations.

Undeniably, modern Christians have committed their share of atrocities. The Serbian massacre of Bosnian Muslims at Srebenica in 1995 remains the largest single crime of its kind in post-1945 Europe. In recent years, though, the pattern of religious conflict has shifted decisively. In the world as a whole, there is no question that the threat of intolerance and persecution chiefly comes from the Islamic side of the equation. Around the world, Islamic states are passing through one of these historic phases of zeal and persecution of the sort just mentioned.

We can discuss at length why this extremism should be occurring. Over the past twenty years, the Muslim world has been caught up in a massive religious revival, and this movement has expressed itself in calls for pure religious states upheld by the full apparatus of Islamic law.[12] Perhaps this idea appeals to people afraid of losing their cultural identity in the face of globalization, or else it might seem to offer a solution for the desperately poor in a world dominated by the wealthy and callous West. If these explanations are correct, then social trends are likely to lead to much greater support for Islamic extremism. According to the U.S. intelligence community, by as early as 2015, "In much of the Middle East, populations will be significantly larger, poorer, more urban, and more disillusioned," and matters could grow still worse by 2050 or so.[13] Looking at matters in social and economic terms does not mean that we should not take the demand for Islamic rule at face value, and accept that people genuinely believe that their faith really does require such a political expression. But whatever the reasons, inter-religious violence in recent years tends to be initiated by Muslims against Christians, and that trend is unlikely to change.

BATTLE FRONTS

To illustrate the dynamics of violence, we can consider some of the main fronts of religious conflict today, all of which occur in countries that will soon be among the world's largest. Perhaps the most brutal conflict has occurred in the Sudan, where religious and racial boundaries coincide. The country is dominated by a northern Muslim population, which speaks Arabic, while the south is Black African, Christian, and animist. According to official statistics, the Sudan has around 25 million Muslims, 2 million Christians, and 8 million animists (by 2050, though, the overall population could be as high as 84 million). Despite this ethnic and cultural balance, the Sudanese government has introduced Islam as the official religion for the whole country, declared Arabic the national language, and established Friday rather than Sunday as the day of rest. Southerners naturally resisted Muslim control. One bloody rebellion raged from 1963 through 1972, and the conflict reerupted in the 1980s, when the government officially applied Muslim religious law, the *Shari'a,* to the whole country.

This has been one of Africa's bloodiest wars, costing a million and a half lives to date. The U.S. State Department has described systematic atrocities against the non-Muslim population, including "indiscriminate bombings, the burning and looting of villages, and the killings, abductions, rapes, and arbitrary arrests and detentions of civilians."[14] Many regions of the Third World have experienced brutal wars of this kind, but what distinguishes the conflict in Sudan is its explicitly religious nature, as Muslim governments have increasingly accepted fundamentalist notions of the religious role of the state. Sudan is also one of the very few countries that still avowedly practices slavery, the other being the Muslim African nation of Mauritania. In both cases, the normal pattern involves lighter-skinned Arabic slave-owners and Black slaves. Often, too, Sudanese slaves are Christian.

We can debate how far the Sudanese experience reflects the inevitable nature of Islamic rule and the Muslim treatment of minorities. Of course, we might argue, backward nations like Sudan and Afghanistan are far more intolerant than wealthy and advanced societies like France or Sweden, but that is a consequence of poverty and backwardness, not of religious traditions. We should not compare apples with oranges. Yet having said this, equally poor Christian-dominated states have not acted anything like as severely toward their religious minorities. At the same time, we find severe intolerance and persecution in much wealthier and more advanced Muslim states, which officially tolerate the existence of minorities but rigidly control the exercise of those faiths. In the very rich state of Saudi Arabia, Christian worship is officially prohibited, although unofficially tolerated.

What is most disturbing about the Sudanese experience is that it shows how, in the new religious climate, existing non-Muslim minorities can be reduced or even eliminated. The same bitter lesson may be in progress in Sudan's far more important neighbor, Egypt, the home of the ancient community of Coptic Christians. The position of the Copts has deteriorated steadily in recent decades, although conditions are nothing like as bad as in the Sudan. During the 1990s, well-armed Islamic guerrillas began attacks on Coptic villages, killing perhaps a hundred victims in all. The violence horrified traditionally minded Muslim neighbors, who denounced the attacks and sought to help Christian victims. But such outbursts of charitable feelings have not prevented communal riots in villages of mixed faiths. In one egregious case in 2000, a row between a merchant and a customer in the village of al-Kosheh led to what in other circumstances would have been called a pogrom, in which twenty Copts died and hundreds of homes were burned. The violence was bad enough in itself, but just as disturbing is the consistently biased attitude of Egyptian authorities. Repeatedly, Copts have been convicted of trumped-up criminal charges, or have suffered severe prison sentences for uttering words supposedly critical of Islam. When Copts suffer acts of mob violence, police regularly ignore the perpetrators, while using the investigation as an excuse to inflict further persecutions on the Christian victims themselves. In the al-Kosheh affair, a judge acquitted Muslim rioters of all charges, and used the opportunity to denounce Coptic clergy for inciting violence. Such episodes raise the long-term question of whether Christians can survive under Islam, even as despised minorities.[15]

NIGERIAN COLLISIONS

The twin experiences of Sudan and Egypt explain why African Christians, so uncomfortably close to the scene of action, should be nervous about any extension of Islamic law and political culture. If Muslims insist that their faith demands the establishment of Islamic states, regardless of the existence of religious minorities, then violence is assuredly going to occur.[16]

This issue becomes acute in the very important nation of Nigeria, which is today about equally divided between Christians and Muslims. Estimates of the exact balance vary: some give Islam a 50–40 predominance, others suggest that each faith claims about 45 percent of Nigerians, with the remaining 10 percent following traditional religions. Complicating this picture is that the religious groups are not equally distributed: the north of the country is chiefly Muslim, the east largely Christian, so each group can aspire to impose its standards in the respective areas. This distribution also means that, as in Sudan, religious allegiances coincide with ethnic, tribal, and geographical loyalties. Of the three major ethnic groupings, the northern Hausa are solidly Muslim, the eastern Igbo are Christian, and the Yoruba are equally divided between the two faiths.[17]

Muslim–Christian rivalries have often led to violence. In 1966, tens of thousands of Christian Igbos were massacred in the north, forcing survivors to flee to safe areas. These events strengthened Muslim hegemony in the north, and reduced the remaining Christians to a clear minority status. Between 1967 and 1970, the Christian east tried unsuccessfully to secede from Nigeria, leading to a bloody civil war that claimed perhaps a million lives. Although religion played an important part in detonating the war, the conflict was not a pure Muslim–Christian affair. Christians made up perhaps half of the federal Nigerian army, and the federal leader was a distinguished lay Christian. But the destruction visited upon the secessionist east, in so-called Biafra, was a catastrophe for the country's Christian population.

The plight of Nigeria's Christian minorities under Muslim rule has always been difficult, and is deteriorating. Local authorities in Muslim-dominated areas hinder the building or repair of churches, while actively sponsoring Islamic causes, paying for pilgrimages and mosque-building. In the 1990s Muslims began imposing *Shari'a* religious law over entire states. By 2001, nine of Nigeria's thirty-six states had imposed *Shari'a* in whole or in part, and others were discussing the idea: *Shari'a* prevailed in all the states along the nation's northern border. The spread of *Shari'a* owed something to growing religious zeal, but can also be seen as a symbolic statement of Muslim identity and tribal pride in a nation then governed by a Yoruba Christian president.[18]

Nigerian Christians understandably fear the prospect of living under *Shari'a*. This reform has many practical consequences for minorities, from the irritating (such as the elimination of alcohol) to the severely oppressive. In extreme cases, non-Muslims might be subjected to the whole battery of

Islamic civil, criminal, and family law, so that Christians could suffer any of the physical punishments, floggings, and mutilations ordained by that tradition. Under *Shari'a* law, the religious activities of non-Muslims are severely constrained. Any kind of Christian evangelism is strictly prohibited, while apostasy from Islam leads to the death penalty.

The effects on gender relations are far-reaching, since women can face restrictions on their ability to move and work freely. In the Muslim stronghold of Kano, a police purge in 2000 resulted in the arrest of several hundred people who had been seen talking to members of the opposite sex in public, leading to investigations for adultery or prostitution. In one international cause célèbre in the northern state of Zamfara, a seventeen-year-old girl who became pregnant before marriage was sentenced to 180 strokes of the cane, although it was conceded that half that number would probably kill her. In 2001, an interfaith crisis developed when a man in the Muslim-ruled province of Kano converted to Islam, and insisted that his daughters accept arranged marriages with Muslim husbands. The daughters, who were both Christians, sought refuge with local Anglican clergy and lay families. The police then intervened, arresting the Christian helpers for kidnapping the girls, and further provoking a worsening political crisis. In the words of the local Anglican bishop, "Life here is increasingly like living under a *jihad*."[19]

In the late 1990s, Nigeria experienced a new wave of communal riots and massacres that recalled the bloodbath of the 1960s, and tension escalated further when *Shari'a* was imposed. In a few weeks in early 2000, some 2,000 people were killed in inter-communal rioting in the Muslim-dominated state of Kaduna; in retaliation, several hundred Muslims were killed in eastern Christian towns. In a sequence of events reminiscent of the horrible 1960s, the remaining Muslims began an exodus from Christian states to return to their home regions, while Christians fled the north. Nigerian religious conflicts spread over the borders into neighboring countries like Niger, which over the past few years have for the first time ever experienced religious-based rioting.[20]

The importance of these events can hardly be exaggerated. Nigeria might have 300 million people by 2050, perhaps a half-billion by the end of the century, and it is a huge oil-producer. Provided the state holds together, and that is an open question, a country of this size and wealth will assuredly be a major regional state, and possibly a global power. Depending on the course of religious conflicts, Nigeria could become a Muslim super-state, or it could fragment into two or three smaller entities, neatly defined by both religious and tribal identity. When in 2000 the U.S. intelligence community sketched the major security threats over the next fifteen years, the explosion of religious and ethnic tensions in Nigeria was prominently listed. Depending on international alignments, the religious fate of Nigeria could be a political fact of immense importance in the new century.[21]

ASIAN THEATERS

In Asia too, religious divisions and persecutions bode ill for the politics of the new century. The progressive hardening of attitudes in recent years is evident from Pakistan, which despite its overwhelmingly Muslim character has a small Christian minority. Christians comprise around 2 percent of Pakistanis, some 3 million people, usually drawn from the humblest classes. While officially tolerated, Christians and other minorities regularly fall prey to legal penalties under provisions theoretically directed against blasphemy and apostasy. Under a 1986 law, anyone who "directly or indirectly by word, gesture, innuendo, or otherwise defiles the name of the holy prophet Muhammad will be punished with death or life imprisonment." These laws offer a potential death sentence for anyone evangelizing Muslims, or even considering conversion, and several Christians have been condemned to death for related offenses. Ordinary Christians are subjected to mob violence, murder, and rape.[22]

Nobody doubts that Pakistan will continue to be a solidly Islamic country, but in other states, religious identity is bitterly contested. Another of the most populous states of the coming century is Indonesia, and as in Nigeria, religious conflicts are aggravated by ethnic divisions. Also as in Nigeria, struggles under way today may be defining the nation's religious politics in the coming century. Although overwhelmingly Muslim, Indonesia has substantial minorities, most significant among which is a Christian community of 21 million: Christians make up 10 percent of the whole. Christians are concentrated in particular regions and ethnic groups. In the cities, Christianity has made inroads among the ethnic Chinese communities who play such a key role in the nation's commercial life. In addition, Christian regions are scattered across the eastern half of the island nation, in areas that, like the Philippines, traditionally looked to Spanish and Portuguese power, or which claimed a strong Dutch heritage. Major Christian centers include Timor, the islands of Sulawesi and Lombok, and Maluku (the Moluccas or Spice Islands).[23]

Since the 1990s, violence between Christians and Muslims has raged through all the eastern regions. Particularly savage was the repression against the Catholic territory of East Timor, which Indonesia invaded and occupied in 1975. This was by no means an exclusively inter-religious struggle, but when the region voted on its independence in 1999, government militias targeted Catholic clergy and faithful for massacre. Recently, the worst violence has occurred in Maluku, where the fighting became so serious in 1999 and 2000 that the government lost control of the area while a civil war raged. Five thousand were killed, the number equally divided between the two communities.[24]

More commonly, though, it is Christians who have been massacred and expelled, as militant political Islam has spread through the region. In one typical incident in 2000, on the island of Halmahera, 200 Christians were massacred in an hour-long killing spree by Muslim paramilitaries of the so-called Laskar Jihad. Two hundred more Christians were wiped out later that year on the island of Saparua. By late 2000, half a million Maluku Christians had been expelled, mainly by Jihad fighters, with the unofficial support of Indonesian armed forces. Thousands of Christians were forced to convert to Islam in public ceremonies, some of which included circumcision for both men and women. Hundreds of Christians were killed for refusing to convert. Large numbers of churches were also destroyed, in a successful act of ethnic/religious cleansing that was largely ignored by Western governments and media. These events raised fears that Christianity would be extirpated across much of eastern Indonesia over the next decade or two. Increasingly, too, religious warfare became national rather than merely regional. Isolated terrorist acts culminated on Christmas Eve of 2000, when bombs exploded during church services in nine cities, killing fifteen worshipers.[25]

Anti-Christian violence has many sources. Partly, the motives are explicitly religious. A new fundamentalist Islam has recently found expression in organized political groups, including vigilantes who destroy bars and supposedly immoral establishments. Hatred also has a nationalist component, since Christianity is strong in areas like Irian Jaya that have powerful secessionist movements. To kill a Christian is to destroy a potential traitor and to reassert national unity. But religious bigotry has a strong economic component. In Indonesia, urban Christianity is associated with the Chinese mercantile community, which has been sporadically attacked since the Indonesian economy went into a tailspin in 1997. This hostility was partly stirred up by the Suharto dictatorship, which was seeking scapegoats for its failed policies. In just a few days in May 1998, some 2,000 Indonesian Chinese perished in mob violence, and hundreds of Chinese women were gang-raped. As in other Asian lands like Malaysia, the more Christianity wins support among ethnic Chinese, the easier it is for agitators to portray the religion as a symbol of the foreign exploiters who keep the nation in poverty. Combining these elements, anti-Christianity looks as varied and as potent an ideology as the populist anti-Semitism that swept Europe in the late nineteenth century, and which would have such parlous consequences in the twentieth. As in Nigeria, the question for Indonesia is whether this vast emerging regional power is to continue as a multiethnic, multireligious nation, or if it is to become a purely Muslim state.[26]

Like Indonesia, the Philippines will soon be one of the Pacific Rim's most populous states, and here too, recent events raise doubts about the possibility of coexistence. Although the Philippines is traditionally a highly Catholic society, a strong Muslim presence exists in the southern island of Mindanao, which culturally looks to its neighbors in Indonesia. Since the 1970s, the Muslim Moro ("Moor") peoples of the southern Philippines have been engaged in a prolonged struggle for autonomy, which culminated in 1996 when the government reached a limited settlement with the largest guerrilla group. Other paramilitary forces, however, kept the struggle alive. In 2000, the long-running revolt suddenly revived, and several hundred soldiers and civilians were killed. This campaign brought to the fore the terrorist Abu Sayyaf group, which seeks a pure Muslim state in Mindanao. The guerrilla movement has engaged in explicitly anti-Christian actions, including the murder of a Catholic bishop outside his cathedral in 1997. In 2001, the group attracted worldwide notoriety for its kidnappings of Christian Filipinos and American missionaries.[27]

CYCLES OF VIOLENCE

The most disturbing feature of contemporary Christian–Muslim conflicts is how very commonplace they have become, how unremarkable. Although the bloodshed in countries like Nigeria and Indonesia receives some coverage in the West, violence of this sort has become almost too widespread to report, even in places like Egypt, which traditionally operated on the principle of live-and-let-live. Just in the past two or three years, Muslim–Christian violence has occurred in places that have long been held up as models of friendship and toleration, including among the Palestinian Arabs and in traditionally peaceful Malaysia. To quote one analyst, "Islam is becoming the defining force in politics in Malaysia and in Indonesia. . . . The pluralistic days are over in Southeast Asia."[28] In bygone years, one of the areas most frequently cited as a model of tolerance was the Indonesian territory of Maluku, where elaborate social customs were designed to encourage respect between the faiths. It was long customary to visit members of the other religion during their respective holiday seasons: Muslims would visit Christian neighbors over Christmas, the visits being repaid over Ramadan. After all the slaughter of the past few years, such relationships lie in ruins.

Similar breakdowns have occurred across Africa, often in places where five or ten years ago no observer would have foreseen religious conflicts. In 2000, mob violence between Muslims and Christians broke out in the Kenyan capital of Nairobi. Even in the Ivory Coast (*Côte d'Ivoire*), which has always been regarded as a sophisticated and tolerant society, religious conflicts have emerged, seemingly from nowhere. The Ivory Coast is a very mixed society, roughly 40 percent Muslim and 33 percent Christian, with the remainder belonging either to traditional African religions, or (a large share) to no religion at all. This last category in itself suggests the country's nonchalance about religious activism: people have no qualms about describing themselves as atheists and secularists. Nevertheless, a coup in 1999 led to political instability, and within just a year, Muslims and Christians were killing each other in the streets. Also for the first time, the two sides were calling for a partition on religious lines, cutting the Muslim north from the Christian south. The conflict has international repercussions, since this Christian-ruled nation finds itself in a tense relationship with its mainly Muslim neighbors, Mali and Burkina Faso. If indeed the Ivory Coast is to become yet another victim of the spreading curse of religious warfare, this is a fact of some importance because this is yet another African country that is growing quickly. Its present population of 16 million should reach 36 million by 2050. If even the Ivory Coast could suffer like this, is any African nation immune?[29]

Another example of such unexpected violence occurred in Europe itself. The savagery that erupted in the former Yugoslavia in the 1990s occurred among communities hitherto famous for their relaxed attitude toward religion. Interfaith marriages and friendships were common among Catholics, Orthodox Christians, and Muslims. When the violence began, though, religious identities reasserted themselves forcefully. The respective groups began to fight and kill on behalf of their faiths, destroying the religious symbols of their enemies in addition to eliminating populations. As a worrying omen of the future direction of other such struggles, international groups took such religious claims very seriously, so that the wars in Bosnia and Kosovo genuinely did turn into international crusades and jihads. They were in religious terms what the Spanish civil war became for Left and Right in the 1930s.[30]

Once it has started, communal violence tends to become self-sustaining. Where communities have historically existed side by side, potential insults and provocations are usually treated with restraint, but once fighting has occurred, the threshold for violence is lowered. The Nairobi riots of 2000 were provoked when youths tore down some shacks that had been erected disrespectfully close to a mosque. When riots displace minority communities, these refugees in turn become detonators for further violence, since they advocate harder-line policies in future conflicts.[31]

Once peoples are primed to believe in the rightness of religious warfare, it becomes easier for outside groups to manipulate public sentiment for their own ends. While we are rightly suspicious of conspiracy theories that imagine sinister clandestine agents trying to stir communal violence, some conspiracies are genuine, and some intelligence agencies do carry out seemingly random attacks as part of a "strategy of tension." Actions of this kind are well documented in the South Africa of the 1980s. More recently, such disruptive strategies have generally been aimed at inciting religious violence, with the goal of discrediting democratic regimes. A common interpretation of the recent upsurge of violence across Indonesia is that it was ignited by agents of that nation's former dictatorship, in order to discredit its democratic successor. At the time of the worst violence in 2000–2001, the nation's elected president was Abdurrahman Wahid, an Islamic scholar who condemned acts of intolerance and forced conversion, and who explicitly blamed the old intelligence agencies for the atrocities. Whatever the truth, it is depressing that the provocateurs found such dry tinder for their efforts, and that once the cycle of violence had begun, it continued with little further encouragement.[32]

EUROPE

Just how inevitable Muslim-Christian conflict is becoming is now, for the first time, a serious question in much of Europe, and not only in the Balkans. Religious rivalries have for some time played at least a marginal role in social conflicts in several Western European nations. In France Muslim North Africans make up a large proportion of the underclass youth who have so often clashed with police in urban rioting since the 1980s. Anti-immigrant protests also have a religious tone. In the 1980s, graffiti in Berlin warned "Yesterday the Jews—tomorrow the Turks" and commemorated "Vienna 1683," the date of the decisive defeat of Turkish Muslim power in Central Europe.

Such sporadic violence acquired a whole new dimension in 1989, when the Iranian regime issued its death sentence, a *fatwa,* against British writer Salman Rushdie. To the astonishment of White Europeans, this campaign against supposed blasphemy mobilized many thousands of Muslim demonstrators in Britain, France, Germany, Belgium, and the Netherlands. Some protesters carried banners with the provocative slogan "Islam—our religion today, your religion tomorrow." The Rushdie affair marked a whole new stage of Muslim political organization and radicalization, and the affair has had later echoes across Europe. In 2000, protests by local Muslim groups forced a Dutch theater to withdraw an opera about Aisha, wife of the Prophet Muhammad. Recently, Italy's Muslims have been galvanized by a protest movement directed against a fifteenth-century fresco of the Last Judgment in Bologna Cathedral. The artwork in question is clearly offensive to Muslims, since it depicts Muhammad being thrown into Hell, naked, with a snake wrapped around his body and attended by a demon: protesters described the piece as even more offensive than Rushdie's *Satanic Verses.* At the same time, it is understandable why Italian Christians resent calls to destroy what is undoubtedly one of the city's greatest treasures. Muslim activism raises the possibility that future campaigns might be mobilized against Europe's literary works, in which Muslims are so often depicted in unflattering terms. Some Muslim activists have further demanded that schools with large immigrant populations not be required to read Dante's *Inferno,* which likewise consigns Muhammad to deepest Hell.[33]

With these precedents in mind, it is quite conceivable that inter-religious violence could erupt in Europe itself: we might even imagine Muslim paramilitary groups waging religious war on French or German soil. We recall that Germany was among the states listed above with a potentially large Muslim minority, and by 2050, France's Muslim minority could be approaching 10 percent of the population. Even if actual violence is avoided, future governments will have to tread delicately to avoid inciting religious conflict, and this should have a dramatic effect on European attitudes toward external politics, above all in the Middle East. This is all the more likely since European nations rely heavily on oil supplies from Muslim Middle Eastern nations.

Interfaith controversies have subtly changed the shape of European debates over immigration, which traditionally were presented in simple racial terms. Now, though, religion is entering the picture. Recently, some conservative Europeans have argued that governments should deliberately promote Christian immigration, as a means of reducing Islamic influence. In Italy in 2000, Bologna's Cardinal Giacomo Biffi made the controversial suggestion that while immigrants were definitely needed, preference should be given to people of Catholic background. "And there are many," he said, "Latin Americans, Filipinos and Eritreans." Although Biffi's ideas reflect familiar concerns about defending traditional notions of European culture, they are far removed from any racist rhetoric.[34] Issues of cross and crescent may in future become ever more important in European political discourse.

CHRISTIAN, MUSLIM, JEW

The question of Christian–Muslim relations becomes all the more sensitive because of the place of Judaism in such a dialogue. In both Europe and the United States, Jews have long been regarded as the chief, almost the sole, religious Other, and the main subject of interfaith dialogue. This raises difficulties when good relations with Jews domestically also require a distinctive foreign policy stance. American Christians have usually followed their government in expressing an absolute and generally uncritical support for the state of Israel. This fact infuriates not just the bulk of the world's Muslims, but also many Third World Christians (not to mention the millions of Arab Christians). Islamic fundamentalism would not have enjoyed the success it has over the past thirty years if it had not been for the continuing provocation of the existence of Israel. The reasons for the West's pro-Israel policy are not hard to seek, grounded as they are in Western guilt over the Holocaust and the failure to rescue Europe's Jews in the 1940s.[35] But the consequences are alarming. Put in the crudest numerical terms, there are rather fewer than 20 million Jews in the world, compared to a billion Muslims, and the disparity is going to grow sharply in coming decades. By 2050, Muslims worldwide should outnumber Jews by over a hundred to one. It has to be asked whether relations between Muslims and Christians can possibly improve as long as the West, and particularly the United States, maintains a Middle East policy which is seen, rightly or wrongly, as virulently anti-Muslim.

A number of different futures suggest themselves. In one, the issue of Israel serves to divide Northern Christians not just from Muslims, but also from the rising churches of the South. Lacking the heritage of guilt that underlies Western attitudes toward Judaism, Christians in Africa and Asia might identify far more with the oppressed Palestinian people than with the Israeli nation, so that in this one area, Southern Christians might align themselves with Muslims. This raises questions about the whole future of Christian-Jewish relations. Quite apart from active anti-Semitism, Christian theology has for most of its history been founded on the idea of supercession, the theory that Christianity perfected and replaced Judaism which was therefore obsolete: the Church is the new Israel. This "replacement theology" became controversial following the Holocaust, and it has become a minority view in Western and particularly North American thought. The idea could well revive in a Southern-dominated church, in areas where actual Jewish communities are quite rare, and in a religious culture founded upon biblical literalism. African and Asian Christians do not necessarily share Northern qualms about blaming the Jews for the death of Jesus, or believing that this guilt should fall upon the whole race. We may once more see the familiar medieval symbols of the vibrant Church trying to enlighten her stubborn sister Synagogue. Outside art and theology, it would not be surprising to see a revival of religious anti-Judaism, directed against the state of Israel.

Alternatively, Southern Christians could find their practical interests in close harmony with those of the Jewish state. Israel has a long record of allying with Christian groups in conflict with Muslim rivals, in order to keep its own Muslim enemies off-balance. As far back as the 1960s, Israeli advisers were supporting Christian rebels in Sudan.[36] With all its military abilities and intelligence capacity, Israel could be a potent ally for African or Asian Christians confronting Muslim neighbors. In that scenario, Israel's continuing struggles with its Arab and Muslim enemies could actually aggravate Christian–Muslim relations well beyond the immediate Middle Eastern theater of conflict.

In either case, though, interactions between not just the two but among the three religions are going to be critical for the foreseeable future. It would be disastrous if American or European policy makers were fully conversant with the ideas and attitudes of Judaism, yet relied on discredited stereotypes to interpret Islam.

NOT JUST ISLAM

Although news reports of religious violence generally focus on Muslim–Christian tensions, this is not the only possible axis of conflict. Christian expansion also threatens to provoke violent reactions from the two other largest world religions, Hinduism and Buddhism, and the issues at stake closely resemble those dividing Christian and Muslim.

The case of Hinduism is critical since India, still home to most members of that faith, will soon surpass China in population. India's population could reach 1.5 billion by 2040 or so, and by 2050, there will be around 1.2 billion Hindus. In recent years, reports of violence against Christian clergy and missionaries have occasionally attracted the attention of the Western media, but usually with little background or explanation. In contrast to their suspicious stereotype of Islam, many Westerners have a benevolent image of Hinduism, which is associated with dreamy mysticism, Gandhian non-violence, and limitless tolerance. In theory, Hinduism should be sufficiently expansive to include almost any theological idea. Why should Jesus not be seen as simply another avatar or manifestation of the divine? Gandhi himself loved the New Testament. Hindu violence against Christianity seems puzzling, not least because the St. Thomas Christians have been a familiar part of the Indian landscape for over 1,500 years. Christian schools are popular with the families of Indian elites, including some of the most reactionary Hindu fundamentalists. Why, then, should Christianity be a source of tension or hatred?[37]

Despite its positive image, Hinduism in India suffers from massive internal tensions, which could conceivably threaten the future of the religion. By far the most significant is the existence of the so-called untouchables, the Dalits, a vast community that today comprises anywhere from 150 million to 250 million people. To put it in perspective, even the lower estimate for Dalit numbers is equivalent to the combined populations of Britain, France, and Italy. Although legal discrimination against these people has been outlawed since 1950, Dalits still suffer from appalling persecution and violence, and there are regular stories of murder, lynching, torture, and rape.[38] It is baffling why a Western world that committed itself so utterly to the plight of Black South Africans under apartheid is so ignorant of the comparable maltreatment of India's far more numerous Dalits. This is, simply, the largest single case of continuing institutional injustice in the world today.

The Dalit issue is also a matter of religious conflict. Successive movements for Dalit rights have threatened to detach the community from the oppressive Hindu system altogether, by converting en masse to some other religion free of the blight of caste, whether that be Islam, Buddhism, or Christianity. In recent decades, Christian missionaries have enjoyed success among the poorest, often people of the lowest castes, or Dalits: many other converts are "tribal" people, who likewise stand on the edge of Hindu society.[39] In the nation as a whole, only 2.3 percent of the present population is officially reportedly to be Christian, but as we noted in chapter 1, that might be a significant underestimate; and even if we accept the official figure, in such a vast country, that figure amounts to a respectable 23 million believers. A great many of these are Dalits. Dalits represent 90 percent of the membership of the Protestant Church of North India, about half that of the Church of South India, as well as 60 percent of India's 16 million Roman Catholics. This success has occurred although the churches themselves are by no means free of caste prejudice. 150 of 156 Catholic bishops in India are of the higher castes, as are the vast majority of Catholic priests. Only gradually are matters changing. In what might be a historic augur of change, the Catholic church in Hyderabad now has a Dalit archbishop.[40]

Fears that Christians might make even deeper inroads among the poorest go far towards explaining the recurrent persecutions and mob violence directed against the churches across India, actions that often occur with the tacit acquiescence of local police and government. Matters have deteriorated sharply since 1997, when Hindu nationalists enjoyed an electoral upsurge. In the most notorious incident to date, Australian missionary Graham Staines and his two young sons were burned to death by a mob in Orissa in 1999. The specific grievance causing this crime was Christian successes in converting tribal peoples on the fringes of Hindu society.[41]

Such well-publicized outbreaks represent only a tiny proportion of actual incidents, of attacks on churches, clergy, and ordinary believers. The state of Gujarat has been the scene of some of the worst violence, and dozens of churches have been destroyed there in the past five years. In one incident in 2000, a mob took over an evangelical church and turned the building into a Hindu temple. Following devastating earthquakes in the same state in 2001, Hindu fundamentalists intercepted relief supplies from Christian activist groups, often relabeling them as their own before distributing them to disaster victims. Survivors were also required to declare loyalty to Hindu causes before receiving food.[42] Lower-class Christian converts can expect a persistent round of low-level bullying and violence. Dalit "converts can point to the wounds they have received, or those who died, in order to establish the right to worship on a Sunday."[43] As elsewhere in Asia, the pervasive current of violence opens the possibility of provocateur attacks. In one case in 2000, a series of bomb attacks against southern Indian churches raised the likelihood of mob violence between Hindus and Christians. Increasing tension was the goal of the perpetrator eventually arrested for the crimes, who proved to be a member of a hard-line Muslim militia.[44]

In addition to ad hoc local vigilantism, there have been repeated calls for official discrimination against Christianity, and such measures are a common platform for fundamentalist Hindu political groups such as the powerful Bharatiya Janata Party (BJP). Individual cities and states have banned conversions, or raised many legal difficulties for potential converts, for instance, by demanding that changes of religion be registered with local authorities. The main target of such measures is evangelism or conversion, even by interfaith marriage. According to Hindu critics, converts are seduced by money payments from Western missionaries. Such an allegation is rhetorically necessary, as it explains why so many Indians would wish to leave the Hindu fold. Interestingly, this position has received the endorsement of the Dalai Lama, one of the West's favorite religious figures: in 2001, he signed a Hindu-inspired declaration opposing "conversions by any religious tradition using various methods of enticement."[45] As we have seen, it is difficult for many liberal Westerners to become too exercised about a ban on conversions or evangelism, since they agree with the basic point that religion is purely a cultural matter. They also agree that it is scarcely proper to visit a clearly extraneous Western religion upon an authentic Third World culture, especially one as idealized as Hinduism.

The fourth of the world's largest religions is Buddhism, which is today rarely cited as a political force, but this will soon change. Viewed over the long span of human history, Buddhism today is at a very atypically low ebb. As recently as 1900, Buddhists claimed the loyalty of 20 percent of the world's people, although that figure now stands closer to 5 percent.[46] The reasons for that decline are not hard to seek, in that the centers of Buddhist faith happened, disastrously, to be at the vortices of anti-religious revolution, in China, Tibet, Mongolia, Vietnam, and Cambodia. The worst era of repression and massacre seems to be ended, and over the next forty or fifty years, Buddhism will be struggling to revert to its historic position as the religion of East and Southeast Asia. The main foci of growth would be in some of the very populous nations, like China, Vietnam, and Thailand. In every case, though, reviving Buddhism will find itself in competition with other expanding religions, above all, Christianity and Islam. It would be tempting to think that a religion founded upon peace and self-sacrifice would not provide an ideological justification for the violence of states and mobs, but the same can also be said of Christianity. Resurgent Buddhism will add another irritant to the religious politics of the coming century.[47]

CROSSING BORDERS

As populations grow in the regions of most intense religious conflict, issues of faith will increasingly shape secular politics, domestic and international. Now, the role of religion in international affairs is open to some debate, and clear-cut faith-based alliances are usually more a matter of rhetoric than reality. Even in early modern Europe, when governments were supposedly motivated by faith, religious boundaries often failed to overcome cynical political calculations. In the sixteenth and seventeenth centuries, when the Turks were threatening to absorb most of eastern and Central Europe, they often acted in close alliance with the Most Christian King of France, who saw the Muslim empire as a necessary counterweight to his fellow-Catholics, the Habsburg rulers. Even popes allied with the sultan when they saw fit. In modern times, some of the bloodiest military conflicts have occurred within or between Muslim states. Such was the civil war that split Pakistan from Bangla Desh in 1971, or the long and messy struggle between Iran and Iraq during the 1980s.

More recently, Western powers have indicated that they make no pre-tense of respecting confessional ties. During the Yugoslav crisis of the 1990s, the United States and Western Europe sided consistently with Muslim inter-ests against the Christian Serbs, to the point of intervening militarily in Kosovo in 1999. Although Western media generally depicted the conflict in very one-sided terms, equating Serbs with German Nazis, such an image could only be sustained by ignoring a great deal of aggression and brutality by Muslim forces, including well-armed international brigades of funda-mentalists. The net result of the Allied intervention was a massive advance of Muslim power and militancy within southeastern Europe, at the expense of ancient Christian communities. At the same time, the oppressed Chris-tians of the Sudan were receiving no support from NATO, or any Western or Christian entity. Even mainstream Western churches were unwilling to be too forthright in denouncing persecution. For Konrad Raiser, head of the World Council of Churches, the main lesson of the massacres in Indonesia and Nigeria was that Christians needed to reassess their missionary endeav-ors, to avoid causing offense to other cultures. For the West at least—if not for Islam—the age of the Crusades is long past.[48]

But having said this, we can easily imagine scenarios in which religion will indeed decide political action. Even without existing religious tensions, demographic change itself will provoke more aggressive international poli-cies, as countries with swollen populations try to expand to acquire living space or natural resources. These actions could be undertaken by govern-ments, or, an even more harrowing prospect, by the kind of ruthless private armies that have marauded over Liberia and Sierra Leone since the 1990s. These extremely destructive wars have been fought by militias made up of uneducated fourteen-year-old boys armed to the teeth, and ready to kill or die for whatever warlord directs them. Border tensions will be very high in regions in which young and expanding populations confront older stagnant nations inhabiting vast geographical spaces. Additionally, growing states with severe domestic tensions might try to unify their discontented peoples by diverting them into foreign adventures. Religious rivalries would provide an obvious justification for external interventions.[49]

Several areas of the globe offer possible settings for future conflicts of this kind. Australian governments have long been nervously aware of the booming Indonesian population just to their north: by 2050, Indonesians will outnumber Australians by around fourteen to one. In this region especially, militant religion might aggravate demographic and economic pressures. We can also look at the former Soviet Union, which often faced serious difficulties over how to accommodate its restive Muslim minority. The breakup of the Soviet Union provided a temporary solution by hiving off the Central Asian republics, but in the long term, this separation also created new political regimes capable of independent action. Sparsely inhabited Russian territory (with its oil wealth) will offer a tempting prize for overpopulated Muslim neighbors to the south and east. If we take the five Central Asian republics together, their current combined population of 57 million should grow to over 100 million by mid-century, a worrying contrast to declining Russia.[50] A similar point could be made about the growth of the former Soviet republics in the Caucasus.

Demography promises to shift the religious balance within these new nation-states. Since Russian and European populations within these countries have far lower birth rates than their Asian-Muslim neighbors, Russians could find themselves in the position of Christian minorities within strict Muslim states. In the post-Soviet successor-state of Kazakhstan, the population is presently divided roughly 50–50 Christian–Muslim, but long-term trends assure a substantial Muslim majority. Muslims outnumber Christians by four to one in Kyrgyzstan, nine to one in Uzbekistan, and the disparities are growing steadily. Currently, most of these governments are deeply hostile to Muslim political activism, but that could change. If Christians in any of these regions complained of religious persecution, the odds of Russia intervening militarily would be high. The disastrous example of the tiny region of Chechnya suggests how bloody such a religious and national conflict might be. Already, Muslim fundamentalist guerrillas are campaigning in Kyrgyzstan, Uzbekistan, and other successor states, with the announced goal of creating a rigidly Islamic state in Central Asia. Religious and racial warfare in the former Soviet Union would be aggravated by the struggle for natural resources, above all oil. Not surprisingly, the U.S. intelligence community has listed Central Asia as a "regional hot spot" in the next decade or two.[51]

If we look at the most populous and fastest-growing states across the

South, we often find Christian and Muslim states standing next to each other, and close to other countries sharply split between the two faiths. Curiously, too, religious minorities are disproportionately likely to reside in areas of rich natural resources, raising the likelihood that religious conflicts might be economically profitable. The fact that minorities are so preferentially located may seem like an odd manifestation of God's sense of humor, but the phenomenon has a sound historical basis. In bygone centuries, religious dissidents were commonly forced to live far removed from the centers of political power, which were located in the more fertile agricultural areas. In order to survive, minorities resorted to remote and marginal lands, which were relatively poor according to the standards of traditional economies. As oil exploration and other extractive industries developed in modern times, these marginal lands often proved to be immensely rich, leaving the minorities in a position of unprecedented influence. This history explains why, for instance, Shi'ite Muslim minorities in the Arab world are so regularly found in oil-rich regions. It also suggests why, religious zeal apart, it is so tempting for a nation to intervene on the behalf of co-religionists who represent a persecuted minority in some neighboring country.

Currently, most of the rising states of Africa and Asia are strictly limited in their capacity to undertake international military operations: witness the disastrous failure of regional African coalitions seeking to end the civil wars in Liberia and Sierra Leone. But this weakness will not continue indefinitely, and African and Asian countries will develop significant military capacities, perhaps based on chemical or biological weapons. If that ever occurred, then regional powers would be under heavy pressure not to stand idly by if co-religionists in nearby countries are threatened with persecution and massacre. We recall the internationalization of the war in former Yugoslavia.

THE WAR OF THE END OF THE WORLD?

We can imagine a future in which Muslim and Christian alliances blunder into conflict, rather as the dual networks of European states reached the point of war in 1914. Several plausible African scenarios should cause strategic planners sleepless nights. Few sub-Saharan states have boundaries that coincide neatly with either ethnic or natural realities. Many ethnic and tribal groupings are scattered over two or more states, though they retain close cultural and religious links, and an insult against one faction can have international ramifications. The massacres in the small nation of Rwanda in 1994 detonated a series of wars and interventions that spilled over into the huge territory of the Congo, what was then Zaire. To date, Angola, Zimbabwe, Namibia, Uganda, and Rwanda have all become directly involved in what has been described as Africa's equivalent of the First World War, and several more nations are watching nervously.[52] Perhaps 2 million Congolese have died in the conflict. Even so, few Westerners know or care about the slaughter, because it occurs so far from centers of media activity, and because there is little risk of superpower involvement, no danger that weapons of mass destruction will be employed. The Congo thus becomes a perpetual war zone reminiscent of Germany during the Thirty Years War.

That analogy should give us pause, because we know in hindsight that Germany would not remain a hapless victim forever, and neither will the growing states of Africa. Let us imagine a near future in which (say) Nigeria, Uganda, and the Congo are all substantial and well-armed regional powers. When Muslims and Christians begin killing each other in another smaller state—in Cameroon, let us say—tribal and religious allies in neighboring lands are swiftly drawn in. Muslim Nigeria demands a cessation of hostilities, and threatens to send in forces. Christian powers respond with their own threats, and the situation escalates, as other major states intervene. Muslim and Christian alliances face off in a model example of cultural and religious confrontation—what Huntington has termed a "fault-line war."[53] Meanwhile, each power tries to destabilize its rivals by stirring up sympathetic minorities within enemy states—Ugandan agents provoke religious rioting across eastern Nigeria, Nigerians reciprocate with terrorist attacks against their rivals. Matters are complicated by the presence of refugees expelled from the zone of conflict, who tell atrocity stories and demand vengeance. As the situation becomes more overtly religious, fundamentalists on each side advocate harder-line positions. Mosques and churches pour forth intemperate propaganda, warning against compromise with the forces of evil.

Worse, religious fundamentalism is sometimes associated with theocratic and authoritarian forms of government, exactly the sort of regime one does not want to be handling delicate international crises. Perhaps the main protagonist nations will themselves be led by religious authorities, by sheikhs or bishops. Some of the likely winners in the religious economy of the new century are precisely those groups who have a strongly apocalyptic mindset, in which the triumph of righteousness is associated with the vision of a world devastated by fire and plague. This could be a perilously convenient ideology for a new international order dominated by countries armed to the teeth with nuclear and biological arsenals. The situation could become so sensitive that a global catastrophe could be provoked by the slightest misjudgment—just like 1914.

A similar conflagration might evolve from an Asian struggle between (say) a vigorously Christian Philippines and a resolutely Muslim Indonesia, especially if each nation offered clandestine support to secessionist groups in its neighbor's territory. Open warfare could develop along this eastern fault-line, and could draw in allied religious powers. Even without the religious factor, this part of the Pacific Rim is going to be one of the major areas of strategic conflict over the next twenty or thirty years. As the People's Republic of China grows militarily, it will project its power in the China Sea, the vast maritime region bounded by Taiwan, the Philippines, Malaysia, and Vietnam. Some Chinese maps are already claiming this area as that nation's territorial waters, which is worrying since the China Sea is the primary route for oil supplies to East Asia's leading industrial nations.[54] Religious-based instability vastly aggravates the potential for great power conflict, especially when (as in Indonesia or Malaysia) anti-Christian violence is directed against ethnic Chinese. The People's Republic might assume a role as the outraged protector of Chinese people everywhere, intervening to save kith and kin from slaughter by Muslim militias. The natural protector and patron of Asia's Christian communities in years to come might not be the United States, Britain, or Australia, but anti-religious China. It would be a curious irony if in this eventuality, the Anglo-Saxon powers found themselves on the other side, fighting alongside Muslim states against a pro-Christian intervention.

The scenarios described here are pure fantasy, but the background is anything but speculative. The countries mentioned will all be significant political players, and they will be at the forefront of growth among both Christians and Muslims. It is conceivable that within a few decades, the two faiths will have agreed on amicable terms of coexistence, but looking at matters as they stand at the start of the twenty-first century, that happy consummation seems highly unlikely. Issues of theocracy and religious law, toleration and minority rights, conversion and apostasy, should be among the most divisive in domestic and international politics for decades to come. It is quite possible to imagine a future Christendom not too different from the old, defined less by any ideological harmony than by its unity against a common outside threat. We must hope that the new *Res Publica Christiana* does not confront an equally militant Muslim world, *Dar al-Islam,* or else we really will have gone full circle back to the worst features of the thirteenth century.

Coming Home

Be nice to whites, they need you to rediscover their humanity.
—*Archbishop Desmond Tutu*

In 1933, Evelyn Waugh's short story, "Out of Depth," told how a magician sent a modern-day Londoner forward in time to the England of the twenty-fifth century. This future England is a primitive peasant society colonized by advanced African nations. At the climax of the story, "in a log-built church at the coast town he was squatting among a native congregation. . . . All around him, dishevelled white men were staring ahead with vague, uncomprehending eyes, to the end of the room where two candles burned. The priest turned towards them his bland, black face. '*Ite, missa est*'"—The Mass is ended.[1] When Waugh wrote, the notion that Africans might someday be rechristianizing Europe would have seemed bizarre, but as the years have gone by, the image seems ever less startling. However fantastic the setting, the story raises a fundamental issue. How will the global North change in response to the rise of a new global Christianity? Will its religious character remain Christian, perhaps with a powerful Southern cast? Or will it entirely lose its Christian character?

Repeatedly throughout church history, observers have noted missionary successes in highly populated parts of the globe, and speculated that the future of Christianity might lie in these mission fields. As Europe was tearing itself apart during the Thirty Years War, St. Vincent de Paul recalled Jesus' promise that his church would continue until the end of days—but he also noted that Jesus had said nothing about the faith necessarily surviving in Europe.[2] The Christian future might well lie in Africa or Asia. Such an insight became all the more probable when set against the religion's long history: the "Christian heartland" has repeatedly shifted as time went on. Syrians and Mesopotamians had once believed that their lands would always be solidly Christian, just like modern Europeans imagine that Christianity will survive on their continent. In 1850, Lord Macaulay warned the then-triumphant British Empire that religion was not the prerogative of any single region, still less a political entity: churches often outlive states and even world empires. In a much-quoted passage, he wrote that the Roman Catholic Church "may still exist in undiminished vigor, when some traveler from New Zealand shall, in the midst of a vast solitude, take his stand on a broken arch of London Bridge to sketch the ruins of St. Paul's."

More recent critics have agreed that Christianity's days in Europe might be numbered. Waugh's story was written during the Great Depression, when Western civilization seemed to be on the verge of collapse. Also in 1933, the great Anglican novelist Charles Williams published his fantasy *Shadows of Ecstasy,* in which the peoples of Africa are inspired to invade a spiritually desolate Europe. As their manifesto declares, "The prophets of Africa have seen that mankind must advance in the future by paths which the white people have neglected and to ends which they have not understood."[3]

No serious observer today expects a literal Southern invasion of Europe or North America, although the numbers involved in peaceful immigration far exceed those of the world's largest armed forces. In religious terms, though, the apocalyptic-sounding visions of St. Vincent, Charles Williams, and the others are sounding ever more credible. While traditional Christianity is weakening in large sections of the North, it is indeed being reinforced and reinvigorated by Southern churches, by means of immigration and evangelization. And the Christianity spread by such means has a predictably Southern cast, conservative and charismatic. How this process develops over the coming century is enormously significant, not just for the future shape of religious alignments, but also for political history. The success of the "prophets of Africa"—and of Asia and Latin America—will determine exactly what kind of North will be confronting a rising South.

FEAR OF A BLACK PLANET

Europeans and North Americans have often felt nervous about population trends that leave Whites such a conspicuous global minority. During the colonial years, writers expressed nightmares that Southern forces might be mobilized by a messianic religious movement that would smash imperial domination and overwhelm Europe and America. Shades of Muhammad's career and the early history of Islam usually lay behind such visions, which seemed more plausible following the rise of native prophets like William Wadé Harris and John Chilembwe. In 1922, Lothrop Stoddard published his epic account of *The Rising Tide of Color Against White World Supremacy*, in which he envisaged the Southern races joining together in a massive anti-White jihad, perhaps led by Islam. The Chilembwe revolt was an early warning sign of this "peculiarly fanatical form of Ethiopianism." In some ways, Williams' *Shadows of Ecstasy* draws on this unsavory tradition, although his work is anything but a racist jeremiad.[4]

The vision of global racial and religious war has continued to galvanize the racist Right. A cult classic in these circles is Jean Raspail's 1973 novel *The Camp of the Saints*, a fantasy of the near future, which describes how the Third World's Black and Brown people invade and overwhelm the White North. The Roman Catholic Church is at the forefront of Raspail's indictment of gutless Western liberalism, because the church preaches subversive messages of racial equality and the evils of imperialism. (It has been thoroughly radicalized and secularized following the "Third Vatican Council.") The pope portrayed in this fantasy is a Brazilian, modeled on Helder Cámara. The familiar nightmare reflected here is that the colonialist trend might be reversed: if there was once a Belgian Congo, could there not someday be a Congolese Belgium? Just as Christianity had spread with the European expansion, so it would collapse with the Fall of the West. The Asian masses of *Camp of the Saints* are explicitly fighting to erase Europe's failed God, and passages from the biblical book of Revelation are scattered throughout the work.[5]

In a perverse way, Raspail really was reflecting the political perceptions of his day, in the sense that liberals and radicals did indeed place their hopes in the southward shift of Christian populations. We have already seen the high hopes that Western Christians placed in the emerging nations of Africa and Asia, and their wholehearted commitment to political liberation movements. On the other side, conservatives loathed the World Council of Churches, never more than when WCC money armed African liberation movements. (The Council is one of Raspail's special targets.) In view of this heritage, it is amazing how favorably many religious conservatives today view the "browning" of world Christianity. In recent debates, it has been the traditionalists who have looked south for allies, in a few cases to the extent of placing themselves under African or Asian ecclesiastical jurisdictions. They almost seem to be awaiting a benevolent *Camp of the Saints* scenario, in which quite genuine saints from Africa or Asia would pour north, not seeking racial revenge, but rather trying to reestablish a proper moral order.

These ideological reversals make better sense if we think of them in terms of political alignments in the contemporary United States. Conservatives generally dislike immigration and the browning of America, and fear the loss of cultural homogeneity. At the same time, though, this process might promote other issues that conservatives do favor. Many of the new immigrants are Christians of a traditionalist bent, with conservative attitudes toward faith and family. They have few qualms about public displays of religion, and show little sympathy for the rigid American separation of church and state. For exactly the same reasons, liberals who generally favor racial diversity will discover that a rainbow America also espouses an uncomfortably traditional kind of religion. Traditional mappings of left and right are ill fitted to comprehend present and future religious changes.

CATHOLICS

The North-South cultural schism is a familiar story within the largest single religious structure on the planet, namely the billion-strong Roman Catholic Church. Although we are not here describing anything like a reevangelization of the North, the Catholic example does show how religion around the world is being transformed by Southern pressures. The conservatism of that Church, so often denounced and derided, must partly be seen as a response to the changing demographics of world religion. It is what it is because it speaks for its members, who are so concentrated in the Third World.

The Catholic Church has long had to deal with trends that other religious communities are only now beginning to face. Back in 1920, Hilaire Belloc not only proclaimed that "Europe is the Faith," but made his boast specifically Catholic: "The Church is Europe; and Europe is The Church."[6] If this was ever true, it has not been so for a good many years. Euro-American Catholics ceased to enjoy majority status a generation ago, and the bulk of the world's Catholics now live in the global South (see table 9.1). The geographical balance is certain to shift even more heavily in coming years.

One suggestive statistic involves baptisms, since regions with the largest number of baptisms are also the centers of the most dynamic growth.[7] Of 18 million Catholic baptisms recorded in 1999, 8 million took place in Central and South America, and no less than 3 million in Africa. Today, the

TABLE 9.1
Catholics Worldwide 2025: A Projection

| | Number of Catholics (in millions) Year | |
Continent	2000	2025
Latin America	461	606
Europe	286	276
Africa	120	228
Asia	110	160
North America	71	81
Oceania	8	11
TOTAL	1056	1,362

Source: David B. Barrett, George T. Kurian, and Todd M. Johnson, eds., *World Christian Encyclopedia,* 2nd ed. (New York: Oxford University Press, 2001), 12.

annual baptismal totals for Nigeria and the Democratic Republic of the Congo are each higher than those for such familiar Catholic lands as Italy, France, Spain, and Poland, which are today the major centers of Catholic population in Europe. Significantly, 37 percent of all baptisms in Africa today are of adults. Observers consider this figure an important gauge of evangelistic efforts, because it means that people are making a deliberate decision to convert from some other faith tradition.[8]

By 2025, Africans and Latin Americans combined will make up about 60 percent of Catholics, and that number should reach 66 percent before 2050. European and Euro-American Catholics will by that point be a small fragment of a church dominated by Filipinos and Mexicans, Vietnamese and Congolese (although of course, the North still provides a hugely disproportionate share of Church finances). The twentieth century was clearly the last in which Whites dominated the Catholic Church: Europe simply is *not* The Church. Latin America may be.

The shift in numbers is increasingly acknowledged at the highest ranks of the Church, among its princes, the cardinals. Although it is not long since that the College of Cardinals was almost wholly European, its composition has now changed thoroughly. Only in 1960 did the College of Cardinals acquire its first African member, Tanzanian Laurian Rugambwa. In 2001, though, when Pope John Paul II elevated forty-four new cardinals, no less than eleven were from Latin America, and two each from India and Africa. Following this infusion of new blood, over 40 percent of the cardinals eligible to vote in papal elections came from Third World nations. It was a new cardinal from Venezuela who drew the obvious conclusion that "the real center of the church is moving from Europe to Latin America." The changes are evident throughout other Church institutions. Although the United States long possessed the largest national province of the Society of Jesus, that honor has now passed to India.[9]

Understanding these numbers goes far toward explaining the Catholic politics of the past forty years or so. Even the election of Pope John Paul II in 1978 owed much to the geographical shift, since Southern Hemisphere cardinals were adamantly opposed to another incumbent from western Europe, and at least the Polish candidate represented a decisive break with tradition. The growing Southern emphasis has also shaped the politics of morality. Repeatedly in recent years, the Catholic hierarchy has become associated with positions that appear conservative or reactionary, to the despair of most Western commentators. The pope and the Vatican have come to symbolize obscurantism on issues of gender, morality, and sexual preference, to the extent that some Catholics see an inevitable schism between the churches of the liberal West and the irredeemably reactionary papacy. The ordination of women to the priesthood is a crucial point of disagreement here, as are matters like contraception and homosexuality. In all these matters, liberal and feminist pressure groups are convinced that their views must triumph in time, once the gerontocracy in the Vatican has faded into history. Indicating this historical confidence, one liberal American pressure group claims for itself the title of FutureChurch.[10]

A global view suggests a quite different interpretation of Catholic behavior, and which part of the church might plausibly claim to speak for the future. The hierarchy knows that the liberal issues dear to American or West European Catholics are irrelevant or worse to the socially traditional societies of the South. While the ordination of women may seem an essential point of justice to Westerners, it is anathema for much of the emerging world. The theological conservatism of the newer Catholic churches is suggested by one of Africa's rising stars, Nigeria's Cardinal Francis Arinze, who in recent years has been touted as a possible future pope. The prospect of a Black African pope understandably excites Christians of all political persuasions, and not just Catholics, but in terms of ideology, an Arinze papacy would probably be a very conservative era. Arinze himself is an Igbo, a people whose Christian roots now run deep. He defines himself as a close follower of Pope John Paul II, and it has been said that "His theology has always been: 'Where does Rome stand? There I stand.'" Among other things, this conservatism shows up in issues of academic freedom, where Arinze's views seem intolerably repressive and restrictive by Western liberal standards. African Catholicism is far more comfortable with notions of authority and charisma than with newer ideas of consultation and democracy.[11]

The question of religious toleration also looks quite different when viewed from the South. In 2000, the Vatican issued another encyclical seemingly designed for the sole purpose of enraging American liberals, when in *Dominus Jesus* it reasserted the exclusive role of Christ and Catholic Christianity as vehicles of salvation. The Vatican warned that "The Church's constant missionary proclamation is endangered today by relativistic theories which seek to justify religious pluralism." Against this position, the document scorned any idea that the Christian message needed to be supplemented by any other faith tradition. "The theory of the limited, incomplete, or imperfect character of the revelation of Jesus Christ, which would be complementary to that found in other religions, is contrary to the Church's faith." All religions simply are not equal.[12]

For the United States or Europe, this material seemed deeply offensive, to Jews in particular. It sabotaged decades of attempts at dialogue with other faiths, and was uncomfortably reminiscent of ancient statements that there was no salvation outside the Church. How could the Church issue such a reactionary rant? In Western parlance, the word "pluralism" is always a good thing. But from an African or East Asian perspective, *Dominus Jesus* addressed crucial issues of daily significance, by warning clergy and believers to observe strict limits in their relations with the other faiths they lived among. It was directed to the faithful in the intense religious atmospheres of Korea, Nigeria, or China, where the terms of interaction with rival religions had to be hammered out afresh each day.[13] In such cases, the Vatican was warning, friendly relations were one thing, but syncretism was quite another, and syncretism was the major theme of the document. The encyclical was not addressed to Northern liberals practicing a dilettantish kind of cafeteria religion, but to fast-growing Southern churches anxious for practical rules to ensure their authenticity. What North Americans did not realize was that the Vatican just was not speaking to them.

The conservative tone of African and Latin American Catholicism suggests why Catholic leaders are less than concerned when Catholics in Boston or Munich threaten schism. In the traditionalist view, adapting to become relevant or sensitive to the needs of Western elites would be suicidal for the long-term prospects of the Church. It is the so-called traditionalists, rather than the liberals, who are playing the political game of the new century. Given their perspective too, we can easily understand how traditionalist Catholics can take in stride all the Northern perceptions that the Church leadership is reactionary and out of touch. Much of the liberal dissidence within Catholicism stems not from the laity but from clergy themselves, and from Catholic universities and teaching institutions. Both priests and institutions are much more likely to be located in the North than the South, so clergy disproportionately reflect European and North American perceptions of the world. Liberal criticism derives especially from only selected regions of the world—and moreover, the very regions in which Catholic numbers are stagnant, or worse.

The relative importance of Northern and Southern interests within Roman Catholicism can be illustrated by the experience of the Netherlands. The Dutch church is one of the most liberal branches of Catholicism, and since the 1960s it has regularly been a thorn in the side of the Vatican. But for all its wealth and activism, the numerical strength of the Dutch Church is tiny. The population of the Netherlands is virtually stable: in 2050, like today, the country will have around 16 or 17 million inhabitants. Church membership, however, is plummeting. About 5 million Dutch people consider themselves Roman Catholics, although only half of these demonstrate any serious commitment to the Church. To put these figures in context, there are about half as many Catholics in the whole of the Netherlands as in (say) just the Manila metropolitan area. Similar stories would emerge if we look at other lands that were once Catholic strongholds in Europe, but where Catholic loyalties are now fading fast. If the church had to choose whether to appeal to the Catholics of Brazil or Belgium, of the Congo or France, then on every occasion, simple self-interest would persuade them to favor the burgeoning Southern community. Of course the leaders of the Roman Catholic Church are so very conservative: they can count.

GENDER AND SEXUALITY

Not just within the Roman Catholic Church, religious conservatives are looking southward with happy expectation. Most of the reasons for this involve disputes over gender and sexuality. Over the past thirty years, religious attitudes in North America and Europe have shifted beyond recognition, with the advance of feminist and progressive causes and the growth of sexual liberalism. The change is symbolized by the general acceptance of women's ordination, and by the free discussion of gay causes within the mainstream Protestant churches. These are the defining issues that separate progressives and conservatives, ecclesiastical Left and Right. They are simply not matters on which it is possible to imagine a church member having no opinion. Although conservatives have suffered repeated defeats in these conflicts, they have been heartened by new support from the global South. Contrary to liberal expectations, churches in Africa and Asia have been highly conservative on moral and sexual issues. As New Left activists of the 1960s often remarked, in a different context, causes that have been lost in Europe or North America might still be won in Africa or Asia.

Just why we are seeing a hemispheric gulf over issues of sexuality needs some explanation. Generally, the newer churches are much more conservative and even reactionary than the Northern mainstream. This may sound curious, since as we have already seen, women are critical to the growth of new churches across the global South. This is evident in Latin American Pentecostalism, and in many of the African independent churches, some of which owe their foundation to female prophets. In some instances, respect for women's spiritual gifts has led to formal leadership positions: the controversial IURD has ordained women since 1993.[14]

Despite these examples, Southern churches are by and large much more comfortable than their Northern neighbors in preaching a traditional role for women. This is especially true in much of Africa, where Muslim notions exercise a powerful cultural influence. Although Christians do not accept the whole Islamic package of mores on this or any issue, they do imbibe a conservatism general to the whole community. While it is difficult to generalize about such diverse cultures, Southern nations tend to be much more patriarchal than Europe or North America. To take a crude guide to social attitudes, abortion is strictly prohibited in almost all African nations, although some nations grant exceptions where the life of the mother is endangered or where a fetus is severely deformed. (Abortions occur in the millions each year across Africa, but the great majority are criminal acts.) A lively debate over abortion law reform rages across the continent, but the state of the law is roughly where it was in Europe or North America in the 1950s. Only liberal and politically sophisticated South Africa permits abortion on request.

Again with the exception of South Africa, organized women's politics are nothing like as developed in most of Africa as in Europe or North America, and that kind of gender balance is inevitably reflected in ecclesiastical life. In every way, Southern churches are far less interested in gender rights issues than are the older denominations of North America or Europe. African churches still lack the kind of activist women's caucuses that are so commonplace in the United States or western Europe. And while believing women are evolving a theology that is both feminist and distinctively African, these ideas have minimal impact when compared with the transformations wrought in the metropolitan countries over the past thirty years or so. Many of the same remarks can be made about the churches of Latin America, in which feminist (*mujerista*) theologies certainly exist, but are commonly viewed as exports from the United States.[15]

By Northern standards, churches in Africa especially appear over-whelmingly male-dominated and often unsympathetic to women's causes and interests. In recent years, some scandalous cases have suggested that these attitudes might have led to widespread sexual exploitation within the churches. In 2001, the U.S. newspaper *National Catholic Reporter* reported on what was alleged to be the commonplace problem of harassment and rape of African nuns and churchwomen by male clergy. According to the stories, drawn from investigations by religious orders themselves, many churchmen have failed to distance themselves from a wider culture of promiscuity and the subordination of women. The general social assump-tion is that maleness is defined by sexual performance and the begetting of children, and that priests, like any other men, are going to be sexually active. In the past, their sexual contacts were casual girlfriends or prosti-tutes, but the threat of AIDS increasingly makes them resort to the safer target of nuns.[16]

These shocking reports should not necessarily be taken at face value, and African clergy deny that the incidents described are at all common or representative. Isolated incidents of abuse should not condemn the whole African priesthood, any more than the churches of Europe or North America should be tainted by over-hyped accounts of child abuse by clergy in those lands. African Catholics have argued that the stories were exaggerated for political reasons, allowing Africa to be "smeared with garbage" so that the American Left can "push forward its own agenda of promoting married priesthood, ordination of women, and attacks on the establishment."[17] At the time of writing, the controversy continues, but the affair has indicated the radically different gender attitudes that prevail in churches North and South.

On issues of homosexuality too, a chasm divides the world's religious communities, nowhere more visibly than in contemporary Africa. Viewed over the span of history, African cultures are no more homogeneous in these matters than those of Europe. Same-sex relationships have often been recorded among different peoples, and the degree of social approval has var-ied enormously according to time and place. As in traditional Europe, most African societies lacked any notion of a "homosexual" as a distinct type, as opposed to an individual who happened to be sexually active with members of the same gender. In recent years, though, the revolutionary change in social attitudes toward homosexuality in Europe and North America has created a social gulf with many Third World societies. As many Northern countries regard gay rights as a fundamental component of human liberty, so homosexuality as such has come to be portrayed as a distinctly Western phenomenon, irrelevant or worse to African or Asian societies.[18]

The virulence of the anti-homosexual reaction has been apparent since the mid-1990s, when Zimbabwe president Robert Mugabe proclaimed that homosexuals were worse than pigs and dogs. Mugabe can be dismissed as a grandstanding demagogue, and his anti-gay tirades were condemned by other African leaders. Some of the harshest responses came from South Africa, where the constitution guarantees freedom of sexual expression. Nevertheless, Mugabe was giving voice to a widespread populist opinion, and his views were widely echoed. Kenyan leader Daniel Arap Moi called homosexuals a "scourge," while the president of Namibia agreed that homosexuality was an "alien practice . . . most of the ardent supporters of these perverts are Europeans, who imagine themselves to be the bulwark of civilization and enlightenment." The presidents of Namibia and Uganda put their rhetoric into practice by ordering severe police crackdowns on gays, to "arrest, deport and imprison" homosexuals.[19] Anti-gay rhetoric combines with anti-Western and anti-imperialist activism, and in this case, gains the backing of religious leaders.

We are not dealing with any kind of ethnic determinism, in the sense that African or Asian societies are intrinsically more hostile either to women's rights or to alternative expressions of sexuality. The main difference is that these communities have not yet experienced the kind of secularizing and modernizing trends that have transformed the West in the past century or so. Southern churches are unlikely to respond to Northern calls to accept general secular trends toward liberalization in these matters, to "join the modern world." They are doubly unlikely to do so, since these same trends are associated with Western cultural imperialism, and are blamed for the decline of religion in Europe and North America. Why should Southerners wish to join this world if they have any chance of remaining separate? If Northerners worry that Southern churches have compromised with traditional paganism, then Southerners accuse Americans and Europeans of selling out Christianity to neo-paganism, in the form of humanistic secular liberalism.

Approaches to both feminism and gay issues also raise the critical issue of authority, of just how different factions justify their opinions. Northern liberals demand that church texts and traditions be viewed in the context of the cultures that produced them, so that it is legitimate and necessary for churches to change in accordance with secular progress. Just because

St. Paul seemed to defend slavery does not justify the practice in the modern world. Southerners, however, demand that all churches respect traditional moral values and gender roles, all the more emphatically when these standards are clearly prescribed in scripture. For charismatic and Pentecostal Christians, contradicting the straightforward words of the biblical text is intolerable. Liberals judge scripture by the standards of the world; conservatives claim to set an absolute value on scripture and religious sources of authority. For the foreseeable future, the newer churches will remain bastions of conservatism on key issues of women's equality and gay rights. (It remains to be seen whether the Southern churches will remain so staunch about these social issues as they evolve and diversify.)

SOUTHERN ALLIES

The moral and sexual conservatism of Southern believers is music to the ears of North Americans or Europeans who find themselves at odds with the progressive leaderships of their own churches. When they suffer an ideological defeat at home—when, for instance, a new denomination approves of same-sex marriages—conservatives are tempted to look South and to say, in effect, "Just you wait." History is on the side of the Southern churches, which will not tolerate this nonsense. These observers echo the hopes of George Canning, the British statesman who looked at the newly independent Latin America of the 1820s and declared that "I called the New World into existence to redress the balance of the old." Finding Southern allies is doubly valuable for traditionalists, since conservative positions stand a much better chance of gaining a hearing in the mainstream media when they are presented by African or Asian religious leaders rather than the familiar roster of White conservatives. Also, Northern traditionalists are tempted to believe that the tides of history are clearly running their way. As the old liberal mainline churches lose their influence in the face of changing world demographics, so their progressive ideas are expected to fade along with them.

Southern influence in sexuality debates has been particularly evident within the Anglican Church. We have already mentioned the 1998 Lambeth Conference of the global Anglican Communion, in which Southern bishops formed a solid bloc to defeat liberal motions on gay rights.[20] The episcopate of what was once the "Church of England" now contains a majority of African and Asian clerics. Of 736 bishops registered at Lambeth, only 316 were from the United States, Canada, and Europe combined, while Africa sent 224 and Asia 95. This body easily passed a forthrightly traditional statement about the evils of homosexuality and the impossibility of reconciling homosexual conduct with Christian ministry. Western responses to the homosexuality statement can best be described as incomprehension mingled with sputtering rage, nowhere more so than in the words of the American Bishop Spong, quoted earlier. Yet the geographical balance within the Anglican Communion promises to shift ever more heavily to the South, and African bishops alone may well comprise a majority by mid-century. Outside Africa too, moral traditionalism is strongly supported by figures like Moses Tay, the Singapore-based archbishop of Southeast Asia, whom we have already seen trying to exorcise Canada's totem poles. Archbishop Tay refuses to attend international Anglican meetings called by clergy who favor gay rights, on the grounds that the liberals are not just ill-advised, but heretical.[21]

The Lambeth debate alerted American conservatives that although they might be isolated within their own church, they had powerful friends overseas. In 2000, some conservative Episcopalians took a step that was remarkable enough at the time, and would have been shocking only a few years earlier. Charles Murphy III and John H. Rodgers Jr. traveled to Singapore, where they were ordained as bishops by Archbishop Tay and the Anglican archbishop of Rwanda, Emmanuel Kolini, as well as several other African and American clerics. By ancient tradition, an archbishop is free to ordain whomever he pleases within his province, so that Rev. Murphy legally became a bishop within the province of Rwanda. In addition, though, these Americans assumed a radical and somewhat controversial new role within North America. They effectively became missionary bishops charged to minister to conservative congregations, where they would support a dissident "virtual province" within the church. They, and their conservative colleagues, were now part of the Anglican Mission in America, sponsored by Archbishop Kolini. The announced goal was to help "lead the Episcopal Church back to its biblical foundations," to restore traditional teachings on issues like the ordination of gay clergy, and blessing same-sex marriages: in short, to combat the "manifest heresy" of the current U.S. church leadership. In 2001, four more American bishops were consecrated to serve what looked increasingly like a new denomination. Again, the service involved overseas archbishops, namely Kolini of Rwanda and Datuk Ping Chung Yong of Southeast Asia.[22]

The established hierarchies of North America were predictably hostile. The presiding bishop of the U.S. Episcopal Church, Frank Griswold, complained about "dangerous fundamentalism," while his Canadian counterpart warned that "Bishops are not intercontinental ballistic missiles, manufactured on one continent and fired into another as an act of aggression."[23] Tay himself was demonized as an agent of intolerance and homophobia, and the bishop of the Canadian province of New Westminster prohibited a planned visit by the Singapore primate. Within both the United States and Canada, though, many rank-and-file Episcopalians expressed sympathy for the new bishops and their international sponsors. As the church became increasingly divided over issues of gender and sexual orientation, North American conservatives found themselves much closer politically to the upstart churches of Africa and Asia than to their own church elites, as they looked to Singapore and Rwanda to defend themselves against New York and Ottawa. Thirty or so conservative Episcopalian congregations physically located in North America are now technically part of the jurisdiction of the Archdiocese of Rwanda—White soldiers following Black and Brown generals.

For these Americans, at least, orthodoxy travels from the South to the North. The story offers a perfect symbol for the termination of the paternalistic relationship between the churches of the Old and New Christian Worlds. After a visit to his distant archdiocesan home in Africa, one American cleric asked wonderingly, "Who should be missionaries to whom?"[24] For many, that question is now thoroughly settled.

EVANGELIZING THE NORTH

In numerical terms, the Episcopalian defection is still very much a fringe phenomenon, but might it be an early sign of a much larger trend? Are we likely to see Southern Christians actually converting or rechristianizing the North? Even today, some denominations draw upon the burgeoning spiritual resources of the South. Within the Roman Catholic Church, Northern dioceses are increasingly likely to use priests from lands in Africa or Latin America, which are still fertile ground for vocations. About one-sixth of the priests currently serving in American parishes have been imported from other countries. African priests are appearing in—of all places—Ireland, that ancient nursery of Catholic devotion. Remarking on this phenomenon, an Irish friend of mine recalled, wryly, how as a child she had been told by the Church to collect pennies to "save Black babies in Africa." She wondered whether some of these babies might have grown up to save Irish souls in recompense. Immigrant communities in Northern lands themselves are also becoming important resources. Although Vietnamese Americans make up only one percent of U.S. Catholics, they provide over 3 percent of the

3,500 men currently studying for the priesthood. Of the seminarians about to be ordained in the United States in 2001, 28 percent have been born outside the country: 5 percent were born in Mexico, 5 percent more in Vietnam.[25]

In Protestant denominations too, Southerners are increasingly visible as clergy and as actual missionaries. In fact, Southern influence grows through two related but distinct phenomena. In some cases, Third World churches undertake actual mission work in secularized North America and especially Europe. Commonly, though, the evangelism is an incidental by-product of the activities of immigrant churches, an important phenomenon given the large African and Asian communities domiciled in Europe.

On the first score, that of deliberate missionary work, Great Britain today plays host to some 1,500 missionaries from fifty nations. Many come from African countries, and they express disbelief at the spiritual desert they encounter in this "green and pagan land." To quote Stephen Tirwomwe, a Ugandan missionary active in the rustbelt north of England: "It was so depressing when I first arrived to find churches empty, and being sold, when in Uganda there is not enough room in our churches for the people. There is a great need for revival in Britain—it has become so secular and people are so inward-looking and individualistic. The country needs reconverting." Announcing a new missionary endeavor, the Anglican primate of Brazil declared that "London is today's field of mission. It's so secular we have to send people for their salvation."[26]

These clerics come from the Anglican tradition, but the independent churches are now beginning to take the lead in evangelism across Europe. Reading their New Testaments, African and Asian Christians encounter the Great Commission that instructs followers to go and make disciples of all nations. They take their claims to catholicity seriously. One active missionary body is the Nigerian-based Redeemed Christian Church of God (RCCG), which was founded in 1952. Its prophetic founder was a veteran of the Cherubim and Seraphim church, part of the Aladura movement. The RCCG has a strong missionary outreach: its statement of beliefs declares that "It is our goal to make heaven. It is our goal to take as many people as possible with us. . . . In order to take as many people with us as possible, we will plant churches within five minutes walking distance in every city and town of developing countries; and within five minutes driving distance in every city and town of developed countries."[27] Since 1981, the RCCG boasts that "an open explosion began with the number of parishes growing in leaps and bounds. At the last count, there are at least about four thousand parishes of the Redeemed Christian Church of God in Nigeria. On the international scene, the church is present in other African nations including Côte D'Ivoire, Ghana, Zambia, Malawi, Zaire, Tanzania, Kenya, Uganda, Gambia, Cameroon, and South Africa. In Europe the church is spread in England, Germany, and France." It is also active in the United States, Haiti, and Jamaica. As the church proclaims, this global presence "is obviously in fulfillment of the vision that had been given to the founder Papa Akinday-omi, that this church would spread to cover the whole earth, and that it would be a viable part of the body of Christ that the Savior would meet here when he returns."[28]

Usually, such independents attract little attention from the media unless they become the focus of scandal, which they do periodically. The Brazilian IURD is one of many bodies expanding its influence into Europe and North America, where it has purchased radio stations and real estate. Like the RCCG, this church too sees a rich potential harvest in the lands of the African diaspora, and the IURD operates missions in southern Africa. Similarly, the EJCSK, the Kimbanguist church, is active in "Republic of Congo (Brazzaville), Congo Democratic (Kinshasa), Angola, Gabon, Central African Republic, Zambia, Zimbabwe, Rwanda, Burundi, South Africa, Nigeria, Madagascar, Spain, Portugal, France, Belgium, Switzerland, England. Many Kimbanguist faithful are all over the world, in U.S.A., in Canada and other countries." The Brazilian-based Sal da Terra (Salt of the Earth) church has missionaries in Britain, Ireland, Portugal, India, and Japan. Such internationally oriented churches use the Internet as a global recruiting tool. The pious surfer can investigate online the IURD, Sal de Terra, the RCCG, EJCSK, the Church of the Lord (Aladura), Celestial Church of Christ, Harrists, and dozens of other like bodies.[29]

The IURD's notoriety distracts attention from the substantial achievements of independent churches on European soil, and from the strong likelihood that they will enjoy major growth. Conditions are ideal, in that most such churches suffer from no substantial language barrier, and they encounter very little competition or resistance from established bodies like the Church of England. The language issue is important: unlike in North America, where the new churches will be overwhelmingly Spanish-speaking, their counterparts in Europe speak the languages of the old colonial powers, English in Britain, French in France. A nice image is offered by Yoweri Museveni, president of Uganda and the person who did the most to end that nation's cycle of bloodshed and repression in the 1980s. Speaking to a British conference in 1997, he remarked, "When we were fighting in the bush, the regime in power got arms from abroad. Our job as guerrillas was simply to wait and grab those arms. You came to our countries and we captured your language. Here I am speaking to you in your own tribal language."[30] Independent churches use these captured languages as the basic tools of evangelism.

Immigrant churches are also crucial, and we have already seen how such congregations make up an ever larger proportion of Christian activity across Europe and Canada. Some are already contemplating outreach to host communities, Black and Brown Christians evangelizing Whites. Although no group is entirely representative, we might look here at one of Britain's most successful Black congregations, London's Kingsway International Christian Centre. Its chief pastor, Matthew Ashimolowo, has recently begun a Breaking Barriers Crusade, with the specific goal of recruiting White members. As he remarked, white converts would feel restive among what he frankly described as "a sea of black faces," and he was anxious to create a hospitable environment.[31]

How feasible is it that this church, or any of its counterparts, might succeed in "breaking barriers," in drawing White Europeans into the world of Southern Christianity? Clearly, this question is enormously significant for the future direction of Christianity. If they do not succeed, then the religion will increasingly be defined as something alien, suspicious, and even hostile. Initially, White recruits are likely to be uncomfortable with the worship style of an African or West Indian church, particularly since British culture is traditionally suspicious of public displays of religious enthusiasm. In an ironic echo of older missionary debates about cultural relevance, Pastor Ashimolowo complains that "The trouble is we are seen as a Black thing and not a God thing." New churches like the KICC have to treat White habits and worldviews with due respect and sensitivity: to practice inculturation, in fact.

As time goes by, Southern-style churches may well make inroads beyond the immigrant population and into the white community. Particularly important as intermediaries are the steadily growing number of mixed race people, who can be expected to draw friends and relatives into the churches. Latin American theologians are exactly right in seeing a pivotal role for such *mestizo* Christians. Just what these new Euro-African and Euro-Asian churches will look like in terms of liturgy and worship style is anybody's guess, but the process of interaction will be fascinating to watch.

Matters should proceed very differently in the United States, since the country has never experienced the same kind of general secularization as Europe, and despite all its critics, American Christianity is very much alive and well. Even so, the country has been designated as mission territory by some Southern churches, which presently evangelize migrant populations.

Both the Brazilian Assemblies of God and the IURD have missions in Los Angeles, and El Shaddai works among Filipino-Americans. Boston offers a neatly symbolic juxtaposition, since a IURD storefront church stands literally just around the corner from the venerable St. Paul's cathedral, a traditional center for the city's bluest-blooded Episcopalians. Another recent example of missionary work involves the churches of the so-called Argentine Revival, a Pentecostal movement that emerged during the social and political disasters that nation experienced in the early 1980s. The Argentine movement believes firmly in concepts of spiritual warfare against the demonic forces that are said to pervade society, and it is characterized by the creation of so-called Lighthouses of Prayer, networks of believers who pray systematically for their neighbors. Since the mid-1990s, the Argentine Revival has sought to evangelize in North America, using Philadelphia as a bridgehead. In 1999, revivalist Carlos Annacondia preached to some 12,000 Philadelphians in the city's first Latino-driven mass crusade.[32]

African and specifically Nigerian churches like the Deeper Life Bible Fellowship have also targeted the United States, and have spreading networks of congregations. With its 80,000 Nigerian residents, the city of Houston plays a pivotal role in these schemes. The RCCG now has "parishes in Dallas, Tallahassee, Houston, New York, Washington, and Chicago, Atlanta, Detroit, Maryland, etc."[33] Another denomination in the process of growth is Christ Apostolic Church which, like the RCCG, has its roots in the Aladura movement. According to the group's official history, its international outreach began in Ibadan, Nigeria, in 1979 when Prophet T. O. Obadare decided "to hold three days of fasting and prayer concerning the situation of Nigerians abroad. After the three day revival, a lady prophesied for almost one hour concerning the same issue of Nigerians abroad. The prophet then went into an additional seven days of prayer and fasting concerning the issue." After forming a CAC church in London, Prophet Obadare moved to Houston in 1981, and then developed a network of congregations across the United States. In less than two decades of existence, Christ Apostolic Church of America has formed congregations in New York, New Jersey, Baltimore, Washington, D.C., Birmingham (Alabama), Chicago, Houston, Dallas, Oklahoma City, and Los Angeles. These are distinct from a number of rival denominations that also claim to be the rightful inheritors of the true CAC tradition, like Christ Apostolic Church Babalola.[34]

Although these newer churches might have a major impact on the United States, particularly on urban communities, the many cultural differences make it unlikely that they will have anything like the transforming effect that we will likely see in Europe. Yet in the United States too, the coming decades should witness a wholly new phase of religious synthesis and hybridization, as immigrant communities Americanize. To take only one ethnic force, a United States with 100 million Latinos is very likely to have a far more Southern religious complexion than anything we can imagine at present.

SOUTHERN MIRRORS

Time and again, when European and American Christians look South, they see what they want to see. A generation ago, liberals saw their own views reflected by the rising masses of the Third World, marching toward socialism and liberation. Today, conservatives have the rosier view. On the basis of population alone, the Southern churches are indeed going to matter far more than they do now, but whether they will continue to have the same political and cultural tone is far from certain. As we have seen, it is likely that as the rising churches mature, their social positions will become quite as diverse as those of their Northern counterparts. Who knows, as Southern societies change, perhaps some of their churches too will someday favor ordaining women, and even blessing the marriages of homosexuals. If a single lesson emerges from all the recent scholarship on the rising churches, it is that they define themselves according to their own standards, despite all the eager efforts to shape them in the mold of the Old Christendom.

Seeing Christianity Again for the First Time

> One of the games to which [the human race] is most
> attached is called 'Keep tomorrow dark', and which
> is also named . . . 'Cheat the prophet'. The players
> listen very carefully and respectfully to all that clever
> men have to say about what is to happen in the next
> generation. The players then wait until all the clever
> men are dead, and bury them nicely. They then go
> and do something else. That is all. For a race of
> simple tastes, however, it is great fun.
>
> —G. K. *Chesterton*, The Napoleon of Notting Hill

If only we had known. . . . Attempts to forecast the future usually derive from more than just intellectual curiosity. Ideally, knowing what is going to happen should better equip us to deal with it, to prevent things we dread. The problem with this approach is that, sometimes, things that are predicted just do not occur; more frequently they do indeed happen, but in forms quite different from what anyone expected. The former difficulty is neatly symbolized by the huge stockpiles of dubious foodstuffs that alarmed Americans collected in order to face the collapse of civilization foretold for January 1, 2000, the onset of the dreaded Y2K bug. In the case of the southward movement of Christianity, we can be quite sure that the event will occur, but interpreting it or preparing for it is quite a different matter. Does our knowledge of future trends allow us to form any appropriate responses? Although precious little perhaps can be done in terms of practical policy, looking at the ways Christianity is now developing tells us a great deal about the essence of the religion. Considering possible futures is so valuable because it can tell us so much about the realities of the present day.

Let us for a moment assume the impossible, that a wormhole in time opened long enough to give us access to something like the *World Christian*

Encyclopedia for the year 2050, complete with detailed population tables of Christian communities worldwide at that future date. Logically, such a treasure would be of huge value for Christian churches in knowing where to allocate resources, how to invest people and funds in particular cities or regions, with the goal of getting in on the ground floor of future population growth. If we knew that a given Asian city that currently had just 500,000 people was going to swell to 20 million by the mid-century, that would seem to present a wonderful opportunity. If churches established themselves there now, planting the kernel of future social services and community networks, then they would be ideally placed to dominate the religious economy of that burgeoning region. People who turned to that church for food and help would likely be loyal members of its congregation, and would build the denomination. In an age of competition between faiths, such a far-sighted policy would be an enormous advantage. In an ideal world, Christians and Muslims, Catholics and Pentecostals, would be engaged in a friendly rivalry as to who could best help the poor, without thought of who was gaining the greatest numbers and influence. This is, however, not an ideal world.

Wormholes may or may not exist, but we do already have much of the information that we would hope to garner from an encyclopedia visited on us from the future. Just to take the example of the cities that will be growing rapidly, we know today where many of these places are going to be, and where an investment of resources could pay off spectacularly. Barring catastrophe, nothing is going to stop African cities like Lagos, Lusaka, Kinshasa, and Kampala from becoming goliaths, from absorbing millions of uprooted rural people. All exist in countries with minimal social service networks, and each stands in a region of lively religious competition. The faith or denomination that builds there today is very likely to be profiting richly in a decade or two. Generally, though, they are not doing this building, or not to anything like the degree we might expect. Why would anyone fail to respond to such obvious future trends?

Of course, some groups are indeed developing a presence across the future centers of growth, but equally striking are the ones that are not. For all their vast wealth, many churches in North America and Europe have far less interest or commitment in the global South than they once had. American mainline churches have dramatically cut back on their budgets for missions. In large measure, this represents a response to charges of cultural imperialism in bygone years, and a guilty sense that there was much justice to the conventional stereotypes of missionary work. Also, Western congregations feel reluctant to interfere in the domains of new native churches, which should be allowed to stand on their own feet. For whatever reason, Western investment in missions has been cut back dramatically at just the point it is most desperately needed, at the peak of the current surge in Christian numbers.

Some Western churches do not wish to respond to the new global challenges. Others, though, are simply unable, because churches face rival demands on scarce resources. This is well illustrated by the Roman Catholic Church, which globally faces very severe challenges from other denominations. Logically, the Church should be responding by reallocating clergy to the regions of greatest need. In practice, the Catholic tradition is highly dependent on its clergy, and the Church is strongest where its priests and religious are ablest and most numerous. Unfortunately, though, the Church faces a massive and growing imbalance between the Catholic faithful and their pastors. Although we can understand the historical circumstances that have led to this situation, it almost seems as if the Church has scientifically assigned its resources to create the minimum possible correlation between priests and the communities that need them most. The Devil himself could scarcely have planned it better. The Catholic example illustrates how badly the North is failing to respond to changing global realities, and the structural reasons why the situation is unlikely to change.

In this matter, as in so many others, the North–South imbalance is quite stark. The Northern world, Europe and North America, presently accounts for 35 percent of Catholic believers and 68 percent of priests; Latin America has 42 percent of believers but only 20 percent of the priests. In terms of the ratio of priests to faithful, the Northern world is four times better supplied with clergy than the global South. To understand what these figures mean, we should recall the endless complaints about priest shortages in Europe and the United States, and the dreadful consequences for parish life. Now let us imagine the circumstances elsewhere in the world, where priests are in far shorter supply. If the North American priest shortage really is such a disaster, as many argue, how can we begin to describe the situation in the South? It is scarcely surprising that the Vatican is so alarmed by evangelical inroads into the ill-shepherded Catholic faithful, or that they see Protestant conversions in terms of sectarian wolves preying on vulnerable believers. In Brazil, Protestant pastors already outnumbered priests by the mid-1980s, and some Catholic parishes notionally had 50,000 members.[1] In Africa, the Church has over the past fifty years enjoyed probably the most rapid numerical expansion in its whole history, but the clergy shortage raises questions about how long this boom can be sustained. For the Church hierarchy, this issue is far more immediately pressing than any social or theological complaints emanating from Northern liberals.

Granted that a severe problem exists, solutions are by no means obvious. It is inconceivable that Northern bishops might seek global equity by shipping half their priests off to the Third World—although the prospect has probably crossed the mind of many a prelate troubled by an obstreperous cleric under his authority. Amazingly enough, the main steps taken so far to remedy priest shortages have been entirely in the opposite direction, namely in importing Third World priests in order to meet shortfalls in North America and Europe. Viewed in a global perspective, such a policy can be described at best as painfully short-sighted, at worst as suicidal for Catholic fortunes. If even an organization as centralized and as globally minded as the Catholic Church cannot mobilize its resources to meet the emerging challenges and opportunities of the global South, what hope there is for any other body?

SEEING CHRISTIANITY AGAIN

Even if we are exactly right in all our predictions, knowing something about the future of Christianity may or may not help any particular church or group to do anything practical to prepare for that future. Still, it might do a great deal in helping us understand the present, so we can act accordingly. If there is one thing we can reliably predict about the twenty-first century, it is that an increasing share of the world's people is going to identify with one of two religions, either Christianity or Islam, and the two have a long and disastrous record of conflict and mutual incomprehension. For the sake of both religion and politics, and perhaps of simple planetary survival, it is vitally necessary for Christian and Jewish Northerners to gain a better understanding of Islam. But odd as it may sound, perhaps the more pressing need is to appreciate that other religious giant, the strangely unfamiliar world of the new Christianity. Southern Christianity, the Third Church, is not just a transplanted version of the familiar religion of the older Christian states: the New Christendom is no mirror image of the Old. It is a truly new and developing entity. Just how different from its predecessor remains to be seen.

Studying Christianity in a predominantly Christian society can pose surprising difficulties. I teach in a Religious Studies program which, like most of its counterparts in universities across the United States, introduces students to the global dimensions of religious experience. In practice, that means providing a wide range of courses on the World Religions, such as Islam, Buddhism, and so on. The main religion that tends to suffer in this package is Christianity, which receives nothing like the attention it merits in terms of its numbers and global scale. Whatever the value of Christian claims to truth, it cannot be considered as just one religion out of many: it is, and will continue to be, by far the largest in existence. A generation ago, the neglect of Christianity in academic teaching made more sense than it does today, in that students could be expected to absorb information about the faith from churches, families, or society at large. Today, though, that is often not a realistic expectation, and one encounters dazzling levels of ignorance about the basic facts of the religion.

If Christianity as such receives short shrift, the situation is still worse when it comes to the religion outside the West. Normally, textbooks discuss the faith in Africa and Asia chiefly in highly negative ways, in the context of genocide, slavery, and imperialism, and the voices of autonomous Southern Christianity are rarely heard. Given the present and future distribution of Christians worldwide, a case can be made that understanding the religion in its non-Western context is a prime necessity for anyone seeking to understand the emerging world. American universities prize the goal of diversity in their teaching, introducing students to the thought-ways of Africa, Asia, and Latin America, often by using texts from non-Western cultures. However strange this may sound in terms of conventional stereotypes, teaching about Christianity would be a wonderful way to teach diversity, all the more so now that particular non-Western religion is returning to its roots. Significantly, though, few Religious Studies departments in public universities offer courses in Pentecostalism, say, compared with the substantial numbers teaching on Buddhism or Islam. Partly, this reflects political prejudices: at least in the humanities, most academics are strongly liberal, and take a dim view of Pentecostalism and fundamentalism. While colleges do discuss Catholicism, the issues involved in these courses are very much those of interest in the liberal West, rather than the lived realities of Catholic practice in Latin America or Africa.

Considering Christianity as a global reality can make us see the whole religion in a radically new perspective, which is startling and, often, uncomfortable. In fact, to adapt a phrase coined by theologian Marcus Borg, it is as if we are seeing Christianity again for the first time.[2] In this encounter, we are forced to see the religion not just for what it is, but what it was in its origins and what it is going to be in future. To take one example of these startling rediscoveries, Christianity is deeply associated with poverty.

Contrary to myth, the typical Christian is not a White fat cat in the United States or western Europe, but rather a poor person, often unimaginably poor by Western standards.

The grim fact of Christian impoverishment becomes all the more true as Africa assumes its place as the religion's principal center. We are dealing with a continent that has endured countless disasters since independence, measured by statistics that become wearying by their unrelieved horror, whether we are looking at life expectancy, child mortality, or deaths from AIDS. Africa contributes less than 2 percent of the world's total GDP, although it is home to 13 percent of world population, and the GDP for the whole of sub-Saharan Africa is equivalent to that of the Netherlands. Since the 1960s, Africa's share of world trade has all but disappeared. Overall, "the continent is slipping out of the Third World into its own bleak category of the *n*th World." Matters are made infinitely worse by the unraveling of several African states, a process attended by unbelievable bloodshed. The U.S. intelligence community sees no chance of improvement in the foreseeable future: "In Sub-Saharan Africa, persistent conflicts and instability, autocratic and corrupt governments, over-dependence on commodities with declining real prices, low levels of education, and widespread infectious diseases will combine to prevent most countries from experiencing rapid economic growth."[3] That is the underlying reality for the Christian masses of the new century.

African and Latin American Christians are people for whom the New Testament Beatitudes have a direct relevance inconceivable for most Christians in Northern societies. When Jesus told the "poor" they were blessed, the word used does not imply relative deprivation, it means total poverty, or destitution. The great majority of Southern Christians (and increasingly, of all Christians) really are the poor, the hungry, the persecuted, even the dehumanized. India has a perfect translation for Jesus' word in the term *Dalit*, literally "crushed" or "oppressed." This is how that country's so-called Untouchables now choose to describe themselves: as we might translate the biblical phrase, blessed are the Untouchables.

Knowing all this should ideally have policy consequences, which are at least as urgent as redistributing church resources to meet the needs of shifting populations. Above all, the disastrous lot of so many Christians worldwide places urgent pressure on the wealthy societies to assist the poor. A quarter of a century ago, Ronald J. Sider published the influential book, *Rich Christians in an Age of Hunger*, which attacked First World hypocrisy in the face of the grinding poverty of the global South. The book could easily be republished today with the still more pointed title *Rich Christians in an Age of Hungry Christians,* and the fact of religious kinship adds enormously to Sider's indictment.[4] When American Christians see the images of starvation from Africa, like the hellish visions from Ethiopia in the 1980s, very few realize that the victims share not just a common humanity, but in many cases the same religion. Those are Christians starving to death.

THE BIBLE IN THE SOUTH

Looking at Southern Christianity gives a surprising new perspective on some other things that might seem to be very familiar. Perhaps the most striking example is how the newer churches can read the Bible in a way that makes that Christianity look like a wholly different religion from the faith of prosperous advanced societies of Europe or North America. We have already seen that Southern churches are quite at home with biblical notions of the supernatural, with ideas like dreams and prophecy. Just as relevant in their eyes are that book's core social and political themes, like martyrdom, oppression, and exile. In the present day, it may be that it is only in the newer churches that the Bible can be read with any authenticity and immediacy, and that the Old Christendom must give priority to Southern voices. If Northern churches cannot help with clergy or missionaries or money, then perhaps they can reinterpret their own religion in light of these experiences.[5]

When we read the New Testament, so many of the basic assumptions seem just as alien in the global North as they do normal and familiar in the South. When Jesus was not talking about exorcism and healing, his recorded words devoted what today seems like an inordinate amount of attention to issues of persecution and martyrdom. He talked about what believers should do when on trial for the faith, how they should respond when expelled and condemned by families, villages, and Jewish religious authorities. A large proportion of the Bible, both Old and New Testaments, addresses the sufferings of God's people in the face of evil secular authorities.

As an intellectual exercise, modern Westerners can understand the historical circumstances that led to this emphasis on bloodshed and confrontation, but the passages concerned have little current relevance. Nor, for many, do the apocalyptic writings that are so closely linked to the theme of persecution and martyrdom, the visions of a coming world in which God will rule, persecutors will perish, and the righteous be vindicated. In recent decades, some New Testament scholars have tried to undermine the emphasis on martyrdom and apocalyptic in the New Testament by suggesting that these ideas did not come from Jesus' mouth, but were rather attributed to him by later generations. The real Jesus, in this view, was a rational Wisdom teacher much more akin to modern Western tastes, a kind of academic gadfly, rather than the ferocious "Doomsday Jesus" of the Synoptic Gospels. From this perspective, Jesus' authentic views are reflected in mystical texts like the *Gospel of Thomas*. For radical Bible critics like the Jesus Seminar, *Thomas* has a much better claim to be included in a revised New Testament than the book of Revelation, which is seen as a pernicious distortion of Christian truth.

For the average Western audience, New Testament passages about standing firm in the face of pagan persecution have little immediate relevance, about as much perhaps as farmyard images of threshing or vine-grafting. Some fundamentalists imagine that the persecutions described might have some future reality, perhaps during the End Times. But for millions of Southern Christians, there is no such need to dig for arcane meanings. Millions of Christians around the world do in fact live in constant danger of persecution or forced conversion, from either governments or local vigilantes. For modern Christians in Nigeria, Egypt, the Sudan, or Indonesia, it is quite conceivable that they might someday find themselves before a tribunal that would demand that they renounce their faith upon pain of death. In all these varied situations, ordinary believers are forced to understand why they are facing these sufferings, and repeatedly they do so in the familiar language of the Bible and of the earliest Christianity. To quote one Christian in Maluku, recent massacres and expulsions in that region are "according to God's plan. Christians are under purification from the Lord."[6] The church in Sudan, the victim of perhaps the most savage religious repression anywhere in the world, has integrated its sufferings into its liturgy and daily practice, and produced some moving literature in the process ("Death has come to reveal the faith / It has begun with us and it will end with us").[7] Churches everywhere preach death and resurrection, but nowhere else are these realities such an immediate prospect. As in several other crisis regions, the oppressors in Sudan are Muslim, but elsewhere, they might be Christians of other denominations. In Guatemala or Rwanda, as in the Sudan, martyrdom is not merely a subject for historical research, it is a real prospect. As we move into the new century, the situation is likely to get worse rather than better.

Persecution is not confined to nations in such a state of extreme violence. Even in situations when actual violence might not have occurred for months or years, there is a pervasive sense of threat, a need to be alert and avoid provocations. Hundreds of millions of Christians live in deeply divided societies, constantly needing to be acutely aware of their relationships with Muslim or Hindu neighbors. Unlike in the West, difficulties in interfaith relations in these settings do not just raise the danger of some angry letters to local newspapers, but might well lead to bloodshed and massacre. In these societies, New Testament warnings about humility and discretion are not just laudable Christian virtues, they can make the difference between life and death.

Just as relevant to current concerns is exile, forcible removal from one's homeland, which forms the subject of so much of the Hebrew Bible. About half the refugees in the world today are in Africa, and millions of these are Christian. The wars that have swept over the Congo and Central Africa over the past decade have been devastating in uprooting communities. Often, it is the churches that provide the refugees with cohesion and community, and offer them hope, so that exile and return acquire powerfully religious symbolism. Themes of exile and return also exercise a powerful appeal for those removed voluntarily from their homelands, the tens of millions of migrant workers who have sought better lives in the richer lands.[8]

Read against the background of martyrdom and exile, it is not surprising that so many Christians look for promises that their sufferings are only temporary, and that God will intervene directly to save the situation. In this context, the book of Revelation looks like true prophecy on an epic scale, however unpopular or discredited it may be for most Americans or Europeans. In the South, Revelation simply makes sense, in its description of a world ruled by monstrous demonic powers. These forces might be literal servants of Satan, or symbols for evil social forces, but in either case, they are indisputably real. To quote one Latin American liberation theologian, Néstor Míguez, "The repulsive spirits of violence, racial hatred, mutilation, and exploitation roam the streets of our Babylons in Latin America (and the globe); their presence is clear once one looks behind the glimmering lights of the neon signs."[9]

Making the biblical text sound even more relevant to modern Third World Christians, the evils described in Revelation are distinctively urban. Then as now, evil sets up its throne in cities. Brazilian scholar Gilberto da Silva Gorgulho remarks that "The Book of Revelation is the favorite book of our popular communities. Here they find the encouragement they need in their struggle, and a criterion for the interpretation of official persecution in our society. . . . The meaning of the church in history is rooted in the witness of the gospel before the state imperialism that destroys the people's life, looming as an idol and caricature of the Holy Trinity."[10] To a Christian living in a Third World dictatorship, the image of the government as

Antichrist is not a bizarre religious fantasy, but a convincing piece of political analysis. Looking at Christianity as a planetary phenomenon, not merely a Western one, makes it impossible to read the New Testament in quite the same way ever again. The Christianity we see through this exercise looks like a very exotic beast indeed, intriguing, exciting, and a little frightening.

Christianity is flourishing wonderfully among the poor and persecuted, while it atrophies among the rich and secure. Using the traditional Marxist view of religion as the opium of the masses, it would be tempting to draw the conclusion that the religion actually does have a connection to underdevelopment and pre-modern cultural ways, and will disappear as society progresses. That conclusion would be fatuous, though, because very enthusiastic kinds of Christianity are also succeeding among professional and highly technologically oriented groups, notably around the Pacific Rim and in the United States.[11] Yet the distribution of modern Christians might well show that the religion does succeed best when it takes very seriously the profound pessimism about the secular world that characterizes the New Testament. If it is not exactly a faith based on the experience of poverty and persecution, then at least it regards these things as normal and expected elements of life. That view is not derived from complex theological reasoning, but is rather a lesson drawn from lived experience. Christianity certainly can succeed in other settings, even amid peace and prosperity, but perhaps it does become harder, as hard as passing through the eye of a needle.

A healthy distrust of worldly power and success is all the more necessary given the remarkable reversals of Christian fortunes over the ages, and the number of times that the faith seemed on the verge of destruction. In 500, Christianity was the religion of empire and domination; in 1000, it was the stubborn faith of exploited subject peoples, or of barbarians on the irrelevant fringes of the great civilizations; in 1900, Christian powers ruled the world. Knowing what the situation will be in 2100 or 2500 would take a truly inspired prophet. But if there is one overarching lesson from this record of changing fortunes, it is that (to adapt the famous adage about Russia) Christianity is never as weak as it appears, nor as strong as it appears.[12] And whether we look backward or forward in history, we can see that time and again, Christianity demonstrates a breathtaking ability to transform weakness into strength.

ABBREVIATIONS

CC	Christian Century
CT	Christianity Today
FEER	Far Eastern Economic Review
IBMR	International Bulletin of Missionary Research
IRM	International Review of Mission
LAT	Los Angeles Times
NCR	National Catholic Reporter
NYT	New York Times
WP	Washington Post
WSJ	Wall Street Journal

NOTES

CHAPTER 1

1. John Mbiti is quoted in Kwame Bediako, *Christianity in Africa* (Edinburgh University Press/ Orbis, 1995), 154. Throughout this book, I will be speaking of the critical hemispheric division between North and South: this is relatively recent terminology, which was popularized only by the Brandt Report of 1980. See *North-South: A Programme for Survival* (Cambridge, MA: MIT, 1980).

2. David B. Barrett, George T. Kurian and Todd M. Johnson, *World Christian Encyclopedia*, 2nd ed. (New York: Oxford University Press, 2001), 12–15. I will be using this book extensively, although in several instances, my figures differ from theirs. My demographic projections are drawn from two sources: the U.S. Census Bureau and the United Nations. U.S. government figures can be found through the U.S. Department of Commerce, Bureau of the Census, International Database, online at http://www.census.gov/ipc/www/idbrank.html. UN figures are online at http://www.popin.org/.

3. The figures given here for Asia should be regarded with some skepticism. Although I will be discussing this issue in more detail later, particularly in chapter 5, I stress here the large disparities that separate estimates about the size of Christian populations, especially in countries in which the religion is officially disapproved. To take a glaring example, the *World Christian Encyclopedia* gives India's current Christian population as 62 million, around 6 percent of the whole. This includes 41 million "professing Christians" and 21 million "crypto-Christians." This overall number is far higher than that reported by Indian census data, which are the figures used by U.S. government agencies. The CIA *Factbook* says there are around 24 million Indian Christians, and this number is reproduced by the U.S. State Department (compare http://www.state.gov/www/global/human_rights/irf/irf_rpt/irf_india.html). Undoubtedly, Indian census counts discriminate against religions held by the underclass, which results in an undercounting of Christian strength. It is far from clear, though, whether that undercount can explain the huge discrepancy (40 million people!) that separates our sources here. In China, similarly, the *World Christian Encyclopedia* gives a figure of 90 million Christians, double what is commonly accepted by other sources. If the current estimates are too high, then any projections of future numbers are necessarily exaggerated. Where such conflicts of evidence occur, I have erred on the side of conservatism, taking an average of

available estimates. This means that my figures often differ from those of the *World Christian Encyclopedia*. See the discussion of this work in Richard N. Ostling, "An Accounting of World's Souls," *WP*, March 17, 2001.

4. Richard J. Neuhaus, "The Religious Century Nears," *WSJ*, July 6, 1995; Dana L. Robert, "Shifting Southward," *IBMR* 24, no. 2 (2000): 50–58. I was struck when I first read Robert's important article, which appeared in April 2000, since she makes many of the same points that I had made in my article on the same subject, "That New Time Religion," which had appeared in *Chronicles* magazine the previous August (pp. 17–19). We also use a number of similar examples. Despite these resemblances, we were of course working quite independently. She first presented her material as a conference paper in January 1999, about the time that I was writing my magazine article. Perhaps we were both inspired by the same event: the previous year's Lambeth Conference of the Anglican Communion, at which African bishops created a stir by outvoting their Northern brethren on key moral issues.

5. Walbert Buhlmann, *The Coming of the Third Church* (Slough, UK: St. Paul, 1976); Edward R. Norman, *Christianity and the World Order* (Oxford University Press, 1979); idem, *Christianity in the Southern Hemisphere* (Oxford University Press, 1981), John Taylor, "The Future of Christianity," in McManners, ed., *The Oxford History of Christianity* (Oxford University Press, 1993), 644–83; Barrett et al., *World Christian Encyclopedia*. The remark about the "third tradition" is from Christopher Fyfe and Andrew Walls, eds., *Christianity in Africa in the 1990s* (Centre of African Studies, University of Edinburgh, 1996), 148; "the standard Christianity" is from the same work (p. 3). Andrew F. Walls, *The Missionary Movement in Christian History* (Maryknoll, NY: Orbis, 1996); idem, "Eusebius Tries Again," *IBMR* 24, no. 3 (2000): 105–11; idem, *The Cross-Cultural Process in Christian History* (Maryknoll, NY: Orbis, 2001); Alex Duval Smith, "Christianity Finds Strength in Africa Due to Adaptability," *CT*, posted to web site July 16, 2001.

6. See *Christian History* 28 (1990) for the "hundred most important events in Church history." The list of the ten most important Christians is from *Christian History* 65 (Winter 2000). William J. Petersen and Randy Petersen, *100 Christian Books That Changed the Century* (Grand Rapids, MI: Baker, 2000); John Wilson, "Big Numbers, Big Problems," *CT*, posted to web site April 16, 2001. For African church statistics, see Bengt Sundkler and Christopher Steed, *A History of the Church in Africa* (Cambridge University Press, 2000), 906. My remark on religious publishers certainly does not apply to the firm of Orbis, which has consistently published Christian authors from Africa and Latin America.

7. Mbiti is quoted in Bediako, *Christianity in Africa*, 154. See also John S. Mbiti, *Introduction to African Religion*, 2nd rev. ed. (Portsmouth, NH: Heinemann Educational, 1991); idem, *Bible and Theology in African Christianity* (Nairobi: Oxford University Press, 1986); Harvey Cox, *Fire from Heaven* (Reading, MA: Addison-Wesley, 1995). Just in the past couple of years, we have a number of ambitious "global histories" of Christianity. See Adrian Hastings, ed., *A World History of*

Christianity (Grand Rapids, MI: Eerdmans, 1999); David Chidester, *Christianity: A Global History* (HarperSan Francisco 2000); Paul R. Spickard and Kevin M. Cragg, *A Global History of Christians* (Grand Rapids, MI: Baker Book House, 2001).

8. Walls, "Eusebius Tries Again."

9. Robert Wuthnow, *Christianity in the Twenty-First Century* (New York: Oxford University Press, 1993); Richard Kew and Roger White, *Towards 2015* (Boston, MA: Cowley, 1997), 118–19, 123. For the Anglican tradition, see also Ian T. Douglas and Pui-Lan Kwok, eds., *Beyond Colonial Anglicanism* (New York: Church, 2001).

10. One major exception to the media's neglect of Southern affairs was the major article by Kenneth Woodward, "The Changing Face of the Church," *Newsweek,* April 16, 2001. Benjamin J. Hubbard, ed., *Reporting Religion* (Sonoma, CA: Polebridge, 1990).

11. Samuel P. Huntington, *The Clash of Civilizations and the Remaking of World Order* (New York: Simon & Schuster, 1996), 65; compare Barrett et al., *World Christian Encyclopedia,* 4.

12. Huntington, *The Clash of Civilizations,* 64–66, 116–19 (the quote is from p. 65); Samuel P. Huntington, *The Third Wave* (Norman: University of Oklahoma Press, 1991); Benjamin R. Barber, *Jihad Vs. McWorld* (New York: Times Books, 1995).

13. James C. Russell, *The Germanization of Early Medieval Christianity* (Oxford University Press, 1996). See, for instance, the portrayal of Jesus as a Germanic warlord in Ronald Murphy, ed., *The Heliand: The Saxon Gospel* (New York: Oxford University Press, 1992).

14. Norman, *Christianity and the World Order;* idem, *Christianity in the Southern Hemisphere.*

15. Barrett et al., *World Christian Encyclopedia,* 4; Teresa Watanabe, "Global Convention Testifies to Pentecostalism's Revival," *LAT,* May 31, 2001.

16. John Spong, *Why Christianity Must Change or Die* (HarperSan Francisco, 1998); John Wilson, "Examining Peacocke's Plumage," *CT,* posted to web site March 12, 2001; Brent L. Staples, *New York Times,* Book Review, November 26, 2000. Compare John Spong, *A New Christianity for a New World* (HarperSanFrancisco, 2001).

17. Gerald R. Cragg, *The Church and the Age of Reason, 1648–1789* (London: Penguin, 1970); Alec Vidler, *The Church in an Age of Revolution* (London: Penguin, 1971).

18. Adriaan Hendrik Bredero, *Christendom and Christianity in the Middle Ages* (Grand Rapids, MI: Eerdmans, 1994); Peter Brown and Jacques Le Goff, eds., *The Rise of Western Christendom* (Oxford: Blackwell, 1997).

19. See, for instance, Douglas John Hall, "Confessing Christ in a Post-Christendom Context," *Ecumenical Review* 52 (2000): 410–17.

20. Benedict Anderson, *Imagined Communities,* rev. ed. (London: Verso, 1991); "Global Trends 2015," online at http://www.cia.gov/cia/publications/globaltrends 2015/.

21. The remark about quasi-states is from Paul Gifford, *African Christianity: Its Public Role* (Bloomington: Indiana University Press, 1998), 9.

22. Hedley Bull, *The Anarchical Society* (New York: Columbia University Press, 1977), 254. Compare Stephen J. Kobrin, "Back to the Future: Neomedievalism and the Postmodern Digital World Economy," *Journal of International Affairs* 51 (1998): 361–86; Paul Lewis, "As Nations Shed Roles, Is Medieval the Future?" *NYT,* January 2, 1999.

23. Norman, *Christianity in the Southern Hemisphere.* For a pioneering encounter between theologians of the two continents, see Sergio Torres and Virginia Fabella, eds., *The Emergent Gospel* (Maryknoll, NY: Orbis, 1978).

CHAPTER 2

1. Kwame Bediako, *Christianity in Africa: The Renewal of a Non-Western Religion* (Edinburgh University Press/ Orbis, 1995).

2. Edward W. Blyden, *Christianity, Islam and the Negro Race* (Edinburgh University Press, 1967); Ronald Segal, *Islam's Black Slaves* (New York: Farrar, Straus and Giroux, 2001); Bernard Lewis, *Race and Slavery in the Middle East* (New York: Oxford University Press, 1990).

3. Andrew F. Walls, "Eusebius Tries Again," *IBMR* 24, no. 3 (2000): 105–11; W. H. C. Frend, *The Rise of Christianity* (Philadelphia: Fortress, 1984).

4. Bengt Sundkler and Christopher Steed, *A History of the Church in Africa* (Cambridge University Press, 2000); Elizabeth Isichei, *A History of Christianity in Africa* (Grand Rapids, MI: Eerdmans, 1995).

5. W. H. C. Frend, *The Rise of the Monophysite Movement* (Cambridge University Press, 1972).

6. Nina G. Garsoïan, *Church and Culture in Early Medieval Armenia* (Brookfield: Ashgate, 1999); Adrian Fortescue, *The Lesser Eastern Churches* (London: Catholic Truth Society, 1913), 383–445.

7. The phrase about the Ark of the Covenant is from Adrian Hastings, *The Church in Africa, 1450–1950* (Oxford: Clarendon, 1996), 4. Taddesse Tamrat, *Church and State in Ethiopia, 1270–1527* (Oxford: Clarendon, 1972); Marilyn Eiseman Heldman, *African Zion* (New Haven: Yale University Press, 1993); Fortescue, *The Lesser Eastern Churches,* 293–321.

8. Hastings, *The Church in Africa, 1450–1950,* 3–45.

9. Sundkler and Steed, *A History of the Church in Africa,* 928; David B. Barrett, George T. Kurian, and Todd M. Johnson, *World Christian Encyclopedia,* 2nd ed. (Oxford University Press, 2001), 265–69.

10. William Dalrymple, *From the Holy Mountain* (New York: Henry Holt, 1997). Robert Brenton Betts, *Christians in the Arab East,* rev. ed. (Atlanta: John

Knox, 1978); Speros Vryonis, *The Decline of Medieval Hellenism in Asia Minor* (Berkeley: University of California Press, 1971).

11. The quote about the Alexandrian primates is from Kenneth Baxter Wolf, *Christian Martyrs in Muslim Spain* (Cambridge University Press, 1988); Jessica A. Coope, *The Martyrs of Córdoba* (Lincoln: University of Nebraska Press, 1995).

12. John H. Watson, *Among the Copts* (Portland, OR: Sussex Academic Press, 2000). For the Coptic language, see Hastings, *The Church in Africa, 1450–1950*, 7. Leonard Ralph Holme, *The Extinction of the Christian Churches in North Africa* (New York: B. Franklin, 1969: reprint of the 1898 edition); Fortescue, *The Lesser Eastern Churches*, 163–290. Barrett et al., *World Christian Encyclopedia*, 250, gives the present-day Christian population of Egypt as 15 percent, which seems high.

13. Dalrymple, *From the Holy Mountain*, 154; Tarek Mitri, "Who are the Christians of the Arab World?" *IRM* 89 (2000): 12–27; Andrea Pacini, ed., *Christian Communities in the Arab World* (Oxford University Press, 1998); Judith Miller, *God Has Ninety-Nine Names* (New York: Simon & Schuster 1996); Kenneth Cragg, *The Arab Christian* (Louisville, KY: Westminster John Knox, 1991); Robert M. Haddad, *Syrian Christians in Muslim Society* (Princeton University Press, 1970).

14. See the estimates of Christian numbers in Betts, *Christians in the Arab East*, 11. For the Jacobites, see Ian Gillman and Hans-Joachim Klimkeit, *Christians in Asia before 1500* (Ann Arbor: University of Michigan Press, 1999), 71. Fortescue, *The Lesser Eastern Churches*.

15. Dalrymple, *From the Holy Mountain*, 154; Benjamin Braude and Bernard Lewis, *Christians and Jews in the Ottoman Empire* (New York: Holmes & Meier, 1982). The *World Christian Encyclopedia* gives Syria's present Christian population as 7.8 percent of the whole (p. 719).

16. Gillman and Klimkeit, *Christians in Asia before 1500*; Samuel H. Moffett, *A History of Christianity in Asia*, 2nd rev. ed. (Maryknoll, NY: Orbis, 1998); Aubrey Russell Vine, *The Nestorian Churches* (New York: AMS, 1980); Fortescue, *The Lesser Eastern Churches*, 54–159.

17. Leslie Brown, *The Indian Christians of St. Thomas* (Cambridge University Press, 1982); Stephen Neill, *A History of Christianity in India: The Beginnings to AD 1707* (Cambridge University Press, 1984); Susan Visvanathan, *The Christians of Kerala* (Oxford University Press, 1993); Antony Kariyil, *Church and Society in Kerala* (New Delhi: Intercultural, 1995); Corinne G. Dempsey, *Kerala Christian Sainthood* (Oxford University Press, 2001). For Prester John, see Elaine Sanceau, *The Land of Prester John* (New York: Knopf, 1944). Undoubtedly, tales of the Ethiopian state also contributed to the legend.

18. David B. Barrett, George T. Kurian, and Todd M. Johnson, *World Christian Encyclopedia*, 2nd ed. (New York: Oxford University Press, 2001).

19. Laurence Edward Browne, *The Eclipse of Christianity in Asia* (Cambridge University Press, 1933); Christopher Dawson, *The Mongol Mission* (New York: Sheed and Ward, 1955); Bat Ye'or, *The Decline of Eastern Christianity under Islam*

(Madison, NJ: Fairleigh Dickinson University Press, 1996). For the 'Ayn Jalut campaign, see Peter Thorau, *The Lion of Egypt,* (London: Longman, 1992).

20. The quote about genocide is from Hastings, *Church in Africa, 1450–1950,* 137; compare 62–70. Frend, *The Rise of Christianity,* 847; Sundkler and Steed, *A History of the Church in Africa,* 73–75.

21. Stephen C. Neill, *A History of Christian Missions* (London: Penguin, 1964); John McManners, "The Expansion of Christianity 1500–1800," in John McManners, ed., *The Oxford History of Christianity* (Oxford University Press, 1993), 310–45.

22. Neill, *A History of Christian Missions,* 170; David Chidester, *Christianity: A Global History* (HarperSan Francisco, 2000), 365; Michael D. Coe, *Breaking the Maya Code,* rev. ed. (New York: Thames & Hudson, 1999); Nicholas Griffiths, *The Cross and the Serpent* (Norman: University of Oklahoma Press, 1996).

23. Lawrence Osborne, "The Numbers Game," *Lingua Franca,* September 1998, 49–58; David P. Henige, *Numbers from Nowhere* (Norman: University of Oklahoma Press, 1998); Nicholas Griffiths and Fernando Cervantes, eds., *Spiritual Encounters* (Lincoln: University of Nebraska Press, 1999).

24. Chidester, *Christianity,* 353–70; Neill, *A History of Christian Missions;* Enrique Dussel, ed., *The Church in Latin America 1492–1992* (Maryknoll, NY: Orbis, 1992); Erick Langer and Robert H. Jackson, eds., *The New Latin American Mission History* (Lincoln: University of Nebraska Press, 1995).

25. Neill, *A History of Christian Missions,* 168–76.

26. The remark about Mvemba Nzinga is from Sundkler and Steed, *A History of the Church in Africa,* 51; the Portuguese priest is quoted from Hastings, *The Church in Africa, 1450–1950,* 83.

27. "A literate elite": John K. Thornton, *The Kongolese Saint Anthony* (Cambridge University Press, 1998), 2.

28. Chidester, *Christianity,* 452–59; Neill, *A History of Christian Missions,* 183–87; idem, *A History of Christianity in India.*

29. Neill, *A History of Christian Missions,* 153–62; Andrew C. Ross, *A Vision Betrayed* (Maryknoll, NY: Orbis, 1994); Robert Lee, *The Clash of Civilizations* (Harrisburg, PA: Trinity Press International, 1999).

30. Chidester, *Christianity,* 434–51; Jonathan D. Spence, *The Memory Palace of Matteo Ricci* (New York: Viking, 1984).

31. The *Propaganda* is quoted in Neill, *A History of Christian Missions,* 179. Ralph Covell, *Confucius, the Buddha, and Christ* (Maryknoll, NY: Orbis, 1986).

32. The emperor is quoted in Lamin O. Sanneh, *West African Christianity* (Maryknoll, NY: Orbis, 1983), 35. George Minamiki, *The Chinese Rites Controversy* (Chicago: Loyola University Press, 1985); Ross, *A Vision Betrayed.*

33. For the origins of the mission movement, see Neill, *A History of Christian Missions,* 261–321; Kevin Ward, Brian Stanley, and Diana K. Witts, eds., *The Church Mission Society and World Christianity, 1799–1999* (Grand Rapids, MI: Eerdmans,

1999); John de Gruchy, ed., *The London Missionary Society in Southern Africa, 1799–1999* (Athens: Ohio University Press, 2000).

34. Throughout this section, I have used Sundkler and Steed, *A History of the Church in Africa*, and Hastings, *The Church in Africa, 1450–1950*. For Christianity in West Africa, see Lamin O. Sanneh, *Abolitionists Abroad* (Cambridge, MA: Harvard University Press, 2000), and idem, *West African Christianity*; J. Kofi Agbeti, *West African Church History*, 2 vols. (Leiden: E. J. Brill, 1986–91); and Peter B. Clarke, *West Africa and Christianity* (London: E. Arnold, 1986).

35. Hastings, *The Church in Africa, 1450–1950*, 385–87.

36. Elizabeth Isichei, *A History of Christianity in Africa* (Grand Rapids, MI: Eerdmans, 1995), 92.

37. Sundkler and Steed, *A History of the Church in Africa*; Joseph Dean O'Donnell, *Lavigerie in Tunisia* (Athens: University of Georgia Press, 1979).

38. Stephen C. Neill, *A History of Christian Missions*, rev. ed. (London: Penguin, 1990), 421.

39. Kevin Ward, "The Development of Anglicanism as a Global Communion," in Andrew Wingate, Kevin Ward, Carrie Pemberton, and Wilson Sitshebo, eds., *Anglicanism: A Global Communion* (New York: Church, 1998), 13–21.

40. F. M. P. Libermann, quoted in Sundkler and Steed, *A History of the Church in Africa*, 103.

41. Frederick Howard Taylor, *Hudson Taylor and the China Inland Mission* (Philadelphia: China Inland Mission, 1934).

42. Hastings, *The Church in Africa, 1450–1950*, 294.

43. For Quaque, see Neill, *A History of Christian Missions* (1964 edition), 239; Hastings, *The Church in Africa, 1450–1950*, 178–79. Crowther is discussed in Neill, *A History of Christian Missions*, 377–79; Sanneh, *West African Christianity*, 168–73; Hastings, *The Church in Africa, 1450–1950*, 338–93. For numbers of native clergy, see Sundkler and Steed, *A History of the Church in Africa*, 627.

44. Sundkler and Steed, *A History of the Church in Africa*, 627, 906.

45. Neill, *A History of Christian Missions*, rev. ed., 473.

CHAPTER 3

1. Robert W. Hefner, ed., *Conversion to Christianity* (Berkeley: University of California Press, 1993); Lewis R. Rambo, *Understanding Religious Conversion* (New Haven: Yale University Press, 1993).

2. *Christianity—The Second Millennium*, Broadcast on Arts and Entertainment Network, December 17–18, 2000.

3. The Gikuyu quote is from Adrian Hastings, *The Church in Africa, 1450–1950* (Oxford: Clarendon, 1996), 485. For the remark attributed to Archbishop Tutu, see, for instance, http://www.bemorecreative.com/one/1455.htm.

4. Chinua Achebe, *Arrow of God* (London: Heinemann, 1964), 105. The "leper"

quote is from p. 51. J. N. Kanyua Mugambi, ed., *Critiques of Christianity in African Literature* (Nairobi, Kenya: East African Educational Publishers, 1992).

5. Mongo Beti, *The Poor Christ of Bomba* (London: Heinemann, 1971), 189. Leslie Marmon Silko, *Almanac of the Dead* (New York: Simon & Schuster, 1991), 416–17.

6. Christopher Hitchens, *The Missionary Position* (New York: Verso, 1997).

7. Peter Mathiessen, *At Play in the Fields of the Lord* (1965; New York: Bantam, 1976); James A. Michener, *Hawaii* (New York: Random House, 1959); Brian Moore, *Black Robe* (New York: Dutton, 1985). As late as 1981, the reverential British film *Chariots of Fire* told the story of Eric Liddell, a man whose life was dedicated to the Chinese missions—although, significantly, the film says virtually nothing about the missionary career.

8. Barbara Kingsolver, *The Poisonwood Bible* (New York: HarperFlamingo, 1998), 13.

9. Ibid., 25–27.

10. Thomas C. Reeves, *The Empty Church* (New York: The Free Press, 1996), 13; Adrian Hastings, *A History of African Christianity, 1950–1975* (Cambridge University Press, 1979).

11. Sathianathan Clarke, *Dalits and Christianity* (Oxford India Paperbacks, 1999), 37–38.

12. Chinua Achebe, *Things Fall Apart* (1959; New York: Fawcett, 1969), 133; Cyril C. Okorocha, *The Meaning of Religious Conversion in Africa* (London: Avebury, 1987); Ogbu Kalu, *The Embattled Gods* (Lagos, Nigeria: Minaj, 1996).

13. Sundkler and Steed, *A History of the Church in Africa*, 470, 88–89.

14. Achebe, *Things Fall Apart*, 137.

15. For Madagascar, see Sundkler and Steed, *A History of the Church in Africa*, 491; Neill, *A History of Christian Missions*, 318.

16. Sundkler and Steed, *A History of the Church in Africa*, 562–93; Hastings, *The Church in Africa, 1450–1950*, 371–85, 464–75.

17. Neill, *A History of Christian Missions*, 415–18.

18. Ngugi wa Thiong'o, *The River Between* (London: Heinemann, 1965), 147. See Elizabeth Isichei, *A History of Christianity in Africa* (Grand Rapids, MI: Eerdmans, 1995), 244–46.

19. Jonathan D. Spence, *God's Chinese Son* (New York: Norton, 1996), 57.

20. Victoria Reifler Bricker, *The Indian Christ, the Indian King* (Austin: University of Texas Press, 1981); Michael Adas, *Prophets of Rebellion* (Chapel Hill: University of North Carolina Press, 1979). For European parallels, see Norman Cohn, *Pursuit of the Millennium*, 3rd ed. (London: Paladin, 1970).

21. Norman, *Christianity in the Southern Hemisphere*, 48–70. For the idea of a messianic role for the Latin American continent, see Thomas M. Cohen, *The Fire of Tongues* (Stanford University Press, 1998). Euclides Da Cunha, *Rebellion in the Backlands* (University of Chicago Press, 1944); Mario Vargas Llosa, *The War of the End of the World* (New York: Farrar, Straus and Giroux, 1984).

22. "The Children of Sandino," http://www.pagusmundi.com/sandino/children. htm#fn15.

23. Sundkler and Steed, *A History of the Church in Africa,* 59. The following account is mainly drawn from John K. Thornton, *The Kongolese Saint Anthony* (New York: Cambridge University Press, 1998).

24. David Chidester, *Christianity: A Global History* (HarperSan Francisco, 2000), 412–33.

25. Deji Ayegboyin and S. Ademola Ishola, *African Indigenous Churches* (Lagos, Nigeria: Greater Heights, 1997); James Amanze, *African Christianity in Botswana* (Gweru, Zimbabwe: Mambo, 1998).

26. Sanneh, *West African Christianity,* 123; Sundkler and Steed, *A History of the Church in Africa,* 198–99; Hastings, *The Church in Africa, 1450–1950,* 443–45, 505–7; Gordon M. Haliburton, *The Prophet Harris* (London: Longman, 1971); Sheila S. Walker, *The Religious Revolution in the Ivory Coast* (Chapel Hill: University of North Carolina Press, 1983).

27. "Let My People Go," television documentary in the *Sword and Spirit* series, made by BBC, 1989.

28. George Shepperson and Thomas Price, *Independent African,* 2nd ed. (Edinburgh University Press, 1987).

29. Hastings, *The Church in Africa, 1450–1950,* 508–35. The prayer is quoted from Sanneh, *West African Christianity,* 207. The Kimbanguist church now has an Internet presence at http://www.kimbanguisme.com/, which applies to the prophet the text of John 14:12.

30. Sundkler and Steed, *A History of the Church in Africa,* 98; Hastings, *The Church in Africa, 1450–1950,* 513–18; Isichei, *History of Christianity in Africa,* 279–83; Sanneh, *West African Christianity,* 168–209; Afe Adogame and Akin Omyajowo, "Anglicanism and the Aladura Churches in Nigeria," in Andrew Wingate, Kevin Ward, Carrie Pemberton, and Wilson Sitshebo, eds., *Anglicanism: A Global Communion* (New York: Church, 1998), 90–97; J. D. Y. Peel, *Aladura* (Oxford: Oxford University Press, 1968). For case-studies of these churches, see Harold W. Turner, *History of an African Independent Church* (Oxford: Clarendon, 1967); J. Akinyele Omoyajowo, *Cherubim and Seraphim* (New York: NOK Publishers International, 1982); Afeosemime U. Adogame, *Celestial Church of Christ* (New York: P. Lang, 1999). The Church of the Lord (Aladura) has a web site at http://www.aladura.de/.

31. Hastings, *The Church in Africa, 1450–1950,* 524–25. Her title is more fully Alice Lenshina Mulenga Mubisha. Isaac Phiri, "Why African Churches Preach Politics," *Journal of Church and State* 41 (1999): 323–47.

32. Harvey Cox, *Fire from Heaven* (Reading, MA: Addison-Wesley, 1995), 243–62; Andrew F. Walls, *The Missionary Movement in Christian History* (Maryknoll, NY: Orbis, 1996), 3–15.

33. Denis Basil M'Passou, *History of African Independent Churches in Southern Africa, 1892–1992* (Mulanje, Malawi: Spot, 1994); Lamin O. Sanneh, *Abolitionists*

Abroad (Harvard University Press, 2000); and idem, *West African Christianity,* 174.

34. Statement by Bishop B. E. Lekganyane at http://www.uct.ac.za/depts/ricsa/commiss/trc/zcc_stat.htm.

35. There is now a huge literature on the independent churches. See, for example, Gerhardus C. Oosthuizen, *Afro-Christian Religions* (Leiden: E. J. Brill, 1979); Marthinus L. Daneel, *Quest for Belonging* (Gweru, Zimbabwe: Mambo, 1987); Harvey J. Sindima, *Drums of Redemption* (Westport, CT: Greenwood, 1994); Ane Marie Bak Rasmussen, *Modern African Spirituality* (London: British Academic Press, 1996); M. C. Kitshoff, *African Independent Churches Today* (Lewiston, NY: Edwin Mellen, 1996); Amanze, *African Christianity in Botswana;* Thomas T. Spear and Isaria N. Kimambo, eds., *East African Expressions of Christianity* (Athens: Ohio University Press, 1999).

CHAPTER 4

1. Dana L. Robert, "Shifting Southward," *IBMR* 24, no. 2 (2000): 50–58.

2. The quote about "organs and sinew" is from ibid. Adrian Hastings, *A History of African Christianity, 1950–1975* (Cambridge University Press, 1979). The quote about "Black Africa today" is from Adrian Hastings, "Christianity in Africa," in Ursula King, ed., *Turning Points in Religious Studies* (Edinburgh: T & T Clark, 1990), 208. See also Bengt Sundkler and Christopher Steed, *A History of the Church in Africa (*Cambridge University Press, 2000), 906; Kwame Bediako, "Africa and Christianity on the Threshold of the Third Millennium," *African Affairs* 99 (2000): 303–23; David B. Barrett, George T. Kurian, and Todd M. Johnson, *World Christian Encyclopedia,* 2nd ed. (Oxford University Press, 2001), 5; Edward Fasholé-Luke et al., eds., *Christianity in Independent Africa* (Bloomington: Indiana University Press, 1978). For the contemporary religious situation in individual countries, I have used the U.S. government's *Annual Reports on International Religious Freedom,* online at http://www.state.gov/www/global/human_rights/irf/irf_rpt/irf_index.html.

3. Kenneth Woodward, "The Changing Face of the Church," *Newsweek,* April 16, 2001.

4. Thomas Hobbes, *Leviathan* (1651), chapter 47; David Martin, *Tongues of Fire* (Oxford: B. Blackwell, 1990), 4.

5. *The Official Catholic Directory,* 1999.

6. Frieder Ludwig, *Church and State in Tanzania* (Leiden, E. J. Brill Academic, 1999), 177–79; Barrett et al., *World Christian Encyclopedia,* 12, 729; Adrian Hastings, *African Catholicism* (London: SCM, 1989); Thomas D. Blakely, Dennis L. Thomson, and Walter E. Van Beek, eds., *Religion in Africa* (London: Heinemann, 1994).

7. Woodward, "The Changing Face of the Church."

8. Adrian Hastings, *African Christianity* (New York: Seabury, 1976); Barrett et

al., *World Christian Encyclopedia,* 4; Andrew Wingate, Kevin Ward, Carrie Pemberton, and Wilson Sitshebo, eds., *Anglicanism: A Global Communion* (New York: Church, 1998); Ian T. Douglas and Pui-Lan Kwok, eds., *Beyond Colonial Anglicanism* (New York: Church, 2001). For the three British-derived faiths in one country, see Akinyele Omoyajowo, ed., *The Anglican Church in Nigeria (1842–1992)* (Lagos: Macmillan Nigeria, 1994); Ogbu U. Kalu, ed., *A Century and a Half of Presbyterian Witness in Nigeria, 1846–1996* (Lagos: Ida-Ivory, 1996); M. M. Familusi, *Methodism in Nigeria, 1842–1992* (Ibadan: NPS Educational Publishers, 1992); Elizabeth Isichei, ed., *Varieties of Christian Experience in Nigeria* (London: Macmillan, 1982).

9. Paul Gifford, *African Christianity: Its Public Role* (Bloomington: Indiana University Press, 1998), 112–80.

10. For the *balokole,* see Hastings, *The Church in Africa, 1450–1950,* 596–600, 608; Elizabeth Isichei, *A History of Christianity in Africa* (Grand Rapids, MI: Eerdmans, 1995), 241–44; Amos Kasibante, "Beyond Revival," in Wingate et al., eds., *Anglicanism: A Global Communion,* 363–68; Allan Anderson, "African Anglicans and/or Pentecostals," in ibid., 34–40; Frieder, *Church and State in Tanzania,* 181–91. For West African parallels, see Afe Adogame and Akin Omyajowo, "Anglicanism and the Aladura Churches in Nigeria," in Wingate et al., eds., *Anglicanism: A Global Communion,* 90–97.

11. Samuel P. Huntington, *The Clash of Civilizations and the Remaking of World Order* (New York: Simon & Schuster, 1996), 96–99.

12. For Guatemala, see Virginia Garrard-Burnett, *Protestantism in Guatemala* (Austin: University of Texas Press, 1998); Amy L. Sherman, *The Soul of Development* (New York: Oxford University Press, 1997); Everett Wilson, "Guatemalan Pentecostals," in Edward L. Cleary and Hannah W. Stewart-Gambino, eds., *Power, Politics, and Pentecostals in Latin America* (Boulder, CO: Westview, 1997), 139–62. For the continuing debate over the size of the evangelical population in different countries, see Edward L. Cleary and Juan Sepúlveda, "Chilean Pentecostalism," in Cleary and Stewart-Gambino, eds., *Power, Politics, and Pentecostals,* 106. Anne Motley Hallum, *Beyond Missionaries* (Lanham, MD: Rowman & Littlefield, 1996).

13. Estimating numbers for any of these denominations is extremely difficult, so my figures for Brazil represent a consensus of several sources: this figure is significantly lower than that proposed by the *World Christian Encyclopedia,* 131. For Pentecostalism elsewhere in Latin America, see, for instance, Daniel Míguez, *To Help You Find God* (Amsterdam: Free University of Amsterdam, 1997); Cornelia Butler Flora, *Pentecostalism in Colombia* (Rutherford, NJ: Fairleigh Dickinson University Press, 1976).

14. David Stoll, *Is Latin America Turning Protestant?* (Berkeley: University of California Press, 1990); Martin, *Tongues of Fire;* Virginia Garrard-Burnett and David Stoll, eds., *Rethinking Protestantism in Latin America* (Philadelphia: Temple University Press, 1993); Guillermo Cook, ed., *New Face of the Church in Latin America* (Maryknoll, NY: Orbis, 1994); Barbara Boudewijnse et al., eds., *More*

than Opium (Lanham, MD: Scarecrow, 1998); Karl-Wilhelm Westmeier, *Protestant Pentecostalism in Latin America* (Madison, NJ: Fairleigh Dickinson University Press/ Associated University Presses, 1999); Christian Smith and Joshua Prokopy, eds., *Latin American Religion in Motion* (New York: Routledge, 1999).

15. For the debate on Latin American religious statistics, see Virginia Garrard-Burnett, "Trustworthy Statistics?" at http://www.providence.edu/las/Trustworthy %20Statistics.htm#Virginia; and David Smilde "What Do the Numbers Mean?" at http://www.providence.edu/las/Trustworthy%20Statistics.htm#David Smilde. The web site http://www.providence.edu/las/ offers rich resources for Latin American religion in general.

16. Edward R. Norman, *Christianity in the Southern Hemisphere* (Oxford University Press, 1981); Martin, *Tongues of Fire,* 93–98; Kurt Derek Bowen, *Evangelism and Apostasy* (Montreal: McGill-Queen's University Press, 1996); Michael J. Mazarr, *Mexico 2005* (Washington, DC: CSIS, 1999).

17. Karla Poewe, ed., *Charismatic Christianity as a Global Culture* (Columbia: University of South Carolina Press, 1994); Harvey Cox, *Fire from Heaven* (Reading, MA: Addison-Wesley, 1995), 161–84; Steve Brouwer, Paul Gifford, and Susan D. Rose, *Exporting the American Gospel* (New York: Routledge, 1996); Ian Cotton, *The Hallelujah Revolution* (Amherst, NY: Prometheus, 1996); "Pentecostals: World Growth at 19 Million a Year," *CT,* November 16, 1998; Allan H. Anderson and Walter J. Hollenweger, eds., *Pentecostals after a Century* (Sheffield: Sheffield Academic, 1999); Richard Shaull and Waldo A. Cesar, *Pentecostalism and the Future of the Christian Churches* (Grand Rapids, MI: Eerdmans, 2000); Simon Coleman, *The Globalisation of Charismatic Christianity* (Cambridge University Press, 2000); André Corten and Ruth Marshall-Fratani, eds., *Between Babel and Pentecost* (Bloomington: Indiana University Press, 2001); David Martin, *Pentecostalism: The World Their Parish* (Oxford: Blackwell, 2001).

18. For attempts to reconcile the two movements, see, for instance, Kenneth MacHarg, "Word and Spirit," *CT,* posted to web site October 2, 2000.

19. Edward L. Cleary, in Cleary and Stewart-Gambino, eds., *Power, Politics, and Pentecostals,* 4; Martin, *Tongues of Fire,* 143; Edith L. Blumhofer, *Restoring the Faith* (Urbana: University of Illinois Press, 1993). For the appeal of Pentecostalism, see Diane J. Austin-Broos and Raymond T. Smith, *Jamaica Genesis* (University of Chicago Press, 1997). For the Jotabeche Methodist Pentecostal church, see http://www.jotabeche.cl/historia.htm.

20. For Brazil, see R. Andrew Chesnut, *Born Again in Brazil* (New Brunswick, NJ: Rutgers University, 1997); David Lehmann, *Struggle for the Spirit* (London: Polity Press/ Blackwell, 1996); Paul Freston, "Brother Votes for Brother," in Garrard-Burnett and Stoll, eds., *Rethinking Protestantism in Latin America,* 68; Paul Freston, "Evangelicalism and Politics," *Transformation* 14 (1997): 23–29; Emilio Willems, *Followers of the New Faith* (Nashville: Vanderbilt University Press, 1967). André Corten, *Pentecostalism in Brazil* (New York: St. Martin's, 1999).

21. For the "52 largest denominations," see Freston, "Evangelicalism and Poli-

tics," 23; Cox, *Fire from Heaven*, 167; Kenneth D. MacHarg, "Brazil's Surging Spirituality," *CT*, December 21, 2000.

22. Chesnut, *Born Again in Brazil*, 45–48; Patricia Birman and Marcia Pereira Leite, "Whatever Happened to What Used to Be the Largest Catholic Country in the World?" *Daedalus* 129 (Spring 2000): 271–90; Stephen Buckley, "'Prosperity Theology' Pulls on Purse Strings," *WP*, February 13, 2001.

23. http://www.igrejauniversal.org.br/. Jeevan Vasagar and Alex Bellos, "Brazilian Sect Buys London Radio Station," *Guardian* (London), August 3, 2000; Maria Alvarez, Laura Italiano, and Luiz C. Ribeiro, "Holy-roller Church Cashes in on Faithful," *New York Post*, July 23, 2000; Laura Italiano and Maria Alvarez, "Ex Member Bids Farewell to COG—and Her Faith," in idem, July 23, 2000; Jeevan Vasagar, "The Death of Anna Climbie," *Guardian*, January 13, 2001; Ken Serbin, "Brazilian Church Builds an International Empire," *CC*, April 10, 1996; Elma Lia Nascimento, "Praise the Lord and Pass the Catch-Up," *Brazzil* magazine, November 1995, at http://www.brazzil.com/cvrnov95.htm.

24. In the U.S. context, the largest ecclesiastical fraud case of the past decade or so was probably that involving Henry Lyons, president of the National Baptist Convention USA. For sexual abuse cases, see Philip Jenkins, *Pedophiles and Priests* (New York: Oxford University Press, 1996).

25. Richard N. Ostling and Joan K. Ostling, *Mormon America* (HarperSan Francisco, 1999).

26. Penny Lernoux, *Cry of the People* (New York: Penguin, 1982); Warren E. Hewitt, *Base Christian Communities and Social Change in Brazil* (Lincoln: University of Nebraska Press, 1991); Cecília Loreto Mariz, *Coping with Poverty* (Philadelphia: Temple University Press, 1994); Madeleine Adriance, *Promised Land* (Albany: State University of New York Press, 1995).

27. http://www.chanrobles.com/elshaddai.htm; Stella O. Gonzales, "Bishops Start Move to Rein in Bro. Mike," *Philippine Daily Inquirer*, September 14, 1999; James Hookway, "In the Philippines, Two Famed Preachers Mix Church, State," *WSJ*, April 11, 2001.

28. For Tanzania, see Ludwig, *Church and State in Tanzania*, 182; Cox, *Fire from Heaven*, 249, 246; Ruth Marshall, "God is not a Democrat," in Paul Gifford, ed., *The Christian Churches and the Democratisation of Africa* (Leiden: E. J. Brill, 1995), 239–60; Paul Gifford, *African Christianity* (Bloomington: Indiana University Press, 1998), 33–39; Allan H. Anderson and Sam Otwang, *Tumelo: The Faith of African Pentecostals in South Africa* (Pretoria: University of South Africa, 1993); Allan H. Anderson, *African Reformation* (Trenton, NJ: Africa World Press, 2001).

29. Richard Elphick and Rodney Davenport, eds., *Christianity in South Africa* (Berkeley: University of California Press, 1998); Martin Prozesky and John De Gruchy, eds., *Living Faiths in South Africa* (New York: Palgrave, 1995). For the emergence of the new sects, see David B. Barrett, *Schism and Renewal in Africa* (Nairobi: Oxford University Press, 1968).

30. Bill Keller, "A Surprising Silent Majority in South Africa," *NYT Magazine*,

April 17, 1994; *Man, God, and Africa,* television documentary made by Channel 4 (UK), 1994; Tangeni Amupadhi, "At Zion City, You Pray—and Pay," *Electronic Mail and Guardian* (South Africa), April 8, 1997; Thokozani Mtshali, "Shembe—The Incredible Whiteness of Being," *Electronic Mail and Guardian,* August 11, 1999, http://www.mg.co.za/mg/news/99aug1/11aug-shembe.html.

31. James Amanze, *African Christianity in Botswana* (Gweru, Zimbabwe: Mambo, 1998).

32. Dickson Kazuo Yagi, "Christ for Asia," *Review and Expositor* 88, no. 4 (1991): 375.

33. Archie R. Crouch, Steven Agoratus, Arthur Emerson, Debra E. Soled, and John King Fairbank, *Christianity in China* (Armonk, NY: M. E. Sharpe, 1989); Edmond Tang and Jean-Paul Wiest, eds., *The Catholic Church in Modern China* (Maryknoll, NY: Orbis, 1993); Alan Hunter and Kim-Kwong Chan, *Protestantism in Contemporary China* (Cambridge University Press, 1993); Daniel H. Bays, ed., *Christianity in China from the Eighteenth Century to the Present* (Stanford University Press, 1996); Richard Madsen, *China's Catholics* (Berkeley: University of California Press, 1998); Timothy C. Morgan, "A Tale of China's Two Churches," *CT,* July 13, 1998, 30–39; Stephen Uhalley and Xiaoxin Wu, eds., *China and Christianity* (M. E. Sharpe, 2000). The possibility of such vast crypto-Christian populations in China obviously excites evangelical writers. See, for instance, Ralph Covell, *The Liberating Gospel in China* (Grand Rapids, MI: Baker Book House, 1995); Tony Lambert, Ross Paterson, and David Pickard, *China's Christian Millions* (London: Monarch, 1999). For State Department figures, see http://www.state.gov/www/global/human_rights/irf/irf_rpt/irf_china.html.

34. Limin Bao, "The Intellectual influence of Christianity in a Changing Maoist Society," *Theology Today* 55 (1999): 532–46; Jon Sawyer, "Spirituality Deepens in China as Communist Party's Role Weakens," *St. Louis Post-Dispatch,* May 25, 2000; Arthur Waldron, "Religion and the Chinese State," in Mark Silk, ed., *Religion on the International News Agenda* (Hartford, CT: Leonard F. Greenberg Center for the Study of Religion in Public Life, 2000), 19–36, at 30.

35. Kenneth Ballhatchet and Helen Ballhatchet, "Asia," in McManners, ed., *The Oxford History of Christianity* (Oxford University Press, 1993), 508–38; Alkman Granitsas, "Back to the Fold," *FEER,* October 12, 2000.

36. Donald N. Clark, *Christianity in Modern Korea* (Lanham, MD: University Press of America, 1986); Wi Jo Kang, *Christ and Caesar in Modern Korea* (Albany: State University of New York Press, 1997); David Chung, *Syncretism: The Religious Context of Christian Beginnings in Korea* (Albany: State University of New York Press, 2001); Cox, *Fire from Heaven,* 213–42; Huntingdon, *Clash of Civilizations,* 96–99.

37. Martin, *Tongues of Fire,* 143–46; Gayle White, "Flourishing Churches in Africa, Asia and Latin America," *Atlanta Journal/Constitution,* December 26, 1999; "Tongues of Fire," television documentary in the *Sword and Spirit* series, made by the BBC, 1989.

38. Murray Hiebert, "Secrets of Repression," *FEER,* November 16, 2000, 34–36; "Large-scale Rural Unrest in Vietnam's Highlands," *Times of India,* March 28, 2001; "Christians Targeted in Vietnam's Highlands," *CT,* posted to web site June 26, 2001.

39. The phrase "post-industrial wanderers" is from Cox, *Fire from Heaven,* 107. For the modern diasporic worlds of international migrants, refugees, and nomads, see Mark Fritz, *Lost on Earth* (New York: Routledge, 2000); Robin Cohen, *Global Diasporas* (Seattle: University of Washington Press, 1997). For the heavy Pentecostal involvement in social ministries, see, for instance, Teresa Watanabe, "Global Convention Testifies to Pentecostalism's Revival," *LAT,* May 31, 2001.

40. Phillip Berryman, *Religion in the Megacity* (Maryknoll, NY: Orbis, 1996).

41. Corrie Cutrer, "Bonnke Returns to Nigeria Year After Tragedy," *CT,* posted to web site November 8, 2000; idem, "Looking for a Miracle," *CT,* posted November 14, 2000; idem, "Come and Receive Your Miracle," *CT,* posted February 2, 2001.

42. Cox, *Fire from Heaven,* 15; Rebecca Pierce Bomann, *Faith in the Barrios* (Boulder, CO: L. Rienner, 1999), 32.

43. Martin is quoted from *Tongues of Fire,* 230.

44. Hannah W. Stewart-Gambino and Everett Wilson, "Latin American Pentecostals," in Cleary and Stewart-Gambino, eds., *Power, Politics, and Pentecostals,* 227–46; Chesnut, *Born Again in Brazil,* 104.

45. John Burdick, *Blessed Anastácia* (New York: Routledge, 1998).

46. Though see John Burdick, "What is the Color of the Holy Spirit?" *Latin American Research Review* 34 (1999): 109–31

47. Joseph M. Murphy, *Working the Spirit* (Boston: Beacon, 1994).

48. Carol Ann Drogus, "Private Power or Public Power," in Cleary and Stewart-Gambino, eds., *Power, Politics, and Pentecostals,* 55–75: quotes are from 55, 57; Martin, *Tongues of Fire,* 181–84; Chesnut, *Born Again in Brazil;* Elizabeth E. Brusco, *The Reformation of Machismo* (Austin: University of Texas Press, 1995). Some scholars take a far less optimistic view of the impact of the new churches on women's lives. See Cecília Loreto Mariz and Maria das Dores Campos Machado, "Pentecostalism and Women in Brazil," in Cleary and Stewart-Gambino, eds., *Power, Politics, and Pentecostals,* 41–54; Martin Riesebrodt and Kelly H. Chong, "Fundamentalisms and Patriarchal Gender Politics," *Journal of Women's History* 10 (1999).

49. Drogus, "Private Power or Public Power," 62. Compare Carol Ann Drogus, *Women, Religion and Social Change in Brazil's Popular Church* (University of Notre Dame Press, 1997).

50. Peter Brown, *The World of Late Antiquity* (London: Thames and Hudson, 1971), 67–68.

51. See, for instance, E. P. Thomson, *The Making of the English Working Class* (New York: Vintage, 1963). In a very different economic setting, there are obvious American parallels: see, for example, Christine Leigh Heyrman, *Southern Cross* (New York: Knopf, 1997).

52. Bomann, *Faith in the Barrios,* 40–41.

53. "Their main appeal": quoted in Ed Gitre, "Pie-in-the-Sky Now," *CT,* posted to web site November 27, 2000; MacHarg, "Brazil's Surging Spirituality"; the Pentecostal pastor is quoted from John Burdick, "Struggling against the Devil," in Garrard-Burnett and Stoll, eds., *Rethinking Protestantism in Latin America,* 23.

54. Chesnut, *Born Again in Brazil,* 51. See chapter 6 below.

55. Wole Soyinka, *Three Short Plays* (Oxford University Press, 1974); Simon Coleman, *The Globalisation of Charismatic Christianity* (Cambridge University Press, 2000); Stephen Buckley, "'Prosperity Theology' Pulls on Purse Strings," *WP,* February 13, 2001.

CHAPTER 5

1. *The World at Six Billion* (Population Division, Department of Economic and Social Affairs, United Nations, 1999); John Bongaarts and Rodolfo A. Bulatao, eds., *Beyond Six Billion* (Washington, DC: National Academy Press, 2000). For shifting population balances by continent, see http://www.undp.org/popin/wdtrends/6billion/t02.htm. As noted earlier, U.S. government figures on individual countries are drawn from Bureau of the Census, International Database, online at http://www.census.gov/ipc/www/idbrank.html. These are somewhat different from the projections employed by the United Nations, although the rank orderings are roughly the same: see http://www.popin.org/pop1998/.

2. Nicholas D. Kristof, "Empty Isles Are Signs Japan's Sun Might Dim," *NYT,* August 1, 1999; W. W. Rostow, *The Great Population Spike and After* (Oxford University Press, 1998).

3. Michael S. Teitelbaum and Jay Winter, *A Question of Numbers* (New York: Hill & Wang, 1998). The eight largest European nations referred to are Russia, Germany, Britain, France, Italy, Ukraine, Poland, and Spain.

4. Michael Wines, "An Ailing Russia Lives a Tough Life That's Getting Shorter," *NYT,* December 3, 2000; Michael S. Gottlieb, "The Future of an Epidemic," *NYT,* June 5, 2001.

5. Michael J. Mazarr, *Global Trends 2005* (New York: St. Martin's, 1999), 25.

6. Ibid., 33. UN figures can be found at http://www.undp.org/popin/wdtrends/6billion/t24.htm. Information about the demographics of individual countries can be found in the *CIA World Fact Book,* online at http://www.odci.gov/cia/publications/factbook/. The names of some African nations have changed in recent decades, causing confusion to outside observers. For present purposes, the most important case is the Democratic Republic of the Congo, which will repeatedly be referred to in this book. The Democratic Republic is a populous and potentially important nation with a large Christian population, and its capital, Kinshasa, is one of Africa's largest cities. From 1908 to 1960, this territory was the Belgian Congo. After independence it changed its name on a number of occasions. It was Zaire from 1971 to 1997, at which point it received its present "Democratic Republic" name.

Adding to an already complex situation is the presence of a neighboring and far smaller country known as the Republic of Congo, with its capital at Brazzaville. This nation is made up of former French territories, and the territory has variously been known as the French Congo and Congo-Brazzaville.

7. Richard N. Ostling and Joan K. Ostling, *Mormon America* (HarperSan Francisco, 1999).

8. See chapter 1 above for a caveat about interpreting figures for countries in which Christianity is officially disapproved, like India or China.

9. The figures offered here are lower than those found in the *World Christian Encyclopedia,* in some cases very much so. In its projections for the year 2025, for instance, this work suggests Christian populations of 135 million for China and 98 million for India; the figures for 2050 would be correspondingly higher. Both countries would therefore rank about the world's top four or five Christian nations by mid-century. These statistics might be reliable, but they are far out of line with other estimates, and therefore I am not using them here. I may be overly cautious in this.

10. See the *Annual Report on Religious Freedom* on Uganda at http://www.state.gov/www/global/human_rights/irf/irf_rpt/irf_uganda.html; David B. Barrett, George T. Kurian, and Todd M. Johnson, *World Christian Encyclopedia,* 2nd ed. (Oxford University Press, 2001), 762.

11. Barrett et al., *World Christian Encyclopedia,* 594–601.

12. *The Official Catholic Directory,* 1999. For the thorough permeation of Filipino life and culture by vernacular Christianity, see Fenella Cannell, *Power and Intimacy in the Christian Philippines* (Cambridge University Press, 1999).

13. Hernando De Soto, *The Mystery of Capital* (New York: Basic, 2000).

14. Stephen Bates, "Decline in Churchgoing Hits C of E Hardest," *Guardian,* April 14, 2001; Grace Davie, *Religion in Britain Since 1945* (Oxford: Blackwell, 1994); Adrian Hastings, *A History of English Christianity, 1920–1990,* 3rd ed. (London: SCM, 1991).

15. "UK is 'Losing' its Religion," BBC World News, November 28, 2000; "Blair Warned over Wooing 'Religious'," BBC World News, March 25, 2001.

16. *Annual Report on Religious Freedom,* online at http://www.state.gov/www/global/human_rights/irf/irf_rpt/irf_germany.html; John L. Allen, "Vatican Laments Weakness in German Church," *NCR,* March 30, 2001; http://www.state.gov/www/global/human_rights/irf/irf_rpt/irf_germany.html. For the current state of the Evangelical Church and its views on contemporary issues, see the materials at its web site, http://www.ekd.de/.

17. Grace Davie, *Religion in Modern Europe* (Oxford: Oxford University Press, 2000); Sandy Tippett-Spirtou, *French Catholicism* (New York: St. Martin's, 1999); Audrey Brassloff, *Religion and Politics in Spain* (New York: St. Martin's, 1998).

18. Barrett et al., *World Christian Encyclopedia,* 4.

19. Anthony Browne, "UK Whites Will Be Minority by 2100," *Guardian,* September 3, 2000.

20. Roger Cohen, "Germany's Uneasy Debate on Immigration Deepens," *NYT,*

May 13, 2001; Ian Black, "Europe 'Should Accept' 75m New Migrants," *Guardian,* July 28, 2000; Barbara Crossette, "Europe Stares at a Future Built by Immigrants," *NYT,* January 2, 2000; "Global Trends 2015," online at http://www.cia.gov/cia/publications/globaltrends2015/.

21. "Global Trends 2015."

22. Christopher Caldwell, "Another French Revolution," *Atlantic Monthly,* November 2000, online at http://www.theatlantic.com/issues/2000/11/caldwell.htm; Roger Cohen, "Germany's Financial Heart Is Open but Wary," *NYT,* December 30, 2000; Roger Cohen, "Austrian School Drama," *NYT,* March 20, 2001. See also Stephen Castles, Heather Booth, and Tina Wallace, *Here for Good* (London: Pluto, 1984); John L. Allen, "Europe's Muslims Worry Bishops," *NCR,* October 22, 1999.

23. Joseph Mudimba Kabongo, "African Churches in Switzerland," *IRM.* 89 (2000): 457–58.

24. Emily Buchanan, "Black Church Celebrates Growth," BBC World Service, July 6, 2000; Jeevan Vasagar, "The Death of Anna Climbie," *Guardian,* January 13, 2001. For the Kingsway Centre, see Victoria Combe, "Black Church in Crusade to Woo Whites," *Electronic Telegraph,* February 16, 2001; Sarah Hall, "Praise Be, It's the Superchurch," *Guardian,* August 24, 1998. The Centre is online at http://www.kicc.org.uk/. For the worship styles of Caribbean religion, see Diane J. Austin-Broos and Raymond T. Smith, *Jamaica Genesis* (University of Chicago Press, 1997); Stephen D. Glazier, ed., *Perspectives on Pentecostalism* (Washington, DC: University Press of America, 1980).

25. Ingrid Peritz, "Quebeckers Crowd Pews But Once a Year," *Globe and Mail* (Canada), December 23, 2000.

26. Corey Takahashi, "Selling to Gen Y," *NYT,* April 8, 2001.

27. Helen R. F. Ebaugh and Janet Saltzman Chafetz, eds., *Religion and the New Immigrants* (Walnut Creek, CA: Altamira, 2000), 29. Mike Davis, *Magical Urbanism* (London: Verso, 2000).

28. Diego Ribadeneira, "The Changing Face of Worship," *Boston Globe,* March 22, 1998. Cindy Rodriguez, "Immigrants Reshaping Black Experience." *Boston Globe,* August 15, 2001. For the kaleidoscopic religious diversity of New York City, see Tony Carnes and Anna Karpathakis, eds., *New York Glory* (New York University Press, 2001).

29. The figure of 3,500 parishes is quoted in Ebaugh and Chafetz, eds., *Religion and the New Immigrants,* 14; Peter Casarella and Raul Gomez, eds., *El Cuerpo de Cristo* (New York: Crossroad, 1998); Timothy Matovina and Gerald Eugene Poyo, eds., *Presente!* (Maryknoll, NY: Orbis, 2000); Ana María Díaz-Stevens and Anthony M. Stevens-Arroyo, *Recognizing the Latino Resurgence in U.S. Religion* (Boulder, CO: Westview, 1998).

30. William Lobdell, "Latino Exodus From Catholic Church Rising, Study Says," *LAT,* May 5, 2001; idem, "Building Respect for Latino Protestantism," *LAT,* June 16, 2001; Hispanic Churches in American Public Life Project, http://www.hcapl.org/; Anna Adams, "*Bricando el Charco:* Jumping the Puddle," in Edward L.

Cleary and Hannah W. Stewart-Gambino, eds., *Power, Politics, and Pentecostals in Latin America* (Boulder, CO: Westview, 1997), 163–78; R. Stephen Warner and Judith G. Wittner, eds., *Gatherings in Diaspora* (Philadelphia: Temple University Press, 1998); Richard W. Flory and Donald E. Miller, eds., *Gen X Religion* (New York: Routledge, 2001). For an example of a U.S. Catholic church adapting Pentecostal worship styles, see David Cho, "Hispanic Priest Builds a Spirited Following," *WP*, June 28, 2001.

31. Fenggang Yang, *Chinese Christians in America* (University Park: Pennsylvania State University Press, 1999); Fenggang Yang, "Chinese Conversion to Evangelical Christianity," *Sociology of Religion* 59 (1998): 237–57; Jeffrey M. Burns, Ellen Skerrett, and Joseph M. White, eds., *Keeping Faith* (Maryknoll, NY: Orbis, 2000); Ebaugh and Chafetz, eds., *Religion and the New Immigrants*.

32. This section is based on Ho Youn Kwon, Kwang Chung Kim, and R. Stephen Warner, eds., *Korean Americans and Their Religions* (University Park: Pennsylvania State University Press, 2001). For growth in one region, see Sajan P. Kuriakos, "The Growth of Korean Churches in Flushing Sparks Community Tensions," *Village Voice*, February 14–20, 2001.

33. Stephen L. Carter, *God's Name in Vain* (New York: Basic, 2000).

34. This is the subtitle of Diana L. Eck's *A New Religious America* (HarperSan Francisco, 2001).

35. Sameer Y. Abraham and Nabeel Abraham, eds., *Arabs in the New World* (Detroit, MI: Wayne State University Press, 1983); Gustav Niebuhr, "Study Finds Number of Mosques Up 25% in 6 Years," *NYT*, April 27, 2001.

CHAPTER 6

1. Ndubisi Innocent Udeafor, *Inculturation* (Lustenau, Austria: Ndubisi Innocent Udeafor, 1994); Emefie Ikenga Metuh, *African Inculturation Theology* (Onitsha, Nigeria: Imico, 1996); J. N. K. Mugambi, "A Fresh Look at Evangelism in Africa," *IRM* 87 (1998): 342–60; Diego Irarràzaval, *Inculturation* (Maryknoll, NY: Orbis, 2000); Andrew F. Walls, *The Cross-Cultural Process in Christian History* (Maryknoll, NY: Orbis, 2001); Steven Kaplan, ed., *Indigenous Responses to Western Christianity* (New York University Press, 1995).

2. "In Black Africa, rhythm is supreme and is everywhere." François Kabasele Lumbala, *Celebrating Jesus Christ in Africa* (Maryknoll, NY: Orbis, 1998), 24.

3. Eugene Hillman, *Polygamy Reconsidered* (Maryknoll, NY: Orbis, 1975); Adrian Hastings, *The Church in Africa, 1450–1950* (Oxford: Clarendon 1996), 318–25; Jeff Guy, *The Heretic* (Johannesburg/ Pietermaritzburg: University of Natal Press, 1983).

4. The quote is from G. C. Waldrep, "The Expansion of Christianity: An Interview with Andrew Walls," *CC*, August 2–August 9, 2000, 792–95; Andrew F. Walls, *The Missionary Movement in Christian History* (Maryknoll, NY: Orbis, 1996), 102–10.

5. For Walls' personal encounters with these issues, see Andrew F. Walls, *The Missionary Movement*, 3–15.

6. Peter Brown, *Authority and the Sacred* (Cambridge University Press, 1997), and idem, *Society and the Holy in Late Antiquity* (Berkeley: University of California Press, 1989); Ramsay MacMullen, *Christianizing the Roman Empire A.D. 100–400* (New Haven: Yale University Press, 1986) and *Christianity and Paganism in the Fourth to Eighth Centuries* (New Haven: Yale University Press, 1999); Averil Cameron, *Christianity and the Rhetoric of Empire* (Berkeley: University of California Press, 1994).

7. Richard Fletcher, *The Barbarian Conversion* (Berkeley, CA: University of California Press, 1999); James C. Russell, *The Germanization of Early Medieval Christianity* (Oxford University Press, 1996); R. A. Markus, *The End of Ancient Christianity* (Cambridge University Press, 1991).

8. Bede, *History of the English Church and People*, I, 30.

9. Gary H. Gossen and Miguel León-Portilla, eds., *South and Meso-American Native Spirituality* (New York: Crossroad, 1993); Ana Castillo, *Goddess of the Americas* (New York: Riverhead, 1996); Manuel M. Marzal et al., *The Indian Face of God in Latin America* (Maryknoll, NY: Orbis, 1996); Guillermo Cook, *Crosscurrents in Indigenous Spirituality* (Leiden: E. J. Brill, 1997); Thomas A. Tweed, *Our Lady of the Exile* (New York: Oxford University Press, 1997); Nicholas Griffiths and Fernando Cervantes, eds., *Spiritual Encounters* (Lincoln: University of Nebraska Press, 1999); David Brading, *Mexican Phoenix* (Cambridge University Press, 2001).

10. Daniel Johnson Fleming, *Each with His Own Brush* (New York: Friendship, 1938); William A. Dyrness, *Christian Art in Asia* (Amsterdam: Rodopi, 1979); Arno Lehmann, *Christian Art in Africa and Asia* (Saint Louis, MO: Concordia, 1969); *Christian Imagery in African Art* (Notre Dame, IN: University of Notre Dame, The Museum, 1980). Volker Küster, *The Many Faces of Jesus Christ* (Maryknoll, NY: Orbis, 2001).

11. Lamin Sanneh, "Pluralism and Christian Commitment," *Theology Today* 45, no. 1 (1988): 27; idem, *Translating the Message* (Maryknoll, NY: Orbis, 1989). Compare Ngugi wa Thiong'o, *Decolonising the Mind* (London: Heinemann, 1986).

12. Lumbala, *Celebrating Jesus Christ in Africa*, 113.

13. Quoted in Kwame Bediako, *Christianity in Africa* (Edinburgh University Press/Orbis, 1995), 59.

14. Quoted in Elizabeth Isichei, *A History of Christianity in Africa* (Grand Rapids, MI: Eerdmans, 1995), 315; Hastings, *The Church in Africa, 1450–1950*, 502–3; G. C. Oosthuizen, *The Theology of a South African Messiah* (Leiden: E. J. Brill, 1967); Irving Hexham and G. O. Oosthuizen, eds., *The Story of Isaiah Shembe* (Lewiston, NY: Edwin Mellen, 1997). For the Ekuphakameni pilgrimage, see Thokozani Mtshali, "Shembe—The Incredible Whiteness of Being," *Electronic Mail and Guardian*, August 11, 1999, at http://www.mg.co.za/mg/news/99aug1/11aug-shembe.html.

15. Andrew Wingate, Kevin Ward, Carrie Pemberton, and Wilson Sitshebo, eds., *Anglicanism: A Global Communion* (New York: Church, 1998), 68.

16. Sundkler and Steed, *A History of the Church in Africa*, 1022–23; Lumbala, *Celebrating Jesus Christ in Africa*, 55–57; Thomas Bamat and Jean-Paul Wiest, eds., *Popular Catholicism in a World Church* (Maryknoll, NY: Orbis, 1999). For Brazil, see, for example, "Good News for the Poor," television documentary in the *Sword and Spirit* series, made by BBC, 1989.

17. The speaker was Namibia's Bonifatius Haushiku, quoted in Alan Cowell, "Africa's Bishops Bring Harsh Realities to Vatican," *NYT*, May 1, 1994.

18. For the idea of Jesus as ancestor, see Bediako, *Christianity in Africa*, 84–85. The extracts from eucharistic prayers are selected from Lumbala, *Celebrating Jesus Christ in Africa*, 36–37. The first two are Gikuyu, the third is Igbo. Patrick Chukwudezie Chibuko, *Paschal Mystery of Christ* (New York: Peter Lang, 1999). For Jesus as physician, see James Amanze, *African Christianity in Botswa* (Gweru, Zimbabwe: Mambo, 1998). For the rise of a distinctive African theology, see S. E. M. Pheko, *Christianity through African eyes* (Lusaka: Daystar, 1969); J. N. Kanyua Mugambi, *African Christian Theology* (Nairobi: Heinemann, 1989); John Parratt, *Reinventing Christianity* (Grand Rapids, MI: Eerdmans/Africa World, 1995); Daniel Carro and Richard F. Wilson, eds., *Contemporary Gospel Accents* (Macon, GA: Mercer University Press, 1996); Priscilla Pope-Levison and John R. Levison, *Jesus in Global Contexts* (Louisville, KY: Westminster/John Knox Press, 1992).

19. "Healers and Ecologists: Pentecostalism in Africa," *CC*, November 9, 1994, 1042–44; Clara Sue Kidwell, Homer Noley, and George E. Tinker, *A Native American Theology* (Maryknoll, NY: Orbis; 2001); Marthinus L. Daneel, *African Earthkeepers* (Maryknoll, NY: Orbis, 2001).

20. Eduardo C. Fernández, *La Cosecha* (Liturgical, 2000); Ada Maria Isasi-Diaz and Fernando F. Segovia, eds., *Hispanic/Latino Theology* (Minneapolis: Fortress, 1996); Roberto S. Goizueta, ed., *We are a People!* (Minneapolis: Fortress, 1992).

21. "The mestizo affirms. . . . " is from Virgilio P. Elizondo, *The Future is Mestizo*, rev. ed. (Boulder: University Press of Colorado, 2000), 84. See also Arturo J. Bañuelas, ed., *Mestizo Christianity* (Maryknoll: Orbis, 1995); Jacques Audinet, *Le Temps du Metissage* (Paris: Les Editions de l'Atelier/Les Editions Ouvrieres, 1999); Manuel A. Vasquez, "Pentecostalism, Collective Identity and Transnationalism among Salvadorans and Peruvians in the US," *Journal of the American Academy of Religion* 67 (1999): 617–36; Daniel Ramirez, "Borderlands Praxis," *Journal of the American Academy of Religion* 67(1999): 573–96; Timothy Matovina, ed., *Beyond Borders* (Maryknoll, NY: Orbis, 2000). For "roots" and "routes," see Paul Gilroy, *The Black Atlantic* (Cambridge, MA: Harvard University Press, 1993). For the new diasporas, Mark Fritz, *Lost on Earth* (New York: Routledge, 2000).

22. Virgilio P. Elizondo, *Galilean Journey* (Maryknoll, NY: Orbis, 2000), 91.

23. Ibid., 133.

24. Ibid., 11; Brading, *Mexican Phoenix*. For messianic ideas surrounding *La Caridad*, see Tweed, *Our Lady of the Exile*.

25. Roberto S. Goizueta, "Why are You Frightened?" in Peter Casarella and Raul Gomez, eds., *El Cuerpo de Cristo* (New York: Crossroad, 1998), 59, Timothy M. Matovina, *Mestizo Worship* (Collegeville, MN: Liturgical, 1998).

26. For the adoption of the figure of Guadelupe by Filipino-Americans, see Margaret Ramirez "Dancing as Prayer," *LAT,* December 9, 2000.

27. Sundkler and Steed, *A History of the Church in Africa,* 970–71, and 924–25 for Zaytoun; Isichei, *A History of Christianity in Africa,* 328; Ferdinand Nwaigbo, *Mary—Mother of the African Church* (New York : P. Lang, 2001).

28. http://www.whidbey.net/~dcloud/fbns/sophia.htm. Hyun Kyung Chung, *Struggle to Be the Sun Again* (Maryknoll, NY: Orbis, 1990).

29. Bengt Sundkler, *Zulu Zion and Some Swazi Zionists* (Oxford University Press, 1976); Bengt Sundkler, *Bantu Prophets in South Africa,* 2nd ed. (Oxford University Press, 1964); Gerhardus C. Oosthuizen, *The Healer-Prophet in Afro-Christian Churches* (Leiden: E. J. Brill, 1992).

30. Oosthuizen, *The Theology of a South African Messiah;* Hexham and Oosthuizen, eds., *The Story of Isaiah Shembe.*

31. Kenneth Woodward, "The Changing Face of the Church," *Newsweek,* April 16, 2001.

32. "Bishop Spong Delivers a Fiery Farewell," *CC,* February 17, 1999.

33. Gerhardus Cornelis Oosthuizen, *Post-Christianity in Africa* (London: C. Hurst, 1968).

34. George Bond, Walton Johnson, and Sheila S. Walker, eds., *African Christianity* (New York: Academic Press, 1979); Nya Kwiawon Taryor, *Impact of the African Tradition on African Christianity* (Chicago: Strugglers' Community, 1984.)

35. Quoted in Sundkler and Steed, *A History of the Church in Africa,* 633. Compare Diedrich Westermann, *Africa and Christianity* (New York: Oxford University Press, 1937).

36. Quoted in David Martin, *Tongues of Fire* (Oxford: B. Blackwell, 1990), 140. David Chung, *Syncretism: The Religious Context of Christian Beginnings in Korea* (Albany: State University of New York Press, 2001); Andrew E. Kim, "Korean Religious Culture and its Affinity to Christianity," *Sociology of Religion* 61 (2000): 117–33; Jung Young Lee, ed., *Ancestor Worship and Christianity in Korea* (Lewiston, NY: Edwin Mellen, 1988).

37. Walls is quoted from Waldrep, "The Expansion of Christianity." Adam Ashforth, *Madumo* (University of Chicago Press, 2000); Isak A. Niehaus, Eliazaar Mohlala, and Kally Shokane, *Witchcraft, Power and Politics* (London: Pluto, 2001). For a recent witch-panic in the Democratic Republic of Congo, see Michael Dynes, "Frenzied Mob Hacks 300 'Witches' to Death," *Times* (London), July 4, 2001.

38. The story is quoted in Bediako, *Christianity in Africa,* 155–56.

39. "Their very life and worship" is quoted from Patrick Chapita and Luka Mwale, "African Churches Heal War Trauma," *Africanews,* May 1996, at http://www.peacelink.it/afrinews/2_issue/p4.htm. The quote about the Cherubim and

Seraphim movement is from Deji Ayegboyin and S. Ademola Ishola, *African Indige-nous Churches* (Lagos, Nigeria: Greater Heights, 1997), 88. Compare J. Akinyele Omoyajowo, *Cherubim and Seraphim* (New York: NOK Publishers International, 1982); Allan Anderson, "Prophetic Healing and the Growth of the Zion Christian Church in South Africa," at http://artsweb.bham.ac.uk/aanderson/Publications/prophetic_healing_&%20the_ZCC.htm.

40. Andrew F. Walls, in Christopher Fyfe and Andrew Walls, eds., *Christianity in Africa in the 1990s* (Edinburgh: Centre of African Studies, University of Edinburgh, 1996), 13; Edward Stourton, *Absolute Truth* (London: Penguin, 1999), 183–91.

41. Alvyn Austin, "Missions Dream Team," *Christian History* 52 (1996).

42. Lamin O. Sanneh, *West African Christianity* (Maryknoll, NY: Orbis, 1983), 184, makes the linkage between the epidemics of these years and the upsurge of healing churches. For the Church of the Lord (Aladura), see Ayegboyin and Ishola, *African Indigenous Churches* 73, 95; Gerhardus C. Oosthuizen and Irving Hexham, eds., *Afro-Christian Religion and Healing in Southern Africa* (Lewiston, NY: Edwin Mellen, 1991); Stephen Owoahene-Acheampong, *Inculturation and African Reli-gion* (New York: Peter Lang, 1998). For the Lutheran example, see Frieder Ludwig, *Church and State in Tanzania* (Leiden: E. J. Brill Academic, 1999), 184.

43. R. Andrew Chesnut, *Born Again in Brazil* (New Brunswick, NJ: Rutgers University Press, 1997), 58, 81.

44. Cox, *Fire from Heaven*, 226; Kim, "Korean Religious Culture and its Affin-ity to Christianity." For Macedo, see Ken Serbin, "Brazilian Church Builds an Inter-national Empire," *CC*, April 10, 1996.

45. Sundkler and Steed, *A History of the Church in Africa*; Timothy C. Morgan, "Have We Become Too Busy with Death?" *CT*, February 7, 2000, 36–44.

46. Wingate et al., *Anglicanism: A Global Communion, 59*; Robert C. Garner, "Safe Sects?" *Journal of Modern African Studies* 38 (2000): 41–69; Anthony Kunda, "Zambia's Churches Win Fight Against Anti-AIDS Ads," *CT*, January 12, 2001. Teresa Malcolm, "African Bishops Reject Condoms to Counter AIDS," *NCR* August 10, 2001.

47. Martin, *Tongues of Fire*, 147.

48. Matthew 11:2–5.

49. Acts 16:9.

50. Martin, *Tongues of Fire*, 146. For Shaull, see Ed Gitre, "Pie-in-the-Sky Now," *CT*, posted to web site November 27, 2000.

51. David A. Shank, quoted in Bediako, *Christianity in Africa*, 104.

52. Quoted in Isichei, *A History of Christianity in Africa*, 256. The Old Testa-ment passage is 1 Samuel 3:1, NIV.

53. Ayegboyin and Ishola, *African Indigenous Churches*, 142.

54. Ephesians 6:12, NRSV.

55. Peter Brown, *The World of Late Antiquity* (London: Thames and Hudson, 1971), 55.

56. Stourton, *Absolute Truth,* 183–91; Niels Christian Hvidt, "Interview with Archbishop Immanuel Milingo" February 14, 1998, online at http://www.hvidt.com/English/Milingo.htm. For the archbishop's marriage, see Dexter Filkins, "Maverick Archbishop Weds in Manhattan," *NYT,* May 28, 2001.

57. Ferdy Baglo, "Canadian Bishop Blocks Asian Church Leader from Visiting his Diocese," *CT,* November 29, 1999.

58. Ayegboyin and Ishola, *African Indigenous Churches,* 114–24; Knut Holter, *Yahweh in Africa* (New York: Peter Lang, 2000); Isichei, *A History of Christianity in Africa,* 289–90.

59. Cedric Pulford, "Debate Continues on Incorporating Animal Sacrifices in Worship," *CT,* October 25, 2000; Lumbala, *Celebrating Jesus Christ in Africa,* 96–98.

60. Thomas E. Sheridan, "The Rarámuri and the Leadville Trail 100," in Thomas E. Sheridan and Nancy J. Parezo, eds., *Paths of Life* (Tucson: University of Arizona Press, 1996), 144–58.

61. Amanze, *African Christianity in Botswana,* 125.

62. Ibid.

63. The vase ritual described here is taken from Lumbala, *Celebrating Jesus Christ in Africa;* compare Allan Anderson, "African Pentecostalism and the Ancestors," *Missionalia* 21, no. 1 (1993): 26–39; Nicholas M. Creary, "African Inculturation of the Catholic Church in Zimbabwe, 1958–1977," *Historian* 61 (1999): 765–81.

64. Sundkler and Steed, *A History of the Church in Africa,* 90–91.

65. Lumbala, *Celebrating Jesus Christ in Africa,* 12–18.

66. The quote is from G. C. Waldrep, "The Expansion of Christianity"; Andrew F. Walls; "Eusebius Tries Again," *IBMR* 24, no. 3 (2000): 105–11.

67. Art Moore, "Spiritual Mapping Gains Credibility Among Leaders," *CT,* January 12, 1998; Jane Lampman, "Targeting Cities with 'Spiritual Mapping,' Prayer," *Christian Science Monitor,* September 23, 1999.

68. Michael W. Cuneo, *American Exorcism* (New York: Doubleday, 2001).

69. These arguments are summarized in Philip Jenkins, *Mystics and Messiahs* (New York: Oxford University Press, 2000).

70. Keith Thomas, *Religion and the Decline of Magic* (New York: Scribner, 1971).

71. Martin, *Tongues of Fire.*

CHAPTER 7

1. Jeffrey Haynes, *Religion in Third World Politics* (Boulder, CO: Lynne Rienner, 1994).

2. David Miller, "Leveling the Playing Field," *CT,* December 7, 2000; Frederick Pike, "Latin America," in John McManners, ed., *The Oxford History of Christianity* (Oxford University Press, 1993), 437–73.

3. Michael A. Burdick, *For God and Fatherland* (Albany: State University of New York Press, 1996); Anthony James Gill, *Rendering Unto Caesar* (University of Chicago Press, 1999).

4. Owen Chadwick, *The Christian Church in the Cold War* (London: Allen Lane, 1992); Edward R. Norman, *Christianity and the World Order* (Oxford University Press, 1979).

5. Penny Lernoux, *Cry of the People* (New York: Penguin, 1982); idem, *People of God* (New York: Penguin, 1989). In Ngugi wa Thiong'o's novel, *A Grain of Wheat*, the Kenyan nationalist revolutionary leader is primarily inspired by the tale of Moses and the Exodus.

6. Doug Struck, "Keeping the Faith," *WP*, April 10, 2001.

7. Anna L. Peterson, *Martyrdom and the Politics of Religion* (Albany: State University of New York Press, 1997); Paul Jeffrey, "Almost Three Years After Bishop's Death, Five Go on Trial," *CT*, posted to web site April 11, 2001.

8. Alain Gheerbrant, *The Rebel Church in Latin America* (London: Penguin, 1974).

9. The Latin American bishops' conference is known as CELAM, the *Consejo Episcopal Latino-Americano*. A major collection of relevant texts can be found at http://www.celam.org/documentos.htm. For Medellín, see Edward Stourton, *Absolute Truth* (London: Penguin, 1999), 113.

10. Gustavo Gutiérrez, *A Theology of Liberation* (Maryknoll, NY: Orbis, 1973); Edward R. Norman, *Christianity and the World Order* (Oxford University Press, 1979), 24; Richard Shaull, *Heralds of a New Reformation* (Maryknoll, NY: Orbis, 1984).

11. Warren E. Hewitt, *Base Christian Communities and Social Change in Brazil* (Lincoln: University of Nebraska Press, 1991); Rowan Ireland, *Kingdoms Come* (Pittsburgh: University of Pittsburgh Press, 1991); John Burdick, *Looking for God in Brazil* (Berkeley: University of California Press, 1993); Cecília Loreto Mariz, *Coping with Poverty* (Philadelphia: Temple University Press, 1994); Madeleine Adriance, *Promised Land* (Albany: State University of New York Press, 1995); Robin Nagle and Jill Nagle, *Claiming the Virgin* (New York: Routledge, 1997); Manuel A. Vasquez, *The Brazilian Popular Church and the Crisis of Modernity* (Cambridge University Press, 1998).

12. German Guzman Campos, *Camilo Torres* (New York: Sheed and Ward, 1969); see also http://www.angelfire.com/md/TobyTerrar/Colombia.html.

13. James R. Brockman, *The Word Remains* (Maryknoll, NY: Orbis, 1982); Hannah Stewart-Gambino, *The Church and Politics in the Chilean Countryside* (Boulder, CO: Westview, 1992). For the progressive church at its height, see Scott Mainwaring and Alexander Wilde, eds., *The Progressive Church in Latin America* (University of Notre Dame Press, 1989). Edward L. Cleary, ed., *Born of the Poor* (University of Notre Dame Press, 1990); Paul E. Sigmund, *Liberation Theology at the Crossroads* (New York: Oxford University Press 1992); Michael Lowy, *The War of Gods* (London: Verso, 1996).

14. Harvey Cox, *The Silencing of Leonardo Boff* (Oak Park, IL: Meyer-Stone Books, 1988); Edward Stourton, *Absolute Truth* (London: Penguin, 1999), 107–49.

15. Barbara J. Fraser, "Peru's New Cardinal Known for Standing with the Powerful," *NCR*, March 23, 2001.

16. John L. Allen, "New Cardinal Symbolizes Direction of Global Catholicism," *NCR*, March 9, 2001; see also http://www.natcath.com/NCR_Online/documents/Rodriguez.htm.

17. Frieder Ludwig, *Church and State in Tanzania* (Leiden: E. J. Brill Academic, 1999), 104, 107; Dana L. Robert; "Shifting Southward," *IBMR*, 24, no. 2 (2000): 50–58; Holger Bernt Hansen and Michael Twaddle, eds., *Religion & Politics in East Africa* (Athens: Ohio University Press, 1995).

18. For the Kairos statement, see http://www.bethel.edu/~letnie/African Christianity/SAKairos.html. The Truth and Reconciliation Commission has a web site at Http://www.truth.org.za/. See also Tristan Anne Borer, *Challenging the State* (University of Notre Dame Press, 1998); James Cochrane, John W. De Gruchy, and Stephen Martin, eds., *Facing the Truth* (Athens: Ohio University Press, 1999); Isaac Phiri, "Proclaiming Peace and Love," *Journal of Church and State* 42 (2000): 781–802.

19. Bengt Sundkler and Christopher Steed, *A History of the Church in Africa* (Cambridge University Press, 2000), 904; for Ugandan affairs, see Paul Gifford, *African Christianity* (Bloomington: Indiana University Press, 1998), 112–80; for Congo-Brazzaville, see Abraham Okoko-Esseau, "The Christian Churches and Democratization in the Congo," in Paul Gifford, ed., *The Christian Churches and the Democratisation of Africa* (Leiden: E. J. Brill, 1995) 148–67. Margaret Ford, *Janani: The Making of a Martyr* (London: Marshall, Morgan and Scott, 1979).

20. See Gifford, *African Christianity*, throughout; Samuel P. Huntington, *The Third Wave* (Norman: University of Oklahoma Press, 1991); Jeffrey Haynes, *Religion and Politics in Africa* (London: Zed, 1996); Phiri, "Proclaiming Peace and Love"; idem, *Proclaiming Political Pluralism* (Westport, Conn.: Praeger, 2001).

21. John L. Allen, "Faith, Hope and Heroes," *NCR*, February 23, 2001. For parallels with ancient bishops, see the account of the collapse of Roman rule along the frontier in what is now Austria, in Eugippius, *The Life of Saint Severin* (Washington, DC: Catholic University of America Press, 1965).

22. Sundkler and Steed, *A History of the Church in Africa*, 966; Gifford, ed., *The Christian Churches and the Democratisation of Africa*, 5; Michael G. Schatzberg, *The Dialectics of Oppression in Zaire* (Bloomington: Indiana University Press, 1988); Michela Wrong, *In the Footsteps of Mr. Kurtz* (New York: HarperCollins, 2001).

23. John N. Schumacher, *Revolutionary Clergy* (Quezon City: Ateneo de Manila University Press, 1981); Benjamin Pimentel, "Battle of Prayers," *San Francisco Chronicle*, December 5, 2000; Sophie Lizares-Bodegon, "Thousands of Filipino Christians Pray for Estrada's Swift Resignation," *CT*, posted to web site December 11, 2000.

24. Robert, "Shifting Southward"; Wi Jo Kang, *Christ and Caesar in Modern Korea* (Albany: State University of New York Press, 1997).

25. David Martin, *Tongues of Fire* (Oxford: B. Blackwell, 1990), 141; Sang-t'aek Yi, *Religion and Social Formation in Korea* (New York: Mouton de Gruyter, 1996); Dennis Coday, "Light and Salt in Korean Society," *NCR,* October 27, 2000. The quote from Kim Dae Jung is taken from "Nobel Winner Has Credited Catholic Faith with Helping Him Survive Torture," *Tidings,* Los Angeles, October 20, 2000, 26.

26. Mark Mitchell, "The Philippines: In God's Country," *FEER,* April 19, 2001.

27. Ralph R. Premdas, *Ethnic Conflict and Development* (Brookfield, VT: Avebury, 1995); Victor Lal, *Fiji: Coups in Paradise* (London: Zed, 1990).

28. Isaac Phiri, "Why African Churches Preach Politics," *Journal of Church and State* 41 (1999): 323–47. For Ivory Coast, see the State Department report online at http://www.state.gov/www/global/human_rights/irf/irf_rpt/irf_cotedivo.html.

29. The Pauline text is Romans 13:1.

30. R. Drew Smith, "Missionaries, Church Movements, and the Shifting Religious Significance of the State in Zambia," *Journal of Church and State* 41 (1999): 525–50. For the abuse of church authority in the service of government, see Paul Gifford, *Christianity and Politics in Doe's Liberia* (Cambridge University Press, 1993). For Zambia, see Isaac Phiri, "Why African Churches Preach Politics"; Odhiambo Okite, "Church Leaders Publicly Oppose Term for Christian President," *CT,* April 23, 2001.

31. Desmond Tutu, "Identity Crisis," in Gifford, ed., *The Christian Churches and the Democratisation of Africa,* 97.

32. Ian Fisher, "Uganda Survivor Tells of When the World Didn't End," *NYT,* April 3, 2000; the Center for the Study of New Religions (CESNUR) offers a huge collection of texts and documents about this incident online at: http://www.cesnur.org/testi/uganda_updates.htm. This archive includes many contemporary media reports from North America, Europe, and Africa.

33. Niels Kastfelt, ed., *The Role of Religion in African Civil Wars* (London: C. Hurst, 2001); Heike Behrend, *Alice Lakwena and the Holy Spirits* (Athens, OH: Ohio University Press, 2000); Stephen Ellis, *The Mask of Anarchy* (New York University Press, 1999); Stephen L. Weigert, *Traditional Religion and Guerilla Warfare in Modern Africa* (London: Macmillan, 1995); Human Rights Watch, "Human Rights Watch Condemns Abduction and Killing of Children by Ugandan Rebel Group," online at http://www.hrw.org/press97/sept/uganda.htm. Chesnut is quoted from Elma Lia Nascimento, "Praise the Lord and Pass the Catch-Up," *Brazzil* magazine, November 1995, at http://www.brazzil.com/cvrnov95.htm.

34. Timothy Paul Longman, "Crisis in Rwanda," in Gifford, ed., *The Christian Churches and the Democratisation of Africa,* 1995; Kastfelt, ed., *The Role of Religion in African Civil Wars;* James C. McKinley, "Church and State: Seeking Complicity in a Genocide," *NYT,* June 10, 2001.

35. The pope is quoted in Hannah W. Stewart-Gambino and Everett Wilson, "Latin American Pentecostals," in Edward L. Cleary and Hannah W. Stewart-

Gambino, eds., *Power, Politics, and Pentecostals in Latin America* (Boulder, CO: Westview, 1997), 228. For the "oil stain," see Kenneth D. MacHarg, "Healing the Violence," *CT,* posted to web site July 25, 2000. Kilian McDonnell, "Pentecostals and Catholics on Evangelism and Sheep-stealing," *America,* March 6, 1999, 11–14.

36. Virginia Garrard-Burnett, *Protestantism in Guatemala* (University of Texas Press, 1998), 21.

37. "The proliferation of Protestantism . . . " is from Virginia Garrard-Burnett, in Virginia Garrard-Burnett and David Stoll, eds., *Rethinking Protestantism in Latin America* (Philadelphia: Temple University Press, 1993), 199; Philip Berryman, *The Religious Roots of Rebellion* (London: SCM, 1984); Daniel H. Levine, "Religion, the Poor, and Politics in Latin America Today," in Daniel H. Levine, ed., *Religion and Political Conflict in Latin America* (Chapel Hill: University of North Carolina Press, 1986); Mark Danner, *The Massacre at El Mozote* (New York: Vintage, 1994); Brian H. Smith, *Religious Politics in Latin America,* (University of Notre Dame Press, 1998); Paul Freston, *Evangelicals and Politics in Asia, Africa and Latin America* (Cambridge University Press, 2001).

38. A classic view of Pentecostal politics in the region is found in Christian Lalive d'Epinay, *Haven of the Masses* (London: Lutterworth, 1969); Frans Kamsteeg, *Prophetic Pentecostalism in Chile* (Lanham, MD: Scarecrow, 1998); Philip J. Williams, "The Sound of Tambourines," in Cleary and Stewart-Gambino, eds., *Power, Politics, and Pentecostals,* 179–200; Hannah W. Stewart-Gambino and Everett Wilson, "Latin American Pentecostals"; John Burdick, "Struggling against the Devil," in Garrard-Burnett and Stoll, eds., *Rethinking Protestantism in Latin America,* 20–44; Rowan Ireland, "The *Crentes* of Campo Alegre," in ibid., 45–65; Ireland, *Kingdoms Come;* Freston, *Evangelicals and Politics in Asia, Africa and Latin America;* idem, "Evangelicalism and Politics," *Transformation* 14 (1997): 23–29; Timothy J. Steigenga, *Politics of the Spirit* (Lanham, MD: Lexington, 2001). For Peru, see Hortensiz Munoz, "Believers and Neighbors," *Journal of InterAmerican Studies and World Affairs* 41 (1999): 73–92.

39. Paul Freston, "Brother Votes for Brother," in Garrard-Burnett and Stoll, eds., *Rethinking Protestantism in Latin America,* 66–110; Freston, "Evangelicalism and Politics"; Thomas W. Walker and Ariel C. Armony, eds., *Repression, Resistance, and Democratic Transition in Central America* (Wilmington, DE: Scholarly Resources, 2000).

40. MacHarg, "Healing the Violence"; Julia Lieblich, "Chiapas Pulses with Crusade for Souls," *Detroit News,* January 17, 1999; Ginger Thompson, "In a Warring Mexican Town, God's Will Is the Issue," *NYT,* August 13, 2000.

41. Nascimento, "Praise the Lord and Pass the Catch-Up"; McDonnell, "Pentecostals and Catholics on Evangelism and Sheep-stealing."

42. "Global Trends 2015," online at http://www.cia.gov/cia/publications/global trends2015/.

43. Rosalind I. J. Hackett, "Religious Freedom and Religious Conflict in Africa," in Mark Silk, ed., *Religion on the International News Agenda* (Hartford, CT:

Leonard F. Greenberg Center for the Study of Religion in Public Life, 2000), 102–14; Benjamin J. Hubbard, ed., *Reporting Religion* (Sonoma, CA: Polebridge, 1990).

CHAPTER 8

1. Samuel P. Huntington, *The Clash of Civilizations and the Remaking of World Order* (New York: Simon & Schuster, 1996), 92–102, 247–72; Gilles Kepel, *The Revenge of God* (University Park: Pennsylvania State University Press, 1994); Peter L. Berger, Jonathan Sacks, David Martin, and Grace Davie, eds., *The Desecularization of the World* (Grand Rapids, MI: Eerdmans, 1999); Armstrong, *The Battle for God* (New York: Knopf, 2000); Mark Juergensmeyer, *Terror in the Mind of God* (Berkeley: University of California Press, 2000).

2. Laurie Goodstein, "Churches Find New Focus in Opposing Persecution," *NYT,* November 9, 1998; Paul Marshall and Lela Gilbert, *Their Blood Cries Out* (Dallas: Word, 1997); Nina Shea, *In the Lion's Den* (Nashville, Tenn: Broadman and Holman, 1997).

3. Arvind Sharma, ed., *Our Religions* (HarperSanFrancisco, 1993).

4. Anto Akkara, "Churches Angry that Indian Census Ignores 14 Million Christian Dalits," *CT,* March 2, 2001.

5. Bengt Sundkler and Christopher Steed, *A History of the Church in Africa* (Cambridge University Press, 2000), 646–49; Nehemia Levtzion and Randall L. Pouwels, eds., *The History of Islam in Africa* (Athens: Ohio University Press, 2000).

6. "Global Trends 2015," online at http://www.cia.gov/cia/publications/global trends2015/.

7. Tarif Khalidi, *The Muslim Jesus* (Cambridge, MA: Harvard University Press, 2001); William E. Phipps, *Muhammad and Jesus* (New York: Continuum, 1996); Geoffrey Parrinder, *Jesus in the Qur'an* (New York: Oxford University Press, 1977).

8. For Africa, see, for instance, Norimitsu Onishi, "Islam Meets Africa and Islam Bows," *NYT,* January 9, 2000; Adeline Masquelier, *Prayer Has Spoiled Everything* (Durham, NC: Duke University Press, 2001). For the Oran case, see John L. Allen, "Faith, Hope and Heroes," *NCR,* February 23, 2001.

9. Laurence Edward Browne, *The Eclipse of Christianity in Asia* (Cambridge University Press, 1933).

10. William Dalrymple, *From the Holy Mountain* (New York: Henry Holt, 1997); Leila Tarazi Fawaz, *An Occasion for War* (Berkeley: University of California Press, 1994). From a vast literature on the Armenian massacres, see, for instance, Richard G. Hovannisian, ed., *The Armenian Genocide* (New York: St. Martin's, 1992); Robert Melson, *Revolution and Genocide* (University of Chicago Press, 1992).

11. The *Kristallnacht* analogy is from Dalrymple, *From the Holy Mountain,* 30–31; Robert Brenton Betts, *Christians in the Arab East,* rev. ed. (Atlanta: John Knox, 1978), 29.

12. Huntington, *The Clash of Civilizations and the Remaking of World Order,* 109–20, 174–79, 209–17; Judith Miller, *God Has Ninety-Nine Names* (New York: Simon & Schuster, 1996); Benjamin R. Barber, *Jihad Vs. McWorld* (New York: Times Books, 1995), 205–17; Francois Burgat, *The Islamic Movement in North Africa* (Austin: University of Texas Press, 1997).

13. "Global Trends 2015."

14. U.S. State Department Annual Report on Religious Freedom 2000, online at http://www.state.gov/www/global/human_rights/irf/irf_rpt/irf_sudan.html; John O. Hunwick, *Religion and National Integration in Africa* (Evanston: Northwestern University Press, 1992); Gino Barsella and Ayuso Guixot Miguel Angel, *Struggling to Be Heard* (Nairobi, Kenya: Paulines Publications Africa, 1998); Ann Mosely Lesch, *The Sudan (*Bloomington: Indiana University Press, 1998).

15. Timothy C. Morgan, "Church of the Martyrs," *CT,* August 11, 1997; Barbara G. Baker, "Egypt Jails Christian for Three Years for 'Insulting Islam,'" *CT,* posted to web site August 9, 2000; Barbara G. Baker, "Egypt Acquits All Muslim Murder Suspects," *CT,* posted to web site February 7, 2001.

16. For relations between the two faiths in Africa, see Lamin O. Sanneh, *The Crown and the Turban* (Boulder, CO: Westview, 1996); idem, *Piety and Power* (Maryknoll, NY: Orbis, 1996). Lissi Rasmussen, *Christian-Muslim Relations in Africa* (London: British Academic Press, 1993); Noel Quinton King, *Christian and Muslim in Africa* (New York: Harper & Row, 1971).

17. Karl Meier, *This House Has Fallen* (London: Allen Lane, 2001); Niels Kastfelt, ed., *The Role of Religion in African Civil Wars* (London: C. Hurst, 2001); Toyin Falola, *Violence in Nigeria* (University of Rochester Press, 1998); Hunwick, *Religion and National Integration in Africa;* Niels Kastfelt, *Religion and Politics in Nigeria* (London: British Academic Press, 1994).

18. Ustaz Yoonus Abdullah, *Sharia in Africa* (Ijebu-Ode, Nigeria: Shebiotimo, 1998); Rosalind I. J. Hackett, "Religious Freedom and Religious Conflict in Africa," in Silk, ed., *Religion on the International News Agenda,* 102–14.

19. Barnaby Phillips, "Nigerians Held for Talking in Public," *BBC World Service,* December 23, 2000; Nathaniel Ikyur, "Sharia Court Acquits Suspects," *Vanguard Daily* (Lagos), January 10, 2001; "Nigerian Woman Lashed for Premarital Sex," Reuters story, *NYT,* January 23, 2001; Alex Duval Smith, "Five Anglicans in Court After Rescuing Teenagers From Arranged Marriages," *CT,* posted to web site June 5, 2001.

20. Norimitsu Onishi, "Deep Political and Religious Rifts Disrupt Harmony of Nigerian Towns," *NYT,* March 26, 2000; idem, "Winds of Militant Islam Disrupt Fragile Frontiers," *NYT,* February 2, 2001.

21. "Global Trends 2015."

22. Mano Ramalshah, "Living as a Minority in Pakistan," in Andrew Wingate, Kevin Ward, Carrie Pemberton, and Wilson Sitshebo, eds., *Anglicanism: A Global Communion* (New York: Church, 1998), 264–70; "Pakistani Bishop's Death Sparks

Riots," *CT,* June 15, 1998; Barry Bearak, "Death to Blasphemers: Islam's Grip on Pakistan," *NYT,* May 12, 2001.

23. Robert W. Hefner, *Civil Islam* (Princeton University Press, 2000); Donald K. Emmerson, ed., *Indonesia beyond Suharto* (Armonk, NY: M. E. Sharpe, 1999).

24. Robert W. Hefner, "Profiles in Pluralism," in Mark Silk, ed., *Religion on the International News Agenda* (Hartford, CT: Leonard F. Greenberg Center for the Study of Religion in Public Life, 2000), 81–98; Anto Akkara, "Daily Life in the Maluku Islands," *CT,* posted to web site August 1, 2000; Mark Kelly, "Indonesian Island Attacks Go Unnoticed," *CT,* posted to web site August 21, 2000; Russell Rankin, "Christians and Muslims Still Fighting, Dying in Ambon," *CT,* posted to web site October 4, 2000.

25. "Hundreds Flee Moluccas Violence," BBC World Service, December 5, 2000; "Reports: Muslims Forcing Converts," Associated Press, December 25, 2000; Alex Spillius, "Indonesian Christians Forced into Islamic Faith," *Daily Telegraph,* February 5, 2001.

26. John McBeth, "Bombs, the Army and Suharto," *FEER,* February 1, 2001; Dini Djalal, "When Might Is Right," *FEER,* March 1, 2001.

27. "Philippine Priest Shot Dead," BBC World Service, December 28, 2000.

28. Rajiv Chandrasekaran, "Southeast Asia Shaken by Rise of Strict Islam," WP, November 5, 2000; Simon Elegant, "Bound by Tradition," *FEER,* July 27, 2000.

29. Geoff Stamp, "Post-election Violence Rocks the Ivory Coast," *CT,* January 5, 2001; "Religious Leaders See State Role in Kenya Clashes," Reuters report in http://www.CNN.com, December 4, 2000.

30. Paul Mojzes, ed., *Religion and the War in Bosnia* (Atlanta: Scholars Press, 1998).

31. "Religious Leaders See State Role in Kenya clashes."

32. Calvin Sims, "As in Manila, So in Jakarta?" *NYT,* January 27, 2001; Mark Landler, "Talk of 'Holy War' From Jakarta Leader's Home Base," *NYT,* April 15, 2001; Djalal, "When Might Is Right"; John McBeth and Dini Djalal, "The Puppet President," *FEER,* August 2, 2001.

33. Malise Ruthven, *A Satanic Affair* (London: Chatto & Windus, 1990); Lars Pedersen, *Newer Islamic Movements in Western Europe* (Aldershot: Ashgate, 1999); Marlise Simmons, "Dutch Group Calls Off an Opera After Muslims Pressure Cast," *NYT,* December 10, 2000; Richard Owen, "Muslims Say Fresco Must Be Destroyed," *Times* (London), June 29, 2001.

34. "Anti-Muslim Remarks Create a Furor," *San Francisco Chronicle,* September 15, 2000; "Cardinal Asks Italy to Favor Catholic Immigrants," *America,* September 30, 2000, 5; John L. Allen, "Europe's Muslims Worry Bishops," *NCR,* October 22, 1999.

35. Peter Novick, *The Holocaust in American Life* (New York: Houghton Mifflin, 1999).

36. Joel Peters, *Israel and Africa* (London: British Academic Press, 1992).

37. For Hindu religious statistics, see David B. Barrett, George T. Kurian, and Todd M. Johnson, *World Christian Encyclopedia,* 2nd ed. (Oxford University Press, 2001), 4.

38. J. Aruldoss, "Dalits and Salvation," in Wingate et al., *Anglicanism,* 294–300; *Broken People: Caste Violence Against India's "Untouchables"* (New York: Human Rights Watch, 1999), online at http://www.hrw.org/reports/1999/india/.

39. John C. B. Webster, *A History of the Dalit Christians in India* (San Francisco: Mellen Research University Press, 1992); John C. B. Webster et al., *From Role to Identity* (Delhi: ISPCK, 1997); Sathianathan Clarke, *Dalits and Christianity* (Oxford India Paperbacks, 1999).

40. T. K. Oommen and Hunter P. Mabry, *The Christian Clergy in India* (Thousand Oaks, CA: Sage, 2000); Anto Akkara, "India's First Dalit Archbishop Holds 'No Grudge' Over Predecessor's Attack," *CT,* posted to web site May 11, 2000; Anto Akkara, "Study of Indian Clergy Exposes Inequalities in Church Leadership," *CT,* October 9, 2000; Thomas C. Fox, "Intolerance in India," *NCR,* May 4, 2001.

41. Michael Fischer, "The Fiery Rise of Hindu Fundamentalism," *CT,* March 1, 1999.

42. Anti-Christian violence in India has become so commonplace as to be rarely noted with any prominence in the media. For a sample of recent media reports, see "Missionary Bashed Up, Stripped," *Times of India,* August 27, 2000; Manpreet Singh, "Justice Delayed for Dalits," *CT,* posted to web site October 19, 2000; Jatindra Dash, "Communal Tension Grips Orissa," *Times of India,* October 19, 2000; Anto Akkara, "Indian Christian Youth Form Protection Group," *CT,* posted to web site November 2, 2000; Manpreet Singh, "Christians Hammered by Pre-Christmas Violence," *CT,* December 22, 2000; Manpreet Singh, "Militant Hindus Assault Christians," *CT,* February 5, 2001; Anto Akkara, "India's Christians Face Continued Threats," *CT,* posted February 15, 2001; Manpreet Singh, "Relief Abuses Rampant," *CT,* April 2, 2001.

43. Aruldoss, "Dalits and Salvation," 295.

44. "Arrest over Indian Church Attacks," BBC World Service, August 17, 2000.

45. Manpreet Singh, "India's Christians Resist Move to Register Conversions," *CT,* May 2, 2000; Anto Akkara, "A Chinese Model for India's Churches?" *CT,* posted to web site October 12, 2000; "Orissa Villages Ban Conversion," *Times of India,* December 29, 2000; "Dalai Lama Condemns Christian, Muslim Practice of Seeking Converts," BBC World Service, January 26, 2001.

46. I differ here from Barrett et al., eds., *World Christian Encyclopedia,* which argues for a world Buddhist population of about 8 percent in 1900. I believe this figure underestimates the historic strength of Buddhism in China, where millions practice multiple faiths simultaneously.

47. For the positive side of the dialogue between the two faiths, see Whalen Lai and Michael von Bruck, *Christianity and Buddhism* (Maryknoll, NY: Orbis, 2001).

48. Gill Donovan, "Leader Says Churches Need to Rethink Missionary Work," *NCR,* May 11, 2001.

49. Robert D. Kaplan, *The Coming Anarchy* (New York: Random House, 2000); Stephen Ellis, *The Mask of Anarchy* (New York University Press, 1999).

50. Ravil Bukharev, *Islam in Russia* (New York: Palgrave, 2000); Yaacov Ro'I, *Islam and the Soviet Union* (New York: Columbia University Press, 2000). The five Central Asian republics are Uzbekistan, Kazakhstan, Turkmenistan, Kyrgyzstan, and Tajikistan.

51. Douglas Frantz, "Central Asia Braces to Fight Islamic Rebels," *NYT,* May 3, 2001; "Global Trends 2015," http://www.cia.gov/cia/publications/globaltrends2015/.

52. Ian Fisher and Norimitsu Onishi, "Chaos in Congo," *NYT,* February 6, 2000.

53. Huntingdon, *The Clash of Civilizations and the Remaking of World Order,* 247–72.

54. Michael Pillsbury, *China Debates the Future Security Environment* (Washington, DC: National Defense University Press, 2000); Michael Pillsbury, ed., *Chinese Views of Future Warfare,* rev. ed. (Washington, DC: National Defense University Press, 1998).

CHAPTER 9

1. *Complete Stories of Evelyn Waugh* (Boston: Little, Brown, 1999), 144: thanks to Chilton Williamson Jr. for drawing my attention to this story.

2. H. Daniel-Rops, *The Church in the Seventeenth Century* (London: Dent, 1963), 46.

3. Charles Williams, *Shadows of Ecstasy* (London: Faber & Faber, 1965), 40.

4. Lothrop T. Stoddard, *The Rising Tide of Color Against White World Supremacy* (New York: C. Scribner's Sons, 1920); John Buchan, *Prester John* (New York: T. Nelson and Sons, 1910); Edward W. Blyden, *Christianity, Islam and the Negro Race* (Edinburgh University Press, 1967).

5. Jean Raspail, *The Camp of the Saints* (New York: Scribner, 1975). In her novel *The Almanac of the Dead* (New York: Simon & Schuster, 1991), Leslie Marmon Silko offers what is almost a left-wing counterpart to *Camp of the Saints,* depicting the native masses of Central and South America pouring north into the ruins of the United States, to overwhelm White civilization and Christianity. The difference from Raspail is that Silko clearly sympathizes with the invaders.

6. Hilaire Belloc, *Europe and the Faith* (New York: Paulist, 1920), ix.

7. All figures are drawn from the *The Official Catholic Directory,* 1999.

8. John L. Allen, "Faith, Hope and Heroes," *NCR,* February 23, 2001.

9. For Cardinal Rugambwa, see Frieder Ludwig, *Church and State in Tanzania* (Leiden: Brill Academic, 1999); Alessandra Stanley, "Shaping a Legacy, Pope Installs 44 Cardinals," *NYT,* February 22, 2001.

10. See Edward Stourton, *Absolute Truth* (London: Penguin, 1999), 66, for the election of Pope John Paul II. For FutureChurch, see http://www.futurechurch.org/. John Cornwell, *Breaking Faith* (New York: Viking, 2001).

11. Ann M. Simmons, "A Potentially Historic Choice," *LAT,* March 17, 2001.

12. *Dominus Jesus,* online at http://www.vatican.va/roman_curia/congregations/cfaith/documents/rc_con_cfaith_doc_20000806_dominus-iesus_en.html.

13. Moonjang Lee, "Experience of Religious Plurality in Korea," *IRM* 88 (1999): 399–413. David Chung, *Syncretism: The Religious Context of Christian Beginnings in Korea* (Albany: State University of New York Press, 2001).

14. Cynthia Hoehler-Fatton, *Women of Fire and Spirit* (Oxford University Press, 1996); Marcy Amba Oduyoye and Musimbi R. A. Kanyoro, eds., *The Will to Arise* (Maryknoll, NY: Orbis, 1992).

15. Letty M. Russell, Katie Geneva Cannon, and Ada Maria Isasi-Diaz, eds., *Inheriting Our Mothers Gardens* (Louisville: Westminster, 1988); Ursula King, *Feminist Theology from the Third World* (Maryknoll, NY: Orbis, 1994); Mercy Amba Oduyoye, *Daughters of Anowa* (Maryknoll, NY: Orbis, 1995); Ada Maria Isasi-Diaz, *Mujerista Theology* (Maryknoll, NY: Orbis, 1996); Musa Dube, *Postcolonial Feminist Interpretation of the Bible* (St. Louis, MO: Chalice, 2000). Gay causes have also made very limited progress in Latin American churches: Paul Jeffrey, "Gay Churches Expand to Latin American Congregations," *CT,* posted to web site September 27, 2000.

16. John L. Allen and Pamela Schaeffer, "Reports of Abuse," *NCR*, March 16, 2001.

17. Charles Muchinshi Chilinda, "Africans Say Continent is 'Easy Prey,'" *NCR,* April 6, 2001.

18. Stephen O. Murray and Will Roscoe, eds., *Boy-Wives and Female-Husbands* (New York: St. Martin's, 1998).

19. Chris McGreal, "Debt? War? Gays Are the Real Evil, Say African Leaders," *Guardian,* October 2, 1999; "Nujoma and Swapo Join Mugabe's Gay-bashing," online at http://www.sn.apc.org/wmail/issues/970214/NEWS58.html.

20. R. William Franklin, "Lambeth 1998 and the Future Mission of the Episcopal Church," *Anglican Theological Review* 81 (1999): 261–69.

21. Ferdy Baglo, "Canadian Bishop Blocks Asian Church Leader from Visiting his Diocese," *CT,* November 29, 1999.

22. Gustav Niebuhr, "Consecrations of U.S. Bishops by Episcopal Officials Overseas Challenges Church Hierarchy," *NYT,* February 2, 2000; Chris Herlinger, "Conservative Anglicans Defy Episcopal Church," *CT,* posted to web site October 5, 2000; D. Aileen Dodd, "Church Losing Priests in Split," *Miami Herald,* October 16, 2000; Stephen Manning, "Maryland Church Rift Sign of Larger Episcopal Divide," Associated Press, June 17, 2001; Joann Loviglio, "Episcopal Parish Levels Criticism Against Pa. Bishop," Associated Press, June 20, 2001; Larry B. Stammer, "Move Hints at Breakaway by Conservative Episcopalians," *LAT,* June 25, 2001. The new movement has a website at http:anglicanmissioninamerica.org.

23. Douglas LeBlanc, "Intercontinental Ballistic Bishops?" *CT,* posted to web site April 25, 2000.

24. Gustav Niebuhr, "Episcopal Dissidents Find African Inspiration," *NYT,* March 6, 2001.

25. Gustav Niebuhr, "Vietnamese Immigrants Swell Catholic Clergy," *NYT,* April 24, 2000; idem, "Immigrant Priests," *NYT,* May 19, 2001.

26. Victoria Combe, "Missionaries Flock to Britain to Revive Passion for Church," *Electronic Telegraph,* January 18, 2001. For the Anglican primate of Brazil, Glauco Soares de Lima, see "Green and Pagan Land," *Economist,* June 21, 2001; "Missionaries to Spread Word in 'Heathen' Britain," *Sunday Times* (London), July 1, 2001.

27. http://www.rccg.org/Church_Ministry/Mission_Statement/mission_statement. htm.

28. The list of nations in which the group is present is from http://www. rccg.org/Church_Ministry/Trustees/history.htm. The second quote ("obviously in fulfillment") is from the web site of the RCCG's congregation in Dallas, Texas, at http://www.dhc.net/rccg/history(1).htm.

29. The note about the Kimbanguist international presence is taken from the church's web site at http://www.kimbanguisme.com/e-option2.htm. The RCCG has a web site at http://www.rccg.org/. For the IURD, see http://www.igrejauniversal. org.br/. For Sal da Terra, see http://www.saldaterra.org.br/missao.htm. The Church of the Lord (Aladura) can be found (on a German server) at http://www.aladura.de/. For the Harrists, see http://www.egliseharriste-ongapa.ci/. The Nigerian-founded Celestial Church of Christ is at http://www.celestialchurch.com/.

30. Andrew Wingate, Kevin Ward, Carrie Pemberton, and Wilson Sitshebo, eds., *Anglicanism: A Global Communion* (New York: Church, 1998), 13.

31. Victoria Combe, "Black Church in Crusade to Woo Whites," *Electronic Telegraph,* February 16, 2001. Refugee communities are also significant. See, for example, Kevin Ward, "Ugandan Christian Communities in Britain," *IRM* 89 (2000): 320–28.

32. R. Andrew Chesnut, *Born Again in Brazil* (New Brunswick, NJ: Rutgers University Press, 1997), 7; Marc Schogol, "Argentinians Pray for a Phila. Revival," *Philadelphia Inquirer,* February 11, 2001; Daniel Míguez, *To Help You Find God* (Amsterdam: Free University of Amsterdam, 1997); Daniel Míguez, *Spiritual Bonfire in Argentina* (Amsterdam: Center for Latin American Studies, 1998).

33. "African Missionaries to U.S.," *CC,* August 13–August 20, 1997, 718–20. The list of RCCG congregations is from http://www.rccg.org/Church_Ministry/ Trustees/history.htm.

34. For the development of the Christ Apostolic Church in North America, see the group's web sites at http://www.christapostolicchurch.org/ and http://www. firstcac.org/bio.html. The list of CAC churches is from http://www.christapostolic church.org/national.html. Compare Maura Kelly, "Praising Lord in So Many Ways," *Chicago Tribune,* March 10, 2000.

CHAPTER 10

1. David Martin, *Tongues of Fire* (Oxford: B. Blackwell, 1990).

2. Marcus J. Borg, *Meeting Jesus Again for the First Time* (HarperSan Francisco;

1995); idem, *Reading the Bible Again for the First Time* (HarperSan Francisco, 2001).

3. The quote about the *"n*th World" is from Paul Gifford, *African Christianity* (Bloomington: Indiana University Press, 1998), 15; "In Sub-Saharan Africa," is from "Global Trends 2015," online at http://www.cia.gov/cia/publications/global trends2015/. Bakut tswah Bakut and Sagarika Dutt, eds., *Africa at the Millennium* (New York: Palgrave, 2000); Ogbu Kalu, *Power, Poverty and Prayer* (New York: Peter Lang, 2000).

4. Ronald J. Sider, *Rich Christians in an Age of Hunger* (Downers Grove, IL: InterVarsity, 1977).

5. R. S. Sugirtharajah, ed., *Voices from the Margin* (Maryknoll, NY: Orbis, 1995); Lamin Sanneh, "Global Christianity and the Re-education of the West," *CC*, July 19, 1995, 715–17; Musimbi Kanyoro, "Reading the Bible from an African Perspective," *Ecumenical Review*, 51 (1999): 18–24; Fernando F. Segovia, *Decolonizing Biblical Studies* (Maryknoll, NY: Orbis, 2000).

6. Doug Bandow, "Letter from Indonesia," *Chronicles*, March 2001, 41.

7. Marc Nikkel, "Death Has Come to Reveal the Faith," in Andrew Wingate, Kevin Ward, Carrie Pemberton, and Wilson Sitshebo, eds., *Anglicanism: A Global Communion* (New York: Church, 1998), 73–78.

8. Mark Fritz, *Lost on Earth* (New York: Routledge, 2000); Jean-Pierre Ruiz, "Biblical Interpretation," in Peter Casarella and Raul Gomez, eds., *El Cuerpo de Cristo* (New York: Crossroad, 1998), 84.

9. Quoted in Ruiz, "Biblical Interpretation," 89–90.

10. Quoted in ibid., 86–87.

11. See, for example, Tony Carnes, "The Silicon Valley Saints," *CT*, August 6, 2001.

12. I have usually seen this phrase attributed to Bismarck, but it has been credited to both Metternich and Winston Churchill.

INDEX